✧Forbes

TRAVEL GUIDE

Formerly Mobil Travel Guide

FLORIDA

2011

ACKNOWLEDGMENTS

We gratefully acknowledge the help of our representatives for their efficient and perceptive inspections of the lodgings listed. Forbes Travel Guide is also grateful to the talented writers who contributed to this book.

Front Cover image: ©iStockphoto.com
All maps: Mapping Specialists

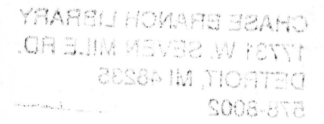

CONTENTS

STAR ATTRACTIONS

If you've been a reader of Mobil Travel Guide, you will have heard that this historic brand partnered in 2009 with another storied media name, Forbes, to create a new entity, Forbes Travel Guide. For more than 50 years, Mobil Travel Guide assisted travelers in making smart decisions about where to stay and dine when traveling. With this new partnership, our mission has not changed: We're committed to the same rigorous inspections of hotels, restaurants and spas—the most comprehensive in the industry with more than 500 standards tested at each property we visit—to help you cut through the clutter and make easy and informed decisions on where to spend your time and travel budget. Our team of anonymous inspectors are constantly on the road, sleeping in hotels, eating in restaurants and making spa appointments, evaluating those exacting standards to determine a property's rating.

What kinds of standards are we looking for when we visit a property? We're looking for more than just high-thread count sheets, pristine spa treatment rooms and white linen-topped tables. We look for service that's attentive, individualized and unforgettable. We note how long it takes to be greeted when you sit down at your table, or to be served when you order room service, or whether the hotel staff can confidently help you when you've forgotten that one essential item that will make or break your trip. Unlike any other travel ratings entity, we visit each place we rate, testing hundreds of attributes to compile our ratings, and our ratings cannot be bought or influenced. The Forbes Five Star rating is the most prestigious achievement in hospitality—while we rate more than 5,000 properties in the U.S., Canada, Hong Kong, Macau and Beijing, for 2011, we have awarded Five Star designations to only 54 hotels, 23 restaurants and 20 spas. When you travel with Forbes, you can travel with confidence, knowing that you'll get the very best experience, no matter who you are.

We understand the importance of making the most of your time. That's why the most trusted name in travel is now Forbes Travel Guide.

STAR RATED HOTELS

Whether you're looking for the ultimate in luxury or the best value for your travel budget, we have a hotel recommendation for you. To help you pinpoint properties that meet your needs, Forbes Travel Guide classifies each lodging by type according to the following characteristics:

★★★★★These exceptional properties provide a memorable experience through virtually flawless service and the finest of amenities. Staff are intuitive, engaging and passionate, and eagerly deliver service above and beyond the guests' expectations. The hotel was designed with the guest's comfort in mind, with particular attention paid to craftsmanship and quality of product. A Five-Star property is a destination unto itself.

★★★★These properties provide a distinctive setting, and a guest will find many interesting and inviting elements to enjoy throughout the property. Attention to detail is prominent throughout the property, from design concept to quality of products provided. Staff are accommodating and take pride in catering to the guest's specific needs throughout their stay.

★★★These well-appointed establishments have enhanced amenities that provide travelers with a strong sense of location, whether for style or function. They may have a distinguishing style and ambience in both the public spaces and guest rooms; or they may be more focused on functionality, providing guests with easy access to local events, meetings or tourism highlights.

Recommended: These hotels are considered clean, comfortable and reliable establishments that have expanded amenities, such as full-service restaurants.

For every property, we also provide pricing information. All prices quoted are accurate at the time of publication; however, prices cannot be guaranteed. Because rates can fluctuate, we list a pricing range rather than specific prices.

STAR RATED RESTAURANTS

Every restaurant in this book has been visited by Forbes Travel Guide's team of experts and comes highly recommended as an outstanding dining experience.

★★★★★Forbes Five-Star restaurants deliver a truly unique and distinctive dining experience. A Five-Star restaurant consistently provides exceptional food, superlative service and elegant décor. An emphasis is placed on originality and personalized, attentive and discreet service. Every detail that surrounds the experience is attended to by a warm and gracious dining room team.

★★★★These are exciting restaurants with often well-known chefs that feature creative and complex foods and emphasize various culinary techniques and a focus on seasonality. A highly-trained dining room staff provides refined personal service and attention.

★★★Three Star restaurants offer skillfully prepared food with a focus on a specific style or cuisine. The dining room staff provides warm and professional service in a comfortable atmosphere. The décor is well-coordinated with quality fixtures and decorative items, and promotes a comfortable ambience.

Recommended: These restaurants serve fresh food in a clean setting with efficient service. Value is considered in this category, as is family friendliness.

Because menu prices can fluctuate, we list a pricing range rather than specific prices. The pricing ranges are per diner, and assume that you order an appetizer or dessert, an entrée and one drink.

STAR RATED SPAS

Forbes Travel Guide's spa ratings are based on objective evaluations of more than 450 attributes. About half of these criteria assess basic expectations, such as staff courtesy, the technical proficiency and skill of the employees and whether the facility is clean and maintained properly. Several standards address issues that impact a guest's physical comfort and convenience, as well as the staff's ability to impart a sense of personalized service. Additional criteria measure the spa's ability to create a completely calming ambience.

★★★★★ Stepping foot in a Five Star Spa will result in an exceptional experience with no detail overlooked. These properties wow their guests with extraordinary design and facilities, and uncompromising service. Expert staff cater to your every whim and pamper you with the most advanced treatments and skin care lines available. These spas often offer exclusive treatments and may emphasize local elements.

★★★★ Four Star spas provide a wonderful experience in an inviting and serene environment. A sense of personalized service is evident from the moment you check in and receive your robe and slippers. The guest's comfort is always of utmost concern to the well-trained staff.

★★★ These spas offer well-appointed facilities with a full complement of staff to ensure that guests' needs are met. The spa facil ties include clean and appealing treatment rooms, changing areas and a welcoming reception desk.

WELCOME TO FLORIDA

THERE'S A REASON VACATIONERS HEAD SOUTH to Florida—blue waters, towering palm trees and a delightfully tropical climate make it an obvious destination for rest and relaxation. Florida is especially appealing to winter-weary Northerners—the state provides a place where beachgoing is not only a favorite recreational activity but a year-round lifestyle option.

Florida is a 450-mile-long and 150-mile-wide peninsula, and from its border with Georgia to its southernmost coast, the state's landscape is unlike any other. The pines near the Georgia border give way to palms and sea grape, then to bougainvillea and hibiscus, and finally to saw grass and mangrove down in the Everglades. With 8,426 miles of coastline (including that of the panhandle), Florida has the largest tidal coastline in the United States. The Gulf Stream flows through the Florida straits between Florida and Cuba, and north up the Atlantic coast, influencing the tropical climate that exists there.

When Ponce de Leon first discovered Florida, he stepped ashore near St. Augustine and mapped the entire coast, but failed to establish a colony. In 1539, Hernando de Soto and his army marched through the tropical land and started what is now the Tampa Bay area. Spanish settlements became rooted in St. Augustine and Pensacola in the 17th century, but in the 18th century, Florida was taken as a British province. Following the defeat of the British in the American Revolution, Spain resumed control, but in 1812, the Americans took over and in 1819 took formal possession of Florida. During the Civil War, Tallahassee was the only Confederate capital east of the Mississippi River to escape capture by Union forces.

Henry Morrison Flagler, a colorful tycoon with a passion for railroads and hotels, transformed Florida from a remote and swampy outpost to a resort destination. Flagler pushed his Florida East Coast Railroad from Jacksonville to Key West, opening one area after another along the coast to tourist and commercial development. On the west coast, Henry Plant, another millionaire railroader, competed with Flagler on a somewhat more modest scale.

Florida is now one of the top four most populated states in the country.

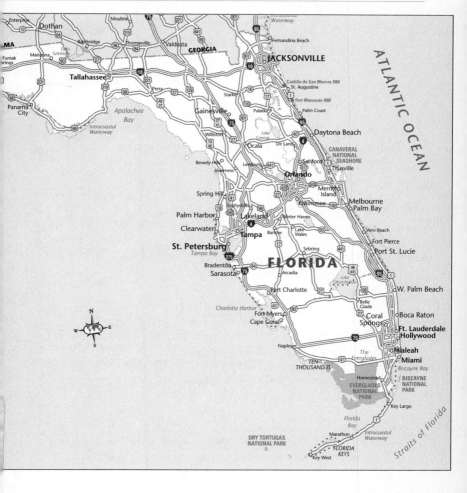

More people retire to Florida than to any other state. Florida's major industry is tourism—it brings in about $41 billion per year. Kennedy Space Center, the launch facility for the Apollo Moon Mission in 1961, brings in more than 1.5 million visitors each year. Walt Disney World has welcomed untold millions since its opening in 1971. With so many things to see and do, Florida is an ideal location to visit—and a place to keep returning to.

BEST ATTRACTIONS

FLORIDA'S BEST ATTRACTIONS

ORLANDO

As the theme-park capital of the world, Orlando is the perfect family destination. Of course, kids will want to see everyone's favorite mouse at Walt Disney World but there's also the new Wizarding World of Harry Potter and the popular Universal Studios.

FORT LAUDERDALE

Everyone from spring breakers to families comes to Fort Lauderdale for fun in the sun. And there are lots of options: Shop along Las Olas Boulevard, hang out at the beach or stroll along the Riverwalk Arts and Entertainment District.

MIAMI AND MIAMI BEACH

Miami and Miami Beach are undoubtedly the hottest spots in Florida. The beautiful people flock here for the trendy clubs in South Beach, striking architecture in the Art Deco District and authentic Cuban in food in Little Havana.

THE KEYS

The Keys offer a rare tropical island paradise in the United States. If the chain of islands inspired singer-songwriter Jimmy Buffett to turn out hits, imagine what the pristine beaches and laid-back vibe will do for you.

TOP HOTELS, RESTAURANTS AND SPAS

HOTELS

★★★★★FIVE STAR
Four Seasons Resort Palm Beach
(Palm Beach)
The Ritz-Carlton, Naples *(Naples)*
The Ritz-Carlton, Palm Beach
(Palm Beach)

★★★★FOUR STAR
Aqualina Resort and Spa on the Beach
(Sunny Isles Beach)
The Breakers, Palm Beach *(Palm Beach)*
Fairmont Turnberry Isle Resort
& Club *(Aventura)*
Four Seasons Hotel Miami *(Miami)*
Loews Miami Beach Hotel
(Miami Beach)
Mandarin Oriental, Miami *(Miami)*
The Peabody Orlando *(Orlando)*
The Ritz-Carlton, Amelia Island
(Amelia Island)
The Ritz-Carlton, Coconut Grove
(Miami)
The Ritz-Carlton, Fort Lauderdale
(Fort Lauderdale)
The Ritz-Carlton Golf Resort, Naples
(Naples)

The Ritz-Carlton, Key Biscayne
(Key Biscayne)
The Ritz-Carlton Orlando, Grande
Lakes *(Orlando)*
The Ritz-Carlton, Sarasota *(Sarasota)*
The Ritz-Carlton, South Beach
(Miami Beach)
The Setai *(Miami Beach)*
Trump International Beach Resort
(Sunny Isles Beach)

RESTAURANTS

★★★★FOUR STAR
Azul *(Miami)*
Blue Door Fish *(Miami Beach)*
Café Boulud *(Palm Beach)*
Palme d'Or *(Coral Gables)*
L'Escalier *(Palm Beach)*
Naoe *(Sunny Isles)*
Norman's *(Orlando)*
The Restaurant, Palm Beach
(Palm Beach)
Vernona Restaurant (Sarasota)
Victoria and Albert's
(Lake Buena Vista)
Wish *(Miami Beach)*

SPAS

★★★★★FIVE STAR
The Spa at Mandarin Oriental, Miami
(Miami)

★★★★FOUR STAR
ESPA at Acqualina Resort & Spa
(Sunny Isles Beach)
Relache at Gaylord Palms Resort
(Kissimmee)
The Ritz-Carlton Members Spa
Club, Sarasota *(Sarasota)*
The Ritz-Carlton Spa, Amelia Island
(Amelia Island)
The Ritz-Carlton Spa, Fort Lauderdale
(Fort Lauderdale)

The Ritz-Carlton Spa, Key Biscayne
(Key Biscayne)
The Ritz-Carlton Spa, Naples *(Naples)*
The Ritz-Carlton Spa Orlando,
Grande Lakes *(Orlando)*
The Ritz-Carlton Spa, South Beach
(Miami Beach)
The Spa at the Breakers *(Palm Beach)*
The Spa at ONE Bal Harbour
(Bal Harbour)
The Spa at the Setai *(Miami Beach)*
Spa Palazzo at Boca Raton Resort
& Club *(Boca Raton)*
SpaTerre at Little Palm Island
(Little Torch Key)
Willow Stream Spa *(Aventura)*

YOUR QUESTIONS ANSWERED

WHEN IS THE BEST TIME TO VIST?

Since Florida is a warm-weather destination, there's really no bad time to visit. Although there's been little activity in recent years, hurricane season runs from June to November. If you decide to go during that time, just be prepared and pay attention to weather reports.

Another factor you may want to take into account is the throngs of spring breakers and tourists. Most spring breaks fall between March and April, and the busiest spots around that time tend to be Daytona Beach, Key West, Miami and Panama City Beach. The peak season for the northern half of the state tends to be the hot summer, while the southern part of Florida sees most of its tourists in the winter. If you travel to the state during the fall, you'll avoid the horrific heat and most of the tourists have gone home by then.

HOW FAR IS IT FROM ORLANDO TO DAYTONA BEACH?

If you are a spring breaker who is flying into Orlando International Airport and need a beach pronto, Daytona Beach is your best option. Daytona Beach is only about an hour's drive east from Orlando. It's an easy drive for families who want to stay in Orlando for its proximity to Walt Disney World and the other theme parks but also would like to hit the sand and surf during their stay.

WHAT IS THE BEST WAY TO TOUR THE KEYS?

South of Miami and off Highway 1, the Florida Keys are America's own tropical islands. A laid-back attitude exists here, dress is always casual and life revolves around the water. The Keys are designated marine wildlife refuges, making them one of Florida's most popular destinations for diving. The Keys stretch for more than 100 miles, beginning with Key Largo. This is the site of John Pennekamp Coral Reef State Park, found at the town's north end, about 40 miles from South Miami. John Pennekamp is known for its snorkeling and glass-bottomed boat tours, but you can also camp and enjoy fishing and other water sports here.

Highway 1 continues south, connecting the islands together on a scenic route known as the Overseas Highway. In Islamorada, 20 miles to the south, kids will enjoy a stop at Theater of the Sea, where they can watch the sea lion and shark shows and participate in the popular dolphin interaction programs.

Manny and Isa's is the place to go for the best home-cooked Cuban food and key lime pie, which is a must if you're visiting the Keys. If you'd rather dine waterside, try Papa Joe's, which is south of town. Long Key Recreation Area, less than 20 miles south of Islamorada, has camping and picnicking on one of the Keys' few good beaches.

Six miles north of Marathon, the Dolphin Research Center conducts educational and interactive programs. Crane Point Hammock, also in Marathon, is a natural history museum with trails, aquariums and a children's museum. Also, check out the Pigeon Key Historic Site. Here, the welcome center occupies a vintage railroad at the very southern edge of town before the Seven Mile Bridge. From here, you take a tram (you can also walk or bicycle) to a historic site that re-creates an old Bahamian-style railroad-builders settlement from the turn of the last century.

Scenic Seven Mile Bridge is the showpiece of Overseas Highway. It takes you to Bahia Honda State Park, eight miles south of the Pigeon Key visitor center. Here you will find the Keys' best beaches, rated among the top in the country. You can snorkel, kayak, swim and fish in the marina. Campgrounds, cabins and beautiful beaches provide a great opportunity to relax. Down the road four miles lies Big Pine Key. It is the second-largest Key and one of the most natural of the islands. It's home to the National Key Deer Refuge, which protects the diminishing diminutive white-tailed deer. Fishing and lobstering are popular pastimes in this community.

A couple of miles south, at Torch Key, find some of the Keys' best snorkeling and diving in an area known as Looe Key National Marine Sanctuary. Continue south about 15 miles to Key West, best known for its sunset celebrations, all-night carousing and festival scene. Its historic Old Town area is full of great dining, shopping, historic sites and museums. Among the most well-known attractions are the Hemingway Home, the Key West Aquarium and the Little White House. Take the Conch Train around town to learn about the island's fascinating history. Check out Fort Zachary Taylor State Historic Site for more history and a beach picnic.

NORTHWEST FLORIDA

White sandy beaches draw visitors to the Northwest region of Florida. Anglers head to Destin, a beach community known for its outstanding fishing that's perched on a narrow strip of land between Choctawhatchee Bay and the Gulf of Mexico. The waters of the Gulf in the Emerald Coast (as Florida's Gulf-facing, panhandle region is called) are full of king mackerel, cobia, marlin, wahoo and sailfish. Spring breakers bring their bikinis and bathing suits to Panama City to party on the 23 miles of beaches. All sun worshippers visit Pensacola, the gateway to "the miracle strip," 100 miles of beach-fringed peninsulas and islands stretching to Panama City. Tallahassee may not be the sun capital of the region, but it is the capital of Florida. It retains the grace of plantation days and the flavor of its rustic pioneer past, which is what attracts travelers. During the Civil War, this city was the only Confederate capital east of the Mississippi not captured by Union forces.

WHAT TO SEE

DESTIN

BIG KAHUNA'S WATER AND ADVENTURE PARK

1007 U.S. Highway 98 E., Destin, 850-837-8319; www.bigkahunas.com

Make a big splash at this seasonal park with water rides for the family. The park offers everything from a gentle lazy river and sprays of water in the Fun Fountain, to rip-roaring rides like the Raging Rhino slide or the Honolulu Half Pipe, in which you can bodyboard on a huge wave. The Adventure Park portion of Big Kahuna's features putt-putt golf and a miniature raceway.

Admission: adults $37, seniors and children $30, children 2 and under free. June-mid-August 10 a.m.-6 p.m.; May, mid-August-September 10 a.m.-5 p.m.

EDEN GARDEN STATE PARK

181 Eden Gardens Road, Point Washington, 850-231-4214; www.floridastateparks.org/edengardens

Overlooking Choctawhatchee Bay, this was once the site of a large sawmill complex. Eden House, built by William Henry Wesley in 1897, is restored and furnished with antiques. There are gardens and a picnic area on the grounds, and tours of the mansion are available (Thursday-Monday, 10 a.m.-3 p.m.).

Admission: Mansion tours: adults $3, children $1.50; park: $3 per vehicle. Daily dawn-dusk.

PANAMA CITY

VISUAL ARTS CENTER OF NORTHWEST FLORIDA

19 E. Fourth St., Panama City, 850-769-4451; www.vac.org.cn

The Visual Arts Center is an art museum that shines a spotlight on local, regional and national artists. There's also an Impressions Gallery for children and a gift shop. Lectures, workshops, a summer youth program and other educational programs are also offered.

Tuesday and Thursday 10 a.m.-8 p.m., Wednesday, Friday, Saturday 10 a.m.- 6 p.m., Sunday 1-5 p.m.

HIGHLIGHTS

WHAT ARE THE TOP THINGS TO DO?

GET WET AT BIG KAHUNA'S WATER AND ADVENTURE PARK

Whether you're a thrill-seeker who wants to free-fall 70 feet down the Jumanji water slide or someone in need of relaxing in the Lazy River, the family friendly Big Kahuna has something for everyone.

JET OVER TO THE NATIONAL MUSEUM OF NAVAL AVIATION

More than 140 historic aircraft are on display at this aviation museum, which is one of the largest of its kind. Check out the Navy's first biplane and the first plane to cross the Atlantic.

MONKEY AROUND THE GULF BREEZE ZOO

More than 700 animals live at this zoo, including one of the largest lowland gorillas in captivity. Be sure to stop by the giraffe-feeding station to give the long-necked mammals a hand during mealtime.

TAKE A LOOK AT THE SPRINGS AT WAKULLA SPRINGS STATE PARK

This park has one of the world's largest and deepest freshwater springs. Get an up-close look by taking a ride on a glass-bottomed boat, which will give you a glimpse of the caverns 120 feet below the surface.

PENSACOLA

GULF BREEZE ZOO

5701 Gulf Breeze Parkway, Gulf Breeze, 850-932-2229; www.gulfbreezezoo.org

This 50-acre zoo and botanical garden has more than 700 animals, including one of the largest lowland gorillas in captivity. Kids will be entertained by the giraffe feeding, the petting zoo and the train rides.

Daily 9 a.m.-5 p.m.

GULF ISLANDS NATIONAL SEASHORE

1400 Fort Pickens Road, Pensacola, 850-934-2600; www.nps.gov/guis

The 1,742 acres include old Fort Pickens, one of the largest masonry forts in the United States, where Geronimo was imprisoned. Swimming, scuba diving,

---

HIGHLIGHT

WHAT ARE TALLAHASSEE'S CANOPY ROADS?

One of the top 10 scenic byways in America, five routes in and around Tallahassee have been termed "canopy roads" for their umbrella of live oaks covered with Spanish moss. The Old St. Augustine Road dates back to the 1600s, when it connected colonial Spanish missions. Centerville and Miccosukee roads travel along old cotton plantations (visit Goodwood Plantation) and into the country (stop at Bradley's Country Store for homemade sausage). Meridian Route begins at the state's Prime Meridian Marker downtown and heads north to the Georgia border. Old Bainbridge Road plunges through archaeological sites of Native American villages and Spanish ranchos. For a driving tour brochure and information on accommodations, call the Tallahassee Visitor Center at 800-628-2866. Approximately 123 miles.

---

fishing, and camping are available. The nearly 1,400 acres of forests provide picnicking, nature trails and a visitor center.

NATIONAL MUSEUM OF NAVAL AVIATION
1750 Radford Blvd., Pensacola, 850-452-3604; www.navalaviationmuseum.org

One of the largest of its kind, this museum features more than 140 historically significant aircraft on display, including the A-1 "Triad," the Navy's first biplane; the NC-4 Flying Boat, the first plane to cross the Atlantic; a vintage 1930s Marine Corps fighter; four A-4 Skyhawks (the Blue Angels) suspended in a diamond formation; and full-size modern-day jets. The museum also includes an IMAX theater.

Daily 9 a.m.-5 p.m.

TALLAHASSEE

ALFRED B. MACLAY GARDENS STATE PARK
3540 Thomasville Road, Tallahassee, 850-487-4556; www.floridastateparks.org

Planned as a private estate garden, the park sits on 308 acres and features azaleas, camellias, dogwood and rare plant species. The site was donated to the state in 1953. The Lake Hall Recreation area and has swimming, fishing, boating, nature trails, biking, picnicking and horseback riding.

Daily dawn-dusk.

GOVERNOR'S MANSION
700 N. Adams St., Tallahassee, 850-488-4661; www.floridagovernorsmansion.com

The historic home was completed in 1956 after the first mansion, which stood for nearly 50 years and was occupied by 11 governors, was torn down because of structural problems. The Governor's Mansion was designed by renowned Palm Beach architect, Marion Sims Wyeth and was built in a Greek Revival architecture style. The central portico was designed to look like the Hermitage, home to Andrew Jackson, in Nashville, Tennessee. Thirty-minute public tours are offered year round. You can also sign up for a guided tour during spring and holiday periods.

Public tours usually take place Monday, Wednesday and Friday from 10 a.m.-noon. Tours by appointment Monday-Friday 10 a.m.-4 p.m.

NATURAL BRIDGE BATTLEFIELD HISTORIC STATE PARK

7502 Natural Bridge Road, Tallahassee, 850-922-6007; www.floridastateparks.org

This 8-acre monument on the St. Marks River marks the spot where a militia of Confederate forces stopped Union troops, barring the way to Tallahassee. The battle, which took place on March 6, 1865, left Tallahassee as the only Confederate capital east of the Mississippi that never fell into Union hands. Picnicking is allowed on the grounds.

Daily dawn-dusk.

SAN MARCOS DE APALACHE HISTORIC STATE PARK

148 Old Fort Road, St. Marks, 850-925-6216; www.floridastateparks.org

This site was first visited by Panfilo de Narvaez in 1527 and Hernando de Soto in 1539. The park includes ruins of a fort and a museum on the site of an old federal marine hospital. You can picnic and walk along nature trails.

STATE CAPITOL

400 S. Monroe St., Tallahassee, 850-488-6167

At the top of Tallahassee's second-highest hill, the modern, 22-story capitol building towers above the city; there is an observation level on the top floor. There are special exhibits and tours are available.

Admission: free (donations). Monday-Friday 9 a.m.-4:30 p.m., Saturday 10 a.m.-4:30 p.m., Sunday noon-4:30 p.m.

TALLAHASSEE MUSEUM OF HISTORY & NATURAL SCIENCE

3945 Museum Drive, Tallahassee, 850-576-1636; www.tallahasseemuseum.org

The museum is on 52 acres with a restored 1880s Big Bend farm and an 1854 plantation house. There is also a gristmill, schoolhouse and church. Kids will enjoy the hands-on Discovery Center and the natural habitat zoo with native wild animals, including the endangered Florida panther.

Monday-Saturday 9 a.m.-5 p.m., Sunday 12:30-5 p.m.

WAKULLA SPRINGS STATE PARK

550 Wakulla Park Drive, Wakulla Springs, 850-926-0700; www.floridastateparks.org

In the heart of this 2,860-acre state park is one of the world's largest and deepest freshwater springs. Glass-bottomed boats allow visitors to see the entrance to the cavern 120 feet below the surface. Wildlife observation boat tours encounter alligators, turtles and a variety of birds.

Daily dawn-dusk.

WHERE TO STAY

DESTIN

★★★HILTON SANDESTIN BEACH GOLF RESORT & SPA

4000 S. Sandestin Blvd., Destin, 850-267-9500, 800-367-1271; www.sandestinbeachhilton.com

The 2,400 acres between the Gulf of Mexico and Choctawatchee Bay are yours at this resort, located 10 miles east of Destin. The all-suite resort offers conference facilities and a private beach. But the best perk is that every suite features a private balcony with an amazing waterfront view. If you're traveling with kids, book one of the Junior Suites, which come with bunk beds.

600 rooms. Restaurant, bar. Business center. Fitness center. Pool. Beach. Golf. Tennis. $151-250

★★★WATERCOLOR INN & RESORT
34 Goldenrod Circle, Santa Rosa Beach, 850-534-5000; www.watercolorinn.com

Architect and designer David Rockwell punches up the classic beach house with a modern, edgy look at Florida's WaterColor Inn & Resort. Snuggled on the sugary-soft beaches of the serene Gulf Coast, this 499-acre mega resort offers something for everyone. Outdoor enthusiasts can kayak, sail, fish or simply splash in the pool (where chilled, mango-scented towels are handed out), while those looking for simple relaxation can head to the spa or shop at the many boutiques. Five restaurants showcase every cuisine.

60 rooms. Restaurant, bar. Fitness center. Pool. Spa. Golf. Tennis. $351 and up

PANAMA CITY

★★★BAY POINT MARRIOTT GOLF RESORT & SPA
4200 Marriott Drive, Panama City Beach, 850-236-6000, 800-644-2650; www.marriottbaypoint.com

Set on 1,100 acres, this resort community overlooks beautiful St. Andrews Bay and has some of the largest meeting spaces in Florida. Try one of the two 18-hole golf courses or water snorkeling, sailing and jet skiing from the white-sand beach.

320 rooms. Restaurant, bar. Business center. Fitness center. Pool. Spa. Golf. Tennis. $61-150

WHERE TO EAT

DESTIN

★★★FISH OUT OF WATER
Watercolor Inn & Resort, 34 Goldenrod Circle, Santa Rosa Beach, 850-534-5008; www.watercolorinn.com

Located within the WaterColor Inn, Fish Out of Water exudes an understated elegance that perfectly complements the beachy, waterfront resort. As its name implies, this restaurant focuses on fish—an ice bar showcases the day's freshest catch, such as panhandle-harvested Apalachicola raw oysters. Sushi is a popular component of the menu, but there are plenty of other tempting dishes, including fresh meats and poultry if you're looking for something besides seafood.

Seafood. Dinner. $36-85

NORTHEAST FLORIDA

The Northeast region offers a little bit of everything. For a beachy getaway, there's Amelia Island, a small barrier island in Florida's northernmost point. It's a quaint spot to enjoy 13 miles of gleaming beaches and unspoiled, natural beauty. Catch views of Cumberland Island and the Georgia coast from Amelia Island. The island itself has a colorful past—it's been part of France, Spain and Mexico, among other countries. On Amelia Island you'll find the charming city of Fernandina Beach, which has a thriving port at its harbor and a 50-block restored Victorian historical district.

For a big-city destination, there's skyscraper-filled Jacksonville. It has everything from the Riverwalk near the St. Johns River, Jacksonville's financial focal point, and the Jacksonville Landing, a festive marketplace with events and entertainment.

HIGHLIGHTS

WHAT ARE THE TOP THINGS TO DO?

HIT MAIN BEACH AT AMELIA ISLAND

Just off the coast of Florida, Amelia Island offers a nice respite thanks to its 13-mile Main Beach. Plant your beach towel in the white sand for the afternoon and when it gets too hot, cool off in the pristine waters.

EXPLORE THE FLORIDA MUSEUM OF NATURAL HISTORY

As the largest natural history center in the southeastern United States, the Florida Museum offers lots to see. Pay a visit to the full-scale North Florida Cave exhibit and the fossil display that boasts 500 remains and artifacts.

GET YOUR GLASS READY FOR THE ANHEUSER-BUSCH JACKSONVILLE BREWERY TOUR

Go behind the scenes on a free tour of this big-name brewery, which makes Budweiser, Busch and Michelob, among other beers. Then comes the best part: when you get a chance to sample some brews.

TAKE IN ART AT THE MUSEUM OF CONTEMPORARY ART JACKSONVILLE

MOCA Jacksonville's permanent collection focuses on work from 1960 onward from noted artists such as Alexander Calder, Alex Katz and Joan Mitchell. One of the highlights is Ed Paschke's futuristic *Malibu*, a portrait with glowing colors and the appearance of a wavering screen.

VISIT THE WORLD GOLF VILLAGE

Duffers will want to spend the day at World Golf Village. There you'll find the World Golf Hall of Fame, championship courses, the PGA Tour Golf Academy, golf-themed restaurants and even a golf IMAX theater

Don't confuse Jacksonville with Jacksonville Beach. About 15 miles east of Jacksonville, "Jax Beach" (as it is often called) has a dual personality; it is a suburban home for many of Jacksonville's commuters, as well as an ocean resort for visitors. With its neighbors—Atlantic Beach, Mayport, Neptune Beach and Ponte Vedra Beach—Jax Beach provides a continuous front of sand and amusement areas.

For an area with a rich past, there's St. Augustine, Florida's most historic city. Spanish towers and steeples, red-capped roofs and low, overhanging balconies are reminders of St. Augustine's four centuries of history. As a symbol of the cultural ties between the United States and Hispanic nations, St. Augustine strives to preserve its Spanish cultural influences.

WHAT TO SEE

AMELIA ISLAND
FERNANDINA BEACH
South 14th Street (between Jasmine Street and Sadler Road), Amelia Island, 904-277-7305; www.fbfl.us

This quaint village within Amelia Island has a long maritime history, which is evident nowadays in its waterfront restaurants and still-thriving shrimping-boat business. The town still boasts lovely Victorian-era architecture, and many of its buildings are listed on the National Register of Historic Places.

GOLFING AT AMELIA ISLAND PLANTATION
6800 First Coast Highway, Amelia Island, 904-261-6161, 888-261-6161; www.aipfl.com

The golfing at the sprawling Amelia Island Plantation resort is a dream for duffers. It features 72 championship holes, and the Tom Fazio-designed, par-72 Long Point course (6,775 yards); the Pete Dye designed, par-72 Oak Marsh course (6,502 yards); and Bobby Weed- and Pete Dye-designed, par-70 Ocean Links course (6,200 yards). Admission: $90-$180, depending on season and number of holes.
Daily 7 a.m.-7 p.m.

MAIN BEACH
Atlantic and N. Fletcher avenues, Amelia Island

This is Amelia Island's longest beach at 13 miles in length. The pretty white sands are a great spot to sunbathe or beachcomb.

FERNANDINA BEACH
AMELIA ISLAND MUSEUM OF HISTORY
233 S. Third St., Fernandina Beach, 904-261-7378; www.ameliamuseum.org

This museum features artifacts and exhibits that recount 400 years of settlement under eight flags. Among the items on display are materials from 17th-century Spanish mission archaeological site, artifacts from 18th-century shipwrecks, and 19th-century "Golden Age" decorative arts and photographs. Docent-guided tours are available.
Admission: adults $7, students and military $4. Monday-Saturday 10 a.m.-4 p.m., Sunday 1-4 p.m.

FERNANDINA BEACH HISTORIC DISTRICT
Bounded by Sixth, Broome, N. Third, Escambia, Seventh, Date and Ash streets, Fernandina Beach; www.ameliaisland.com

This district has been on the National Register of Historic Places since 1973, thanks to its 50-plus blocks of architecturally significant buildings. Highlights include the Fernandina Beach Courthouse (Atlantic Avenue at Fifth Street),

HIGHLIGHT

WHAT IS THERE TO DO ON AMELIA ISLAND?

Amelia Island is best known for its bluff-height dunes and white, wide beaches. The best way to get there is to travel north via Route A1A, which involves taking a car ferry across the mouth of the St. Johns River at the naval town of Mayport. Before you reach Mayport, stop at Kathryn Abbey Hanna Park (904-249-4700), where you can play in the ocean, picnic, kayak, go lake fishing and camp. Past Mayport about two miles on Route A1A, turn off at Fort George Island to see Kingsley Plantation Historic Site (www.nps.gov). Learn how cotton was farmed and tabby houses were built. Little Talbot Island State Park (www.floridastateparks.org) lies a few miles to the north if you are looking for a place on the beach away from the crowds. Be sure to check out the hiking trails previously traveled by early explorers and colonists. Up A1A about six miles, cross the bridge to Amelia Island. Fort Clinch State Park (www.floridastateparks.org), at the island's north end along Route A1A, is a good place to visit the beach and experience some of the island's history. Civil War soldier re-enactors bring history to life and weekend candlelight tours are a hit with visitors. From the fort's embankments, you can see long sweeps of beach and Georgia's Cumberland Island. To reach downtown Fernandina Beach (www. fbfl.us), head west on Atlantic Avenue, which turns into Centre Street, the heart of the historic district. This well-preserved pirate seaport and former playground of the rich showcases a Victorian influence and is known for its bed and breakfast inns. Learn the history on a visit or specialty tour from Amelia Island Museum of History (www.amelia-museum. org) in the old jail. Check out the Palace Saloon, shop in the unique boutiques and fill up on white shrimp, a local specialty. Hook up with a local kayak tour of the salt marshes on the islands leeward side or hire a fishing captain and see what you can catch. *Approximately 55 miles.*

one of the best-preserved Victorian courthouses in Florida, and the entire block of houses at 100 N. Sixth St., which is often referred to as the "Silk Stocking District." The area received the moniker because the original women who lived there were the only ones who could afford expensive silk stockings.

FORT CLINCH STATE PARK
2601 Atlantic Ave., Fernandina Beach, 904-277-7274; www.floridastateparks.org
Found at Florida's most northeastern point, this 1,100-acre park features an old fort with brick ramparts that offer a view of the Georgia shoreline and the Atlantic Ocean. A living history interpretation is provided by park rangers dressed as Union soldiers from the 1864 garrison. Visitors can partake in swimming; fishing from a 1,500-foot pier, the shore and jetties; nature trails, picnicking; and camping.
Admission: $4 per single-occupant vehicle. Daily dawn-dusk.

GAINESVILLE
DEVIL'S MILLHOPPER STATE GEOLOGICAL SITE
4732 Millhopper Road, Gainesville, 352-955-2008; www.floridastateparks.org
This giant sinkhole, at 500 feet wide and 120 feet deep, formed when the roof

of an underground limestone cavern collapsed. The cool environment allows growth of unique lush vegetation. Access to the bottom is by wooden walkway. Nearby is San Felasco Hammock State Preserve, which is home to rare flora and fauna; there are nature trails here as well.

Admission: $2 per vehicle. Wednesday-Sunday 9 a.m.-5 p.m.

FLORIDA MUSEUM OF NATURAL HISTORY

University of Florida, Hull Road at S.W. 34th Street, Gainesville, 352-846-2000; www.flmnh.ufl.edu

This facility is one of the largest museums of natural history in the southeastern United States. It features a full-scale North Florida Cave exhibit, as well as a butterfly aviary (extra fee is charged for entry) and a fossils exhibit where visitors can see 500 fossilized remains and artifacts.

Admission: adults $6, seniors and students $4, children 3-12 $2, children 2 and under free. Monday-Saturday 10 a.m.-5 p.m., Sunday 1-5 p.m.

GINNIE SPRINGS

7300 N.E. Ginnie Springs Road, Gainesville, 386-454-7188; www.ginniespringsoutdoors.com

These springs are a tranquil spot in which to camp or hike. For an extra dose of relaxation, rent tubes and float down the natural lazy river—it takes about two hours to leisurely glide from beginning to end.

Admission: adults $12, children 7-14 $3, children 6 and under free. Monday-Thursday 8 a.m.-6 p.m., Friday-Saturday 8 a.m.-10 p.m., Sunday 8 a.m.-7 p.m.

KANAPAHA BOTANICAL GARDENS

4700 S.W. 58th Drive, Gainesville, 352-372-4981; www.kanapaha.org

Stroll around this 62-acre botanical garden to see a butterfly garden, an expansive bamboo garden, a hummingbird garden, a large herb garden and more. The gardens burst into their most colorful June to September; during that time, gorgeous Asian plants such as huge water lilies can be seen.

Admission: adults $6, children 6-13 $3, children 6 and under free. Monday-Wednesday, Friday 9 a.m.-5 p.m., Saturday-Sunday 9 a.m.-dusk.

JACKSONVILLE

ANHEUSER-BUSCH JACKSONVILLE BREWERY TOUR

111 Busch Drive, Jacksonville, 904-696-8373; www.budweisertours.com

Tampa might have Busch Gardens, but Jacksonville is home to this beer-making giant's Florida brewing operations. The complimentary tour takes visitors behind the scenes at this Anheuser-Busch brewery, and anyone older than 21 can sample beer in the Hospitality Room, where you can sample beers, including seasonal brews and new products.

January-December, Monday-Saturday 10 a.m.-4 p.m.

ATLANTIC BEACH

Beach Avenue between Atlantic Boulevard and 19th Street, Atlantic Beach; www.ci.atlantic-beach.fl.us

Atlantic Beach—a shimmering stretch of sand located in the Jacksonville suburb of the same name—is a pretty place for catching rays or playing in the tranquil surf.

CUMMER MUSEUM OF ART & GARDENS

829 Riverside Ave., Jacksonville, 904-356-6857; www.cummer.org

This museum contains 14 galleries and the Tudor Room from the original Cummer Mansion. The mansion's formal gardens were retained as the setting for the gallery. The collection ranges from ancient Egypt to the 20th century and features 700 pieces of early Meissen porcelain and important American paintings. There are also interactive exhibits on hand.

Admission: adults $10, seniors, students and military $6, children 5 and under free. Free Tuesday 4-9 p.m. Tuesday, Thursday 10 a.m.-9 p.m., Wednesday, Friday-Saturday 10 a.m.-5 p.m., Sunday noon-5 p.m.

JACKSONVILLE JAGUARS

Jacksonville Municipal Stadium, 1 Stadium Place, Jacksonville, 904-633-6000; www.jaguars.com

Jacksonville's professional NFL football team calls Jacksonville Municipal Stadium home.

Admission: varies by game; check website for pricing and schedule.

THE JACKSONVILLE LANDING

2 Independent Drive, Jacksonville, 904-353-1188; www.jacksonvillelanding.com

This dining, shopping and entertainment complex sits along the north bank of the St. Johns River. The complex features more than 60 stores and restaurants, plus a courtyard with a stage where live music shows are staged weekly. You'll find shops such as a Nine West Outlet, The Toy Factory and soaps store Lina M. Bath Boutique.

Mall: Monday-Thursday 10 a.m.-8 p.m., Friday-Saturday 10 a.m.-9 p.m., Sunday noon-5:30 p.m.; restaurants and bars: varies by location.

JACKSONVILLE ZOO AND GARDENS

8605 Zoo Parkway, Jacksonville, 904-757-4462; www.jaxzoo.org

This zoo is home to more than 700 mammals, birds and reptiles, all inhabiting natural environments along the Trout River. There are daily animal shows, plus a restaurant on the premises. Be sure to stop by Tuxedo Coast to see the cute Magellanic penguins splash around. The Botanical Gardens feature flora in beautifully manicured landscapes, such as the Asian Bamboo Garden and the Themed Pocket Gardens, which are tied to the animal exhibits of the zoo.

Admission: adults $13, seniors $11, children 3-12 $8, children 2 and under free. Daily 9 a.m.-5 p.m.

KINGSLEY PLANTATION

11676 Palmetto Ave., Jacksonville, 904-251-3537; www.nps.gov

This plantation house was built in the 1790s by slave trader Zephaniah Kingsley. You can tour the house and grounds, which include the slave quarters, a barn and gardens, all of which reflect 19th-century life on a Sea Island cotton plantation.

Daily 9 a.m.-5 p.m.

KONA SKATEPARK

8739 Kona Ave., Jacksonville, 904-725-8770, 866-758-5662; www.konaskatepark.com

For the X-treme games-obsessed, it doesn't get better than this skate park. It was built in 1977, and remains one of most popular parks in Florida, thanks to its challenging amenities, such as an 80-foot-wide ramp and snake runs, among others. No wonder the park has been name-checked by skateboarder Tony

Hawk. You can in-line skate, or rent equipment.

Admission: $5-10, free for seniors. Monday-Friday 1-10 p.m., Saturday 10 a.m.-10 p.m., Sunday noon-9 p.m.

LITTLE TALBOT ISLAND STATE PARK

12157 Heckscher Drive, Jacksonville, 904-251-2320; www.floridastateparks.org

More than 2,500 acres of wide Atlantic beaches and extensive salt marshes teem with life, including migrating birds and sea turtles. The disparate terrain includes sand dunes and forests. Swimming, surfing, fishing, picnicking, playground, camping are all allowed onsite.

MUSEUM OF CONTEMPORARY ART JACKSONVILLE

333 N. Laura St., Jacksonville, 904-366-6911; www.mocajacksonville.org

MOCA Jacksonville showcases modern art from international and regional artists. The museum is inside a rehabbed Western Union Telegraph Building and features a permanent collection as well as rotating exhibits. Artists on view in the permanent collection include Alexander Calder, Alex Katz, James Rosenquist and Joan Mitchell.

Admission: adults $8, seniors, students and military $5, children 2 and under free. Free Sunday and first Wednesday of the month from 5-9 p.m. for Artwalk. Tuesday-Saturday 10 a.m.-4 p.m., Thursday 10 a.m.-8 p.m., Sunday noon-4 p.m.

MUSEUM OF SCIENCE AND HISTORY

1025 Museum Circle, Jacksonville, 904-396-6674; www.themosh.org

This museum features interactive exhibits on science, marine mammals and north Florida history, including the natural and physical sciences, wildlife and Native Americans. Check out the Civil War artifacts from battleship Maple Leaf. Entry includes reduced admission to the planetarium, and science shows.

Admission: adults $9, seniors and military $7.50, children 3-12 $7. Monday-Friday 10 a.m.-5 p.m., Saturday 10 a.m.-6 p.m., Sunday 1-6 p.m.

JACKSONVILLE BEACH

ADVENTURE LANDING AND SHIPWRECK ISLAND WATERPARK

1944 Beach Blvd., Jacksonville Beach, 904-246-4386; www.adventurelanding.com

This theme park takes a two-prong approach to fun: Adventure Landing offers mini golf, laser tag and go-karts year-round, while Shipwreck Island Waterpark boasts tons of water slides and rides to keep you cool in summer.

Admission: Adventure Landing: varies by attraction; Shipwreck Island Waterpark: adults $30, children $25, children 3 and under free. Hours vary by season.

ST. AUGUSTINE

CASTILLO DE SAN MARCOS NATIONAL MONUMENT

1 S. Castillo Drive, St. Augustine, 904-829-6506; www.nps.gov

This massive masonry structure constructed between 1672 and 1695 was built to permanently replace a succession of nine wooden fortifications. Hispanic artisans and convicts, Native American laborers, black royal slaves and English prisoners erected walls 26 feet high, 14 feet thick at the base, 9 feet at the top and 4 feet at the parapet. Before completion in 1683, Castillo served as St. Augustine's citadel during a pirate raid.

FOUNTAIN OF YOUTH

11 Magnolia Ave., St. Augustine, 904-829-3168, 800-356-8222; www.fountainofyouthflorida.com

This 15-acre tropical setting is thought to be the first recorded North American landmark. While this place likely won't ward off wrinkles, it does have Native American burial grounds, a planetarium and a discovery globe (both featuring continuous shows), a museum and a swan pool. In keeping with history of the spot, there is also a Ponce de Leon statue on the grounds.

Daily 9 a.m.-5 p.m.

LIGHTNER MUSEUM

75 King St., St. Augustine, 904-824-2874; www.lightnermuseum.org

This museum celebrating the Victorian era is set in the restored 300-room former Hotel Alcazar, a Spanish Renaissance-style structure built in 1887 by the architects who went on to build the New York Public Library and the U.S. Senate building. The museum offers natural science exhibits, a Victorian village as well as collections of art, porcelain, 19th-century musical instruments, needlework, ceramics, Tiffany glass, furniture and dolls.

Daily 9 a.m.-5 p.m.

MISSION OF NOMBRE DE DIOS

27 Ocean Ave., St. Augustine, 904-824-2809, 800-342-6529; www.missionandshrine.org

A 208-foot stainless-steel cross marks the site of the founding of St. Augustine on September 8, 1565. You'll also find the Shrine of Our Lady of La Leche, established in 1603 and dedicated to the Motherhood of Mary.

ST. AUGUSTINE ALLIGATOR FARM

999 Anastasia Blvd., St. Augustine, 904-824-3337; www.alligatorfarm.com

This farm, established in 1893, has tropical birds, monkeys, deer and ducks. But the reason to visit is that it provides close-up views of huge alligators and crocodiles.

Daily 9 a.m.-5 p.m.

ST. AUGUSTINE LIGHTHOUSE AND MUSEUM

81 Lighthouse Ave., St. Augustine, 904-829-0745; www.staugustinelighthouse.com

The property allows tours of the restored lightkeeper's house. There is also a coastal museum with exhibits. Climb to the top of lighthouse tower for a nice view.

THE WORLD GOLF VILLAGE

1 World Golf Place, St. Augustine Beach, 904-940-4000; www.wgv.com

Home to the World Golf Hall of Fame, this venue is a golfer's mecca, with interactive exhibits, an IMAX golf theater, a golf school and a golf course and resort. There are also souvenir shops and restaurants.

WHERE TO STAY

★★★AMELIA ISLAND PLANTATION INN

6800 First Coast Highway, Amelia Island, 904-261-6161, 888-261-6161; www.aipfl.com

This 1,350-acre resort with panoramic views of the Atlantic Ocean is not just pretty—it's also green. Environmentally friendly initiatives range from energy-efficient light bulbs to recycling options in all rooms. To further pay homage to Mother Earth, there's even a nature center on the grounds. The resort features guest rooms and separate villas, as well as individualized recreation programs. Speaking of recreation, the resort offers 72 championship holes of golf. But kids will be more interested in the game room with air hockey, billiards, foosball and arcade games.

905 rooms. Restaurant, bar. Business center. Fitness center. Pool. Spa. Golf. Tennis. $151-250

★★★ELIZABETH POINTE LODGE
98 S. Fletcher Ave., Amelia Island, 904-277-4851, 800-772-3359; www.elizabethpointelodge.com

The oceanfront main house at this popular inn is 1890s "Nantucket Shingle" style, with a wraparound porch and plenty of rocking chairs. Sway back and forth on the chairs while watching the tide roll in or sipping some lemonade, which is served each afternoon on the porch and beach. In the evenings, you can switch to the complimentary wine and hors d'oeuvres. The cozy living room features floor-to-ceiling bookcases and an old stone fireplace. The Ocean House has large, luxurious suites, and the property is just minutes from historic Fernandina Beach.

20 rooms. Complimentary breakfast. Beach. $251-350

★★★FLORIDA HOUSE INN
20-22 S. Third St., Fernandina Beach, 904-261-3300, 800-258-3301; www.floridahouseinn.com

This inn, located in the historic Fernandina Beach district of Amelia Island, is Florida's oldest hotel still in operation—in fact, it is on the National Register of Historic Places. Open since 1857, the inn features rooms decorated with antiques but updated with crisp white linens and colorful quilts. Some rooms even boast fireplaces and antique claw-foot baths, and all have access to spacious porches. What's more, guests can look into the hotel's complimentary scooter service for a charming ride on the town. Get back just in time for cocktails at the small pub, the Frisky Mermaid.

25 rooms. Restaurant, bar. Pets accepted. $251-350

★★★★THE RITZ-CARLTON, AMELIA ISLAND
4750 Amelia Island Parkway, Amelia Island, 904-277-1100, 800-241-3333; www.ritzcarlton.com

This resort captures the essence of magical Amelia Island, where time seems to stand still. The guest rooms are decorated with Florida-chic floral prints, and all offer gorgeous coastal or ocean views. Spend the day by the beach, or try tennis, golf, horseback riding or sailing, which the concierge desk can help you arrange. Fernandina Beach, Amelia Island's quaint Victorian-era neighborhood with specialty boutiques, is just down the road. The resort's outstanding restaurants (including one with a poolside veranda) and lounges serve up a variety of specialties with a focus on seafood.

444 rooms. Restaurant, bar. Business center. Fitness center. Pool. Spa. Golf. $251-350

FERNANDINA BEACH
★★★GREYFIELD INN
6 N. Second St., Fernandina Beach, 904-261-6408, 866-410-8051; www.greyfieldinn.com

To truly get away from it all, escape to the historic Greyfield Inn, built in 1900. Accessible by private ferry from Fernandina Beach, this inn is a tranquil place to enjoy Cumberland Island's natural beauty and abundant wildlife, including wild horses and many species of birds. Furnished with family heirlooms and antiques, the guest rooms and suites vary (not all have private baths). Room rates include breakfast, picnic lunch, gourmet dinner (jacket required) and snacks throughout the day, as well as unlimited use of the inn's sporting, fishing and beach equipment. A two-night minimum stay is required.

17 rooms. Restaurant, bar. Fitness center. No children under 6 years. $351 and up

JACKSONVILLE
★★★CROWNE PLAZA
1201 Riverplace Blvd., Jacksonville, 904-398-8800; www.crowneplaza.com

Conveniently located on the south bank of the St. Johns River on Riverplace Boulevard, this 10-story downtown hotel is just a short stroll from many area attractions. The simply decorated, elegantly furnished rooms feature walkout balconies and large, comfortable beds. The square-shaped pool overlooks the St. Johns River and has its own seasonal bar, Breezers.

292 rooms. Restaurant, bar. Business center. Fitness center. Pool. $151-250

★★★OMNI JACKSONVILLE HOTEL
245 Water St., Jacksonville, 904-355-6664, 800-843-6664; www.omnihotels.com

The heated rooftop pool and sundeck overlooking the St. Johns River are not to be missed during a stay at this high-rise hotel in downtown Jacksonville. Luxuriously decorated rooms have pillow-top mattresses, duvets, velvet pillows and plush chairs. You can take a water taxi to nearby attractions, and the hotel is close to The Jacksonville Landing shopping center. The large guest rooms feature comfortable bedding and plush bathrobes, plus your choice of foam or feather pillows.

354 rooms. Restaurant, bar. Business center. Fitness center. Pool. Pets accepted. $151-250

JACKSONVILLE BEACH
★★★THE LODGE & CLUB AT PONTE VEDRA BEACH
607 Ponte Vedra Blvd., Ponte Vedra Beach, 904-273-9500, 800-243-4304; www.pvresorts.com

Capitalizing on the historic charm of the coastal community of Ponte Vedra Beach, The Lodge &

WHAT ARE THE BEST BEACHFRONT HOTELS?

Amelia Island Plantation Inn:
You'll get great views of the Atlantic Ocean at this resort. If you really want to take in all of the natural beauty around the hotel, take an environmental tour with one of the on-staff naturalists.

Elizabeth Pointe Lodge:
At Elizabeth Pointe Lodge, there's a number of ways to enjoy the beautiful view: Sit in the big rocking chairs in the wrap-around porch, eat breakfast in the sunroom or use the complimentary beach chairs and umbrellas to spend the day in the sand.

Ponte Vedra Inn & Club:
This 300-acre resort sits along picturesque Ponte Vedra Beach. Even if you don't feel like going in the ocean, you can enjoy the scenery from one of the resort's four oceanfront pools.

The Ritz-Carlton, Amelia Island:
The Ritz-Carlton overlooks Amelia Island's 13 miles of lovely beaches. What's even better is that every room comes a private balcony that offers stunning coastal or ocean views.

Club at Ponte Vedra Beach is designed to resemble a European seaside resort. This sister property to the Ponte Vedra Inn & Club has a Mediterranean flair—all of the rooms and suites overlook the ocean and feature patios or balconies with striking views of the water. Rooms and suites are large, and feature lovely touches, such as four-poster beds and drapes made from imported European fabrics. A sophisticated selection of restaurants and bars awaits diners at the Lodge.

66 rooms. Restaurant, bar. Business center. Fitness center. Pool. Spa. Golf. Tennis. $61-150

★★★PONTE VEDRA INN & CLUB

200 Ponte Vedra Blvd., Ponte Vedra Beach, 904-285-1111, 800-234-7842; www.pvresorts.com

Open since 1928, this inn, part of the 300-acre Ponte Vedra Resort (which also includes the Lodge & Club), is a traditionalist's haven. The guest rooms and suites pay tribute to classic Floridian décor, with pastel tones, light woods and floral fabrics. The resort offers tennis, golf, horseback riding, water sports, cycling, fishing and sailing. Spend the day sunning by one of the four ocean-front pools or indulging in a treatment at the spa. Multiple restaurants offer everything from snacks and cocktails to gourmet meals.

250 rooms. Restaurant, bar. Business center. Fitness center. Pool. Spa. Golf. Tennis. $151-250

★★★SAWGRASS MARRIOTT RESORT & BEACH/CLUB

1000 PGA Tour Blvd., Ponte Vedra Beach, 904-285-7777, 800-457-4653; www.marriott.com

A getaway for the entire family, this resort offers 99 holes of golf and is the official course of the Players Championship. Rooms have large beds, with mounds of plush pillows and floor-to-ceiling windows that let in plenty of sunshine. After a day out on the green, take some time for yourself at the day spa, which features East Indian-inspired treatments like the Bindi, an exfoliation using Ayurvedic oils and herbs. The location is convenient to historic St. Augustine and Jacksonville.

485 rooms. Restaurant, bar. Business center. Fitness center. Pool. Spa. Pets accepted. Golf. Tennis. $61-150

ST. AUGUSTINE

★★★CASA MONICA HOTEL

95 Cordova St., St. Augustine, 904-827-1888, 800-648-1888; www.casamonica.com

Part of Marriott's new autograph collection of hotels, this Spanish-style hotel dates back to 1888 but has been restored to its former glory. Moorish details enhance the rooms and suites, and all accommodations are outfitted with the amenities to make you feel like you're at home, like triple-sheeted beds, bathrobes and a Bose sound system with CDs. The city-center location does not preclude a visit to the beach because all guests are granted privileges at the nearby Serenata Beach Club. Tee times at local courses can also be easily arranged.

138 rooms. Restaurant, bar. Fitness center. Pool. $151-250

★★★GRANDE VILLAS AT WORLD GOLF VILLAGE

100 Front Nine Drive, St. Augustine, 904-940-2000; www.wgv.com

Golf fanatics will deem this hotel up to par. It's part of the World Golf Village complex, which is also home to the World Golf Hall of Fame, courses designed by Hall of Famers and the PGA Tour Golf Academy, where you can get lessons from the pros. The hotel has one- or two-bedroom villas with fully equipped kitchens as well as washers and dryers. Rooms overlook the 17th and 18th holes of the famed Slammer and Squire golf course.

104 rooms. Restaurant, bar. Business center. Fitness center. Pool. Spa. $61-150

★★★RENAISSANCE WORLD GOLF VILLAGE RESORT

500 S. Legacy Trail, St. Augustine, 904-940-8000, 888-740-7020; www.worldgolfrenaissance.com

The atrium lobby and rooms at this sprawling hotel have an Asian influence. The rooms come with 37-inch flat-panel television, wet bars and refrigerators. But the hotel's best amenity is that it has the only course to be codesigned by Jack Nicklaus and Arnold Palmer. The World Golf Hall of Fame also is on the premises.

301 rooms. Restaurant, bar. Business center. Fitness center. Pool. $151-250

WHERE TO EAT

AMELIA ISLAND

★★★SALT: THE GRILL AT THE RITZ-CARLTON

4750 Amelia Island Parkway, Amelia Island, 904-277-1028, 800-241-3333; www.ritzcarlton.com

A restaurant with the word "grill" in its name may sound like a local joint where burgers and fries are the specialties. The food at Salt, however, is decidedly more refined. The menu changes weekly, but it's typically full of seasonal, regional American fare tinged with global flavors with plenty of grilled fish, meat and vegetarian options. The formal dining room has views of the Atlantic, which makes a seat at a window table a worthwhile choice. The wine list features approximately 500 selections to match any taste.

Contemporary American. Dinner, Sunday brunch. Bar. Reservations recommended. Closed Monday. $36-85

FERNANDINA BEACH

★★★BEECH STREET GRILL

801 Beech St., Fernandina Beach, 904-277-3662; www.beechstreetgrill.com

Built in 1889, the house in which this restaurant is located has been fully restored, and contains many intimate dining areas and fireplaces. Beech Street's menu also boasts fresh local seafood and seasonal ingredients, which blend together nicely in outstanding dishes like the herb-citrus panko-crusted Chilean sea bass, seared tuna served over jasmine-coconut sticky rice, and seared peppered lamb loin with black-truffle butter. There's live piano on Saturday, which pairs nicely with the extensive wine list and cocktails.

Seafood. Dinner. Children's menu. Bar. $36-85

JACKSONVILLE

★★★BISTRO AIX

1440 San Marco Blvd., Jacksonville, 904-398-1949; www.bistrox.com

Watch chefs at work in the exhibition kitchen at this restaurant, where the menu changes seasonally. Recently, the menu included items such as mussels and lamb shank, alongside wood-fired pizzas like the scampi with shrimp, pesto, sweet onions, tomatoes and spinach. Located in the historic downtown San Marco district of Jacksonville, the restaurant has an authentic French bistro feel.

Mediterranean, French. Lunch, dinner. Outdoor seating. Bar. $36-85

★★★MATTHEW'S
2107 Hendricks Ave., Jacksonville, 904-396-9922; www.matthewsrestaurant.com

Treat yourself to a meal at chef/owner Matthew Medure's namesake restaurant and experience the palate-pleasing European-influenced food that has been drawing diners for more than 10 years. The sleek dining room, decorated in soft moss tones with terrazzo floors inlaid with bronze, was originally built as a bank in the 1920s. The chef selects organically grown vegetables and attempts to source most produce and meat from local boutique farms. The resulting food is thoughtful and complex. The wine list offers more than 420 selections, and the staff is gifted at helping with pairings.

Mediterranean. Dinner. Closed Sunday. Reservations recommended. Bar. $36-85

★★★MORTON'S, THE STEAKHOUSE
1510 Riverplace Blvd., Jacksonville, 904-399-3933; www.mortons.com

This popular steak house, a chain started in Chicago, offers dark wood paneling, gold fabric-designed booths and glass signature windows that separate the dining area from the bar. Wine displays and the golf art on the walls add to the steak house décor. Pick any of the steaks on the menu—chances are, whether you order the Chicago-style bone-in rib-eye, the porterhouse steak or double-cut filet mignon, the beef will be done to perfection and brought out by efficient, attentive waiters. Save room for dessert—the ones at Morton's are rich and decadent, just like the entrées.

Steak, seafood. Dinner. Reservations recommended. Bar. $36-85

SPA

AMELIA ISLAND
★★★★THE RITZ-CARLTON SPA, AMELIA ISLAND
The Ritz-Carlton, Amelia Island, 4750 Amelia Island Parkway, Amelia Island, 904-277-1087; www.ritzcarlton.com

You're simply bound to relax at this tranquil spa. The 27,500-square-foot space utilizes the private sanctuary that is Amelia Island to create a peaceful and luxurious oasis. Details are meticulously accounted for, from a plunge pool with underwater music to spa butlers on hand. If you're in the mood for a rubdown but hesitate to give up your beachfront perch, try the Heaven in a Hammock massage, where a therapist will work out tension while the ocean breeze lulls you into an even more restful state. Other treatments include a signature Sea Creations facial, which uses sea silk, pearl proteins and other oceanic elements to combat aging, and a honey butter wrap that incorporates a soothing warm oil scalp massage. You'll also find seasonal indulges such as champagne treatments during the holidays and chocolate ones come February.

JACKSONVILLE BEACH
★★★THE SPA AT PONTE VEDRA INN & CLUB
200 Ponte Vedra Blvd., Ponte Vedra Beach, 904-273-7700; www.pvresorts.com

When your golf or tennis game has worn you out, the Spa at Ponte Vedra is a perfect place to unwind. This spa is a celebration of the classics. An extensive spa menu has 100 different options, from massages and body therapies to facials and salon services. Treat tired muscles to a Swedish, an aromatherapy, a maternity or a reflexology massage. Pampering manicures and pedicures incorporate pressure-point therapy, exfoliating sea salts or paraffin dips.

TAMPA BAY AREA

The Tampa Bay area is chockfull of things to do. Travelers come for the golf, museums, shopping and even its big theme park. Located on the Manatee River, Bradenton provides access to river, bay and Gulf fishing, as well as 20 miles of white-sand beaches. The town is mostly residential, and it's a good jumping-off point for visiting several national parks.

Clearwater is the smallest of the cities in the Tampa Bay area, though it is still a destination for tourists who flock here for its white-sand beaches. It has retained its quiet feel despite a rapid population growth in the past several years. Clearwater is the perfect jumping-off point for exploring neighbor cities St. Petersburg and Tampa. Folks head to the latter two to check out major attractions such as Busch Gardens, Tampa Bay and Adventure Island.

Just west of Clearwater is Clearwater Beach, a four-mile-long island of white-sand beaches that's connected to the mainland by Memorial Causeway. The beach extends the length of the island and varies between 350 and 1,700 feet wide. There is a fishing pier, and the marina has slips, docks, boat rentals, sailing and a sports-fishing fleet. Skin diving and shelling are also popular activities.

The fourth-largest city in the state and second only to Miami as a winter resort, St. Petersburg hosts more than a million visitors each year. It draws golf and boating enthusiasts throughout the year but also has the appeal of a larger city with its service and nearby high-tech industries. St. Petersburg has a fringe of beaches, parks and yacht basins along Tampa Bay and a string of resort-occupied islands (connected to the mainland by causeways) on the Gulf side, across Boca Ciega Bay. These islands form the St. Pete Beach Area.

Tourism is the main industry in Sarasota—and that has been true since the days before a single house was built, when anglers used to pitch tents on the beach. The standard Florida attractions of beach, fishing, golf and sunbathing are available here, and the city has more than earned its claim as "the cradle of golf" since the first Florida course was laid out here in 1886 by Col. J. Hamilton Gillespie. But ever since John Ringling selected the Sarasota as winter quarters for his circus (1929-1959), the two have become synonymous. Ringling did much to develop and beautify the area and surrounding islands.

The business and vacation hub of Florida's West Coast, Tampa is Florida's third-largest city. Within it you'll find Ybor City, a Spanish, Cuban and Italian enclave of narrow streets and cigar makers.

WHAT TO SEE

BRADENTON
DE SOTO NATIONAL MEMORIAL
De Soto Memorial Highway and 83rd Street N.W., Bradenton, 941-792-0458; www.nps.gov
At a spot believed to be somewhere near this memorial, Don Hernando de Soto

landed on May 30, 1539, with more than 600 conquistadors to begin the first European expedition into the interior of what is now the Southeastern United States. In a 4,000-mile, four-year wilderness odyssey, de Soto and his army explored beyond the Mississippi, staking out claims to a vast empire for Spain. The visitor center has weapons, armor and a film depicting the de Soto era.

Daily 9 a.m.-5 p.m.

GAMBLE PLANTATION HISTORIC STATE PARK

3708 Patten Ave., Ellenton, 941-723-4536; www.floridastateparks.org

This park is home to a Confederate memorial and the only surviving antebellum house in South Florida. Major Robert Gamble ran a 3,500-acre sugar plantation and refinery here. In May 1865, Judah P. Benjamin, secretary of state to the Confederacy, fled to the plantation to hide from Union troops. The restored mansion, which you can access only during tours, is furnished with period pieces.

Tours: adults $5, children $3. Daily 9 a.m.-5 p.m.

MANATEE VILLAGE HISTORICAL PARK

1404 Manatee Ave. E., Bradenton, 941-741-4075; www.manateeclerk.com

This park contains renovated historic buildings from the 19th and early-20th centuries, such as Manatee County's first courthouse, the Old Meeting Church, a one-room schoolhouse, a potter barn, a smokehouse and a sugar mill. The Stephens House, built in the "cracker Gothic" architectural style, is a good example of a pre-World War I Florida rural farmhouse.

Monday-Friday, and second and fourth Saturday of the month 9 a.m.-4:30 p.m.

CLEARWATER

CALADESI ISLAND STATE PARK

El Dorado and Mandalay avenues, Clearwater; www.floridastateparks.org

Caladesi is well-known for its gorgeous shores, frequently topping lists as one of the U.S.'s best beaches. It's also one of the few natural islands on Florida's west coast. Aside from sunbathing, visitors can fish from their boats, kayak through mangroves or hike three-mile-long wildlife trail. The park is one mile west of Dunedin off the Gulf Coast.

Admission: $4. Daily 8 a.m.-dusk.

CLEARWATER BEACH

Two miles west of downtown on State Road 60; www.myclearwater.com

This outstanding city beach is lauded as one of the best in the country. It's actually on a small island between the Gulf of Mexico and the Clearwater Harbor. The beach itself is three miles long, and home to Pier 60, which extends 300 yards into the Gulf and hosts a free sundown event nightly with buskers, live music and artisans. To make the most of the water, you can charter a deep-sea fishing boat, rent fishing rods or sign up for an adventure or dinner cruise.

Daily until dark; 9:30 a.m.-4:30 p.m.

FLORIDA BOTANICAL GARDENS

Pinewood Cultural Park, 12520 Ulmerton Road, Largo, 727-582-2100; www.flbg.org

Although these gardens are a little bit out of the way from Clearwater, it's worth a drive just to take in the tropical Gulf Coast foliage. The grounds are home

HIGHLIGHTS

WHAT ARE THE TOP MUSEUMS?

RINGLING MUSEUM OF ART AND RINGLING RESIDENCE

Here you'll find the estate of circus maestro John Ringling, as in Ringling Bros. and Barnum & Bailey. Within the grounds there's also a Circus Museum with old costumes and other big-top memorabilia.

SALVADOR DALI MUSEUM

This new building is a work of art itself, with a geodesic glass shell running along the concrete façade. Inside it, you'll find the world's largest and most highly acclaimed works by surrealist master Salvador Dali.

SARASOTA CLASSIC CAR MUSEUM

More than 100 antique rides are parked here, the second-oldest continuously operating antique car museum in the U.S. It showcases antique, exotic, European and one-of-a-kind classics in rotating exhibits. Check out John Lennon's '56 Bentley.

to more than 30 acres of landscaped gardens and 90 acres of local natural habitats like wetlands. The grounds include a butterfly garden, palm garden, tropical courtyard and more. Kids can look for wildlife using binoculars and learn about fruit in the fruit garden. The free admission also makes it a family friendly activity.
Daily 7 a.m.-7 p.m.

HERITAGE VILLAGE

Pinewood Cultural Park, 11909 125th St. N., Largo, 727-582-2123; www.pinellascounty.org

Touting itself as a "living history museum," this 21-acre, open-air compound features more than 28 historic buildings such as a school, church and sponge warehouse. There are also live demonstrations throughout the grounds, such as palm-frond weaving and rope-making. The visitor center showcases historical artifacts, and the library houses 3,500 books, periodicals and photographs that shed light on local history.
Tuesday-Saturday 10 a.m.-4 p.m., Sunday 1-4 p.m.

MOCCASIN LAKE NATURE PARK

2750 Park Trail Lane, Clearwater, 727-462-6024; www.myclearwater.com

This environmental and energy education center consists of a 51-acre wilderness preserve, a five-acre lake, nature trails and boardwalks. Partake in bird walks and bird-watching tours, and see native wildlife and plant exhibits, such as a songbird aviary and a butterfly garden. Guided tours are available by appointment.

Admission: adults $3, children 3-12 $2, children 3 and under free. Tuesday-Friday 9 a.m.-5 p.m., Saturday 10 a.m.-6 p.m.

SAND KEY BEACH AND PARK
South of Clearwater Pass Bridge, off Gulf Boulevard; www.pinellascounty.org

Sand Key is the 14-mile stretch of land dotted with several beaches, including Clearwater Beach. Sand Key Beach features a wide swath of white sand and the calm waters of the Gulf, plus cabana-rental facilities, nine outdoor showers and two bath houses. The park portion of Sand Key has a picnic area, grills and even a dog park, providing for a much more outdoorsy experience.

7 a.m.-sunset.

CLEARWATER BEACH
CLEARWATER MARINE AQUARIUM
249 Windward Passage, Clearwater Beach, 727-441-1790, 888-239-9414; www.seewinter.com

This is one of only three facilities on Florida's expansive west coast equipped for the rescue and treatment of marine mammals and sea turtles. You can learn about the aquarium's rescue work with a film in the Atlantis Theater. But you can see the recuperating critters up close as well. Visit the dolphins, otters, sharks and sea turtles in the aquarium. The aquarium also has research laboratories and educational programs.

Admission: adults $11, seniors $9, children 3-12 $7.50. Monday-Thursday 9 a.m.-5 p.m., Friday-Saturday 9 a.m.-7 p.m., Sunday 10 a.m.-5 p.m.

SUNSETS AT PIER 60
Pier 60 Park, Clearwater Beach, 727-449-1036; www.sunsetsatpier60.com

This event began as a casual sundown get-together in 1994, but by 1998, it was a nightly affair. Nowadays, you can catch artists, crafters, performers and musicians any day of the week at Pier 60 as they celebrate the setting of the sun.

Daily, 3:30-7:30 p.m.

ST. PETERSBURG
THE PIER
800 Second Ave. N.E., St. Petersburg, 727-821-6164; www.stpete-pier.com

A five-story inverted pyramid at the end of this quarter-mile pier contains an observation deck with views of the city, restaurants, shops and an aquarium. The pier offers special events and daily entertainment. Activities include fishing, boating and water sports.

Monday-Thursday 10 a.m.-8 p.m., Friday-Saturday 10 a.m.-9 p.m., Sunday 11 a.m.-7 p.m.

ST. PETERSBURG MUSEUM OF FINE ARTS
255 Beach Drive N.E., St. Petersburg, 727-896-2667; www.fine-arts.org

The museum features pre-Columbian, European, American, Asian, African paintings and sculpture, decorative arts and photography. One of its most popular pieces is Georgia O'Keeffe's bold *Poppy*. Be sure to check out the galleries devoted to photography and Steuben glass and the sculpture gardens.

Admission: adults $16, seniors $14, children $10, children 6 and under free. Tuesday-Saturday 10 a.m.-5 p.m., Sunday 1-5 p.m.

SALVADOR DALI MUSEUM

1000 Third St. S., St. Petersburg, 727-823-3767; www.salvadordalimuseum.org

This new museum overlooking Tampa Bay houses the world's largest and most highly acclaimed collection of works by famous Spanish artist Salvador Dalí. The ultramodern building befits the surrealist masterpieces inside of it. A geodesic glass shell snakes along the large concrete structure's façade and is a sight unto itself. The museum features oils, drawings, watercolors, graphics and sculptures from 1914 to 1980, and you can catch Dalí's films inside an onsite theater.

Admission: adults $17, seniors $14.50, children $4, children 4 and under free. Monday-Wednesday 10 a.m.-5:30 p.m., Thursday 10 a.m.-8 p.m., Friday-Saturday 10:30 a.m.-5:30 p.m., Sunday noon-5:30 p.m.

SUNKEN GARDENS

1825 Fourth St. N., St. Petersburg, 727-551-3102; www.stpete.org/sunken

Stroll among waterfalls, gardens and more than 50,000 tropical plants and flowers in Florida's oldest living museum. The more than 100-year-old garden is home to some of the oldest tropical plants in the region. Stop by the butterfly garden to see colorful swarms of the fluttering insects.

Admission: adults $8, seniors $6, children $4, children under 2 free. Monday-Saturday 10 a.m.-4:30 p.m., Sunday noon-4:30 p.m.

SARASOTA

RINGLING MUSEUM OF ART AND RINGLING RESIDENCE (CA'D'ZAN)

5401 Bay Shore Road, Sarasota, 941-359-5700; www.ringling.org

The "Ringling" of this museum's name is courtesy of John Ringling, the person responsible for uniting the Ringling Bros. and Barnum & Bailey circuses into the "Greatest Show on Earth." In the Circus Museum, you'll find big-top memorabilia, including performers' costumes and retro circus posters. But the 66-acre Ringling estate isn't just a freak show. It's a cultural complex that features the family's elaborate Venetian Gothic mansion, an art museum filled with works from Old Masters like El Greco, a sculpture courtyard and a rose garden.

Admission: adults $25, seniors $20, children $10, children under 6 free. Daily 10 a.m.-5:30 p.m.

SARASOTA ART GALLERY

707 N. Tamiami Trail, Sarasota, 941-365-2032; www.artsarasota.org

This Italian Renaissance-style villa was created by local crafters with shiploads of columns, doorways, roof sculptures and marble collected in Italy by John Ringling. The gallery features one of the most distinguished collections of Baroque art in the Western Hemisphere. There is also contemporary art, a Rubens collection and sculpture garden in courtyard.

Tuesday-Saturday 10 a.m.-4 p.m.

SARASOTA CLASSIC CAR MUSEUM

5500 N. Tamiami Trail, Sarasota, 941-355-6228; www.sarasotacarmuseum.org

Built in 1952, the museum houses more than 100 restored antique classic cars. Get a look at John Lennon's psychedelic '56 Bentley and Paul McCartney's Mini

Cooper. If you don't have a need for speed, the museum has 2,000 mechanical antique music boxes and machines. A turn-of-the-century arcade is also onsite. Tours run every half hour.

Admission: adults $8.50, seniors $7.50, children $6.50, children 5 and under free. Daily 9 a.m.-6 p.m.

SARASOTA JUNGLE GARDENS

3701 Bay Shore Road, Sarasota, 941-355-5305, 877-861-6547; www.sarasotajunglegardens.com

Here tropical birds frolic in a jungle paradise featuring more than 5,000 varieties of plants, wild jungle trails and even formal gardens. Flamingos, swans, peacocks and pelicans roam free. Take a break from the animal action at the Flamingo Café, which serves delicious sandwiches, ice cream and snacks.

Daily 10 a.m.-5 p.m.

TAMPA

ADVENTURE ISLAND

10001 McKinley Drive, Tampa, 888-800-5447; www.adventureisland.com

This 30-acre water theme park is jammed with rides: four speed slides, an inner tube slide, a slow-winding tube ride, a water-sled ride, 16 water flumes, diving platforms, a pool that creates three- to five-foot waves for body and raft surfing, a large children's water play section and lifeguards. The park also includes a restaurant, picnicking, games and a gift shop.

BUSCH GARDENS TAMPA

3000 E. Busch Blvd., Tampa, 813-987-5082; www.buschgardens.com

This 335-acre theme park re-creates some of the sites and sounds of Africa, with the addition of roller coasters and water rides. The area is divided into eight different regions. The Timbuktu section has a dolphin theater, rides, a German restaurant and an entertainment center; the Myombe Reserve has gorillas and chimpanzees; and visitors can go on safari in the Serengeti Plain.

March-December, schedule varies. Need to fill this out.

DAVID A. STRAZ, JR. CENTER FOR THE PERFORMING ARTS

1010 N.W.C. MacInnes Place, Tampa, 813-229-7827, 800-955-1045; www.tbpac.org

This arts complex includes the 2,500-seat Festival Hall, 1,000-seat Playhouse Hall, 300-seat Robert and Lorena Jaeb Theater and 100-seat Off Center Theater. The Florida Orchestra performs classical and pop concerts here September-May, and the Tampa Opera belts it out in the theater November-May.

FLORIDA AQUARIUM

701 Channelside Drive, Tampa, 813-273-4000; www.flaquarium.org

Exhibit areas replicate the state's water environments (mangrove estuary, fresh-water, beach, marine and coral reef). The Swim with the Fishes attraction offers scuba diving for those ages six and older. Saltwater and freshwater tanks house species like the Bonnethead shark and the spiny lobster. Frights of the Forest contains some of the world's most dangerous wetland creatures—vampire bats, poison dart frogs, leeches and scorpions.

Admission: adults $19.95, seniors $16.95, children $14.95, children 2 and under free. Daily 9:30 a.m.-5 p.m.

YBOR CITY

Two miles east of downtown, between I-4, 1600 E. Eighth Ave., Nebraska Avenue and 22nd Street; 813-242-0398; www.ybor.org

A link between the past and present, Florida's Latin Quarter retains some of the atmosphere of the original Cuban settlement. Spanish and Italian are spoken as much as English. Head here for Spanish restaurants, coffeehouses, funky boutiques and cigar factories. Fill this out by mentioning some of the most popular ones.

WHERE TO STAY

CLEARWATER

★★★SAFETY HARBOR RESORT AND SPA

105 N. Bayshore Drive, Safety Harbor, 727-726-1161, 888-237-8772; www.safetyharborspa.com

This retreat on Tampa Bay offers extensive spa treatments and salon services, plus a lovely indoor pool and Jacuzzis. Rooms are spacious and airy thanks to all-white bedding and floor-to-ceiling glass doors, which in some rooms lead out to balconies. But the real appeal—other than lounging along the 28 miles of white sand on the Gulf or catching a show in the 300-seat theater—are the Espirito Santo Mineral Springs, 2,000-year-old springs on the premises that provide mineral water to guests. Once thought to be the Fountain of Youth, the springs supposedly have healing properties.

189 rooms. Restaurant, bar. Business center. Fitness center. Pool. Pets accepted. Tennis. $251-350

CLEARWATER BEACH

★★★HILTON CLEARWATER BEACH RESORT

400 Mandalay Ave., Clearwater Beach, 727-461-3222, 800-753-3954; www.clearwaterbeachresort.com

Overlooking Clearwater Harbor, this family-friendly hotel is situated on 10 acres of sandy white beaches and is right in the center of all of the action—the surf, the sand, shopping and dining are just steps away. Guest rooms have a contemporary, light feel and feature balconies with views of the Gulf of Mexico. If you tire of the beach, hang out in the pool area, where you can soak in the Jacuzzi or two heated pools, or dine poolside at the Sand Bar & Grill. Kids can go to there for hourly activities and crafts.

416 rooms. Restaurant, bar. Business center. Fitness center. Pool. Pets accepted. Beach. $251-350

★★★SHERATON SAND KEY RESORT

1160 Gulf Blvd., Clearwater Beach, 727-595-1611, 800-456-7263; www.sheratonsandkey.com

The Sheraton Sand Key Resort is in a quiet spot, just slightly off the main drag of Clearwater Beach. The well-landscaped beachfront property faces Clearwater Bay and offers 10 acres to roam (and more, if you consider the adjacent Sand Key Park). Guest rooms feature calming beige walls and ocean-blue bedding, flat-screen TVs, and high-quality linens in which you can stretch out after a long day at the beach.

375 rooms. Restaurant, bar. Business center. Fitness center. Pool. Pets accepted. Beach. Tennis. $151-250

ST. PETE BEACH

★★★THE DON CESAR, A LOEWS HOTEL

3400 Gulf Blvd., St. Pete Beach, 727-360-1881, 800-282-1116; www.loewshotels.com

Affectionately known as the pink palace for its distinctive hue, this 1920s-era resort rests on a stretch of white sand at St. Pete Beach. All guest rooms offer a Gulf view and feature crisp white bed linens and white wrought-iron headboards. The resort's restaurants and bars capitalize on the seaside setting by filling their menus with seafood and tropical cocktails.

277 rooms. Restaurants, bar. Business center. Fitness center. Pool. Spa. Pets accepted. Beach. $251-350

★★★DOUBLETREE BEACH RESORT

17120 Gulf Blvd., North Redington Beach, 727-391-4000, 800-678-3832; www.doubletreebeachresort.com

This beachfront resort overlooks the Boca Ciega Intracoastal Waterway and the Gulf. Each of the 125 guest rooms feature private balconies to best soak up the views. The prime location keeps you on the beach but relatively close to all the area attractions. Upon check-in, you'll get a freshly baked chocolate chip cookie. But if that's not enough to fill you, dine along the water on the veranda at Mango's restaurant and their seasonal Florida/Caribbean cuisine. Of course no visit is complete without a sunset cocktail at the The Beachside Tiki Bar.

125 rooms. Restaurant, bar. Pool. Beach. $151-250

★★★TRADEWINDS ISLAND GRAND BEACH RESORT

5500 Gulf Blvd., St. Pete Beach, 727-367-6461, 800-360-4016; www.tradewindsresort.com

Sister to the Tradewinds Sandpiper Hotel & Suites, this 18-acre, Gulf-front resort features a Floridian-styled lobby and guest rooms decorated with white furniture, colorful artwork and shuttered windows. Many rooms also offer views of the Gulf. The property offers water sport rentals, beach cabanas and chairs, nine-hole mini-golf and a life-size chessboard. Paddleboats are also available for use on the quarter-mile waterway that meanders through the property.

585 rooms. Restaurant, bar. Business center. Fitness center. Pool. Beach. Tennis. $251-350

★★★TRADEWINDS SANDPIPER HOTEL & SUITES

6000 Gulf Blvd., St. Pete Beach, 727-360-5551, 800-360-4016; www.tradewindsresort.com

Sitting on acres of white sandy beachfront, the Tradewinds Sandpiper offers recreation and relaxation like its sister property the Tradewinds Island Grand Beach Resort. The rooms have amenities you'll find in your home kitchen: refrigerators, microwaves, coffee makers and toasters.

211 rooms. Restaurant, bar. Business center. Fitness center. Pool. Beach. $151-250

ST. PETERSBURG

★★★HILTON ST. PETERSBURG BAYFRONT

333 First St. S., St. Petersburg, 727-894-5000, 866-454-8338; www.stpetersburg.hilton.com

This downtown corporate and convention hotel is across from the Mahaffey Theater and 15 minutes from the airport. Enjoy views of the local marina from the patio deck and pool. Room perks include 42-inch HD flat-panel televisions, alarm clocks with iPod docking stations and Lavazza coffee.

333 rooms. Restaurant, bar. Business center. Fitness center. Pool. $61-150

★★★RENAISSANCE VINOY RESORT AND GOLF CLUB
501 Fifth Ave. N.E., St. Petersburg, 727-894-1000, 888-303-4430; www.renaissancehotels.com

The waterfront Vinoy Resort and Golf Club boasts an 18-hole golf course, 12 tennis courts and a private marina, all within a short distance from St. Petersburg. This historic hotel has Mediterranean Revival architecture and elegant, rich décor. Hiking and jogging trails are right on the property.

361 rooms. Restaurant, bar. Business center. Fitness center. Pool. Golf. Tennis. $251-350

SARASOTA
★★★HYATT SARASOTA
1000 Boulevard of the Arts, Sarasota, 941-953-1234, 800-233-1234; www.sarasota.hyatt.com

On the Sarasota Quay waterfront and minutes from beaches and shopping at St. Armand's Circle, this property remains a popular convention site. Dine inside or out at the Boathouse, taking in views of the private Hyatt marina. Or lounge at the lagoon-style pool and waterfalls amid the palm trees. Inside the hotel, you'll find newly remodeled rooms from Lilly Pulitzer, who added bursts of bright pink and lime to the airy spaces.

294 rooms. Restaurant, bar. Business center. Fitness center. Pool. Pets accepted. $251-350

★★★★THE RITZ-CARLTON, SARASOTA
1111 Ritz-Carlton Drive, Sarasota, 941-309-2000, 800-241-3333; www.ritzcarlton.com

Located in the city's cultural district overlooking Sarasota Bay, the Ritz-Carlton is close to the boutiques and galleries of the city but maintains a resort feel. Rooms feature rich colors, sumptuous fabrics and antiques. You will sleep soundly in the featherbeds, which come with feather duvets, goose-down pillows, Egyptian cotton linens and Italian wool throws. The hotel also offers an 18-hole Tom Fazio–designed golf course. From the butlers on call to assist with computer woes to the bath drawn by the bath butlers, service is superlative. But lest you think the property borders on stuffiness, there's a burger bar where you can get dine alfresco while sipping a glazed doughnut shake.

266 rooms. Restaurant, bar. Business center. Fitness center. Pool. Spa. Pets accepted. Beach. Golf. Tennis. $251-350

TAMPA
★★★GRAND HYATT TAMPA BAY
2900 Bayport Drive, Tampa, 813-874-1234, 800-633-7313; www.grandtampabay.hyatt.com

Situated on a 35-acre wildlife preserve on the shores of Tampa Bay, this hotel boasts the finest views in the city. The lobby is airy and decorated in pastel tones, and the guest rooms feature comfortable bedding, overstuffed chairs and work desks. Armani's, an upscale northern Italian restaurant on the top floor of the hotel, is a sophisticated spot with exceptional views.

445 rooms. Restaurant, bar. Business center. Fitness center. Pool. Pets accepted. Tennis. $151-250

★★★HYATT REGENCY TAMPA
211 N. Tampa St., Tampa, 813-225-1234, 888-591-1234; www.hyattregencytampa.com

This downtown hotel is just minutes from the Florida Aquarium, Ybor City and the convention center. Guest rooms are contemporary in décor and feature work desks, sitting areas and Portico bath amenities. Some rooms offer views of the pool on the fifth floor.

521 rooms. Restaurant, bar. Business center. Fitness center. Pool. $151-250

★★★INTERCONTINENTAL TAMPA

4860 W. Kennedy Blvd., Tampa, 813-286-4400, 866-402-0758; www.intercontampa.com

This sleek downtown hotel, with a curved glass façade, is connected to Tampa's Urban Center office complex by 11-story atriums filled with exotic foliage. The ever-popular Shula's Steakhouse is in the lobby.

322 rooms. Restaurant, bar. Business center. Fitness center. Pool. $251-350

★★★SADDLEBROOK RESORT TAMPA

5700 Saddlebrook Way, Wesley Chapel, 813-973-1111, 800-729-8383; www.saddlebrookresort.com

This resort near Tampa is a great destination for outdoor enthusiasts. The complex includes a sports village with a state-of-the-art fitness center, volleyball courts, a basketball court and a sports field. Two 18-hole Arnold Palmer-designed golf courses are onsite—Saddlebrook is the world headquarters for the prestigious Arnold Palmer Golf Academy. Tennis players will love the 45-court center that offers professional instruction.

800 rooms. Restaurant, bar. Fitness center. Business center. Pool. Spa. Golf. Tennis. $151-250

★★★WESTIN HARBOUR ISLAND HOTEL

725 S. Harbour Island Blvd., Tampa 813-229-5000, 800-937-8461; www.westin.com

The downtown Westin Harbour Island Hotel sits in the business district adjacent to the Tampa Convention Center, a central location for business travelers. Wide hallways with nicely framed, colorful art lead guests to their comfortable rooms, which feature Heavenly beds, marble baths and Starbucks coffee.

299 rooms. Restaurant, bar. Business center. Fitness center. Pool. Pets accepted. $251-350

WHERE TO EAT

BRADENTON

★★★BEACH BISTRO

6600 Gulf Drive, Holmes Beach, 941-778-6444; www.beachbistro.com

It doesn't get much more romantic than this: beachfront breezes, a single red rose in a vase at your table, delicious regional fare and views of lovely Gulf Coast sunsets. Beach Bistro, located on Anna Maria Island, is a popular destination for locals for its consistently good contemporary Floribbean fare, which includes dishes such as the bouillabaisse, grouper with toasted-coconut crust, and buttery "lobsterscargot."

Contemporary American. Dinner. Reservations recommended. Outdoor seating. Bar. $36-85

CLEARWATER

★★★ALFANO'S

1702 Clearwater/Largo Road, Clearwater, 727-584-2125; www.alfanosrestaurant.com

A local favorite since 1984, this family-owned restaurant features classic Italian fare, available à la carte or as a three-course prix fixe meal, as well as a number of selections to suit everyone from vegetarians to carnivores. Entrées such as filet mignon, manicotti and striped Maine lobster ravioli are nicely complemented by the award-winning wine list. Live jazz fills the lounge on Wednesday nights, and a pianist performs on Friday and Saturday evenings.

Italian. Lunch, dinner. Closed Sunday from mid-May-November. Reservations recommended. Outdoor seating. Children's menu. Bar. $16-35

ST. PETE BEACH
★★★THE LOBSTER POT
17814 Gulf Blvd., Redington Shores, 727-391-8592; www.lobsterpotrestaurant.com

Opened in 1978, this seafood restaurant is known for its Maine lobster, Alaskan king crab and other tempting dishes from the ocean, although the steak dishes will not disappoint. A free cocktail or glass of wine is offered with every dinner. When dining on the weekends, be sure to check out the live jazz in the newly opened Martini Lounge.

Seafood. Dinner. Children's menu. $36-85

★★★THE MARITANA GRILLE
The Don Cesar, 3400 Gulf Blvd., St. Pete Beach, 727-360-1882; www.doncesar.com

This elegant restaurant inside the historic Don Cesar resort serves a seafood menu of local favorites. Pan-seared yellow snapper is accompanied by lemongrass shrimp dumplings while pan-seared scallops come with a creamy lobster risotto. The cozy setting has several salt water aquariums throughout so you can see first hand the fresh seafood offered. An extensive and wine list rounds out the distinctive dining experience.

American. Dinner. Reservations recommended. Children's menu. Bar. $36-85

★★★PALM COURT ITALIAN GRILL
Tradewinds Island Beach Resort, 5500 Gulf Blvd., St. Pete Beach, 727-367-6461; www.tradewindsresort.com

This intimate St. Pete Beach dining room is located at the Tradewinds Island Beach Resort and serves a traditional American and seafood menu with eclectic touches. The décor is cozy and features an outdoor patio. A great spot to celebrate a special occasion or romantic dinner, the restaurant also serves lunch and Sunday brunch.

American, seafood. Lunch, dinner, Sunday brunch. Reservations recommended. Outdoor seating. Bar $16-35

★★★WINE CELLAR
17307 Gulf Blvd., North Redington Beach, 727-393-3491; www.thewinecellar.com

More than 20 years old, this perennial favorite in a country-style house serves satisfying continental cuisine. Monday nights feature a buffet with Angus beef carving stations, a make-your-own-pasta bar and a selection of fresh seafood. The wine list is extensive as the family has been collecting since 1976 when the restaurant opened.

Continental. Dinner. Children's menu. Bar. $36-85

SARASOTA
★★★BIJOU CAFÉ
1287 First St., Sarasota, 941-366-8111; www.bijoucafe.net

This noisy, eclectic restaurant with country French décor is a converted 1930s gas station. If you're headed to the nearby Opera House, dine pre-theater on hearty options like braised lamb shank with wild mushrooms or roast duckling with dried cherry and apricot bread pudding.

International. Lunch, dinner. Closed Sunday in summer. Reservations recommended. Outdoor seating. Bar. $16-35

★★★MICHAEL'S ON EAST

1212 East Ave. S., Sarasota, 941-366-0007; www.michaelsoneast.com

This contemporary restaurant showcases fresh, seasonal and organic ingredients in dishes such as local Atlantic swordfish with red potatoes and onions. The cozy, onsite piano bar offers a comfortable place to sample hors d'oeuvres, such as fresh tomato bruschetta, and classic cocktails.

American. Lunch, dinner. Closed Sunday. Reservations recommended. Bar. $36-85

★★★★VERNONA RESTAURANT

The Ritz-Carlton, Sarasota, 1111 Ritz-Carlton Drive, Sarasota, 941-309-2008, 800-241-3333; www.ritzcarlton.com

The ambience at this restaurant inside the Ritz-Carlton resembles that of a Tuscan villa, complete with crystal chandeliers and elegantly arched windows. The menu, though, is contemporary American and features locally sourced organic ingredients. Signature favorites include lobster macaroni and cheese and olive oil-poached prime beef tenderloin. Save room for the Sarasota key lime pie.

American. Breakfast, lunch, dinner, Sunday brunch. Reservations recommended. Children's menu. Bar. $36-85

TAMPA

★★★ARMANI'S

Grand Hyatt Tampa Bay, 2900 Bayport Drive, Tampa, 813-207-6800; www.armanisrestaurant.com

Located high atop the Grand Hyatt Tampa Bay, Armani's offers views of the sunset over Tampa Bay as well as of planes taking off and landing at the nearby airport. The outdoor terrace is the perfect spot for a twilight cocktail, and the restaurant is elegant and refined. The centerpiece of the restaurant is its antipasto bar, which features an extensive selection of grilled vegetables, smoked meats, pastas, olives, cheeses and other Italian treats. Armani's impressive Northern Italian menu includes something for everyone.

Italian. Dinner. Closed Sunday. Reservations recommended. Outdoor seating. Bar. $36-85

★★★BERN'S STEAK HOUSE

1208 S. Howard Ave., Tampa, 813-251-2421; www.bernssteakhouse.com

Bern's is nothing if not different. Inside the themed dining rooms, you'll see an assortment of antiques. The wine list—a five-pound document chained to the table—is mind-boggling. The steak—dry-aged for two weeks—is superb. Don't miss dessert, served upstairs in an area reserved for sweet treats. There, you'll sit in private pods wired with closed-circuit TVs and jukeboxes.

Steak. Dinner. Reservations recommended. Bar. $36-85

★★★COLUMBIA RESTAURANT

2117 E. Seventh Ave., Tampa, 813-248-4961; www.columbiarestaurant.com

Opened in 1905, this is supposedly Florida's oldest restaurant. Owned and operated by the fourth and fifth generations of the Hernandez/Gonzmart family, the extensive Spanish menu includes both tapas and full entrées. There is a $6 cover charge for the dining room when the flamenco show is performed. A jazz band in the lounge entertains Tuesday through Saturday evenings. The wine cellar features California and Spanish reds.

Spanish. Lunch, dinner. Reservations recommended. Children's menu. Bar. $16-35

★★★DONATELLO
232 N. Dale Mabry Highway, Tampa, 813-875-6660; www.donatellorestaurant.com

Named after the famous Florentine sculptor, this authentic Italian restaurant has been around since 1984. The menu features flavorful homemade pastas, fresh fish and several chicken and veal dishes, and there is live music in the lounge every night.

Italian. Lunch, dinner. Reservations recommended. Bar. $36-85

★★★MISE EN PLACE
442 W. Kennedy Blvd., Tampa, 813-254-5373; www.miseonline.com

Located across the street from the University of Tampa's historic Tampa Hotel, this downtown restaurant is popular for its modern American cuisine, which includes dishes such as grilled chicken with polenta fries and Kobe rib-eye with mac and cheese. There's also a cozy lounge and private spaces that are good for business dinners.

American. Lunch, dinner, late-night. Closed Sunday-Monday. Reservations recommended. Bar. $36-85

★★★RUSTY PELICAN
2425 N. Rocky Point Drive, Tampa, 813-281-1943; www.therustypelican.com

This restaurant, which also has a location in Key Biscayne, is a favorite for fresh seafood. Views of Tampa Bay make for an ideal setting for enjoying fresh grilled lobster, tuna or the specialty dessert, bananas Foster.

American. Lunch, dinner. Children's menu. Bar. $36-85

★★★RUTH'S CHRIS STEAK HOUSE
1700 N. Westshore Blvd., Tampa, 813-282-1118; www.ruthschris.com

This tried-and-true outpost of the national steak house chain is a popular choice for business and

---

WHICH RESTAURANTS HAVE THE BEST SEAFOOD?

The Lobster Pot:
If you couldn't tell from its name, The Lobster Pot is known for its delicious lobster. Lobster tails, whole lobster and lobster bisque are all on the menu here. Whether or not you order an entrée with the crustacean, every dinner comes with a free cocktail or glass of wine.

The Maritana Grille:
This is a favorite among seafood lovers. The ocean-plucked goodies get top billing: Pan-seared scallops come with creamy lobster risotto and osetra caviar, and the orange habanero barbecue grouper with papaya-banana ravioli.

Michael's on East:
Fresh, seasonal, organic ingredients create tasty dishes at this contempo-rary restaurant. Try the local Atlantic swordfish, the espresso-crusted yellowfin tuna or the pan-roasted bluefin crab cakes. Then stop by the piano bar for a tune and drink.

Rusty Pelican:
Come here for fresh seafood like blackened swordfish, grouper, seared sesame ahi or lobster tails.

leisure travelers. The clubby interior is richly decorated and dimly lit. The restaurant offers seafood, chicken, veal and vegetarian dishes. But obviously the stars on the menu are the different cuts of steak. For a filling meal, grab a companion and try the 40-ounce porterhouse for two.

Steak. Dinner. Bar. Reservations recommended. $36-85

★★★SIDEBERN'S

2208 W. Morrison Ave., Tampa, 813-258-2233; www.bernssteakhouse.com

Dining in Tampa doesn't get any more creative and fun than at this contemporary offshoot of Bern's Steak House. The sleek dining space is the perfect place to enjoy items like the autumn coleslaw with cabbage, figs, prosciutto and thyme vinaigrette, beer cheese soup and oxtail ravioli. It is both surprising and delicious.

International. Dinner. Closed Sunday. Reservations recommended. Outdoor seating. Bar. $36-85

RECOMMENDED

SHULA'S STEAK HOUSE

4860 W. Kennedy Blvd., Tampa, 813-286-4366; www.donshula.com

Famous not only for its owner, University of Miami coach Don Shula, but also for its massive 48-ounce porterhouse, this restaurant attracts a large crowd every night of the week. Menus are printed on leather footballs, and there is plenty of pigskin memorabilia throughout. The atmosphere is both lively and intimate.

Steak. Lunch, dinner. Reservations recommended. Bar. $36-85

SPA

SARASOTA

★★★★THE RITZ-CARLTON MEMBERS SPA CLUB, SARASOTA

1111 Ritz-Carlton Drive, Sarasota, 941-309-2000, 800-241-3333; www.rcmcsarasota.com

This exclusive spa, for use only by guests of the resort and members of the Ritz-Carlton Members Club, combines state-of-the-art design with European technique. More than 100 treatments make up the comprehensive menu, but massages, masks, scrubs and body treatments are the specialties. Hand and foot treatments go beyond the basic manicure or pedicure to include citrus antiaging manis and mineral powder pedis. Salon services include hair care and styling, as well as makeup application and lessons.

EAST CENTRAL FLORIDA

The kid-friendly attractions in East Central Florida lure in lots of families. They go to delicious-sounding Cocoa Beach and Cocoa on the mainland for their proximity to Space Coast destinations like Cape Canaveral and Kennedy Space Center. As one of the oldest Floridian resort areas, Daytona Beach is a year-round vacation spot that's especially popular with students during spring break and families the rest of the year. Kissimmee is also a choice spot for vacationers, since it's the gateway to Walt Disney World (theme parks are around 30 minutes away) and several other central Florida attractions.

HIGHLIGHTS

WHAT ARE THE BEST THEME PARKS?

DAYTONA 500 EXPERIENCE
This is like Disney World for NASCAR fans. Ride in a stock car along with a pro instructor in the Richard Petty Experience, tour the Speedway or see if your hand matches Dale Earnhardt Jr.'s concrete print in the Walk of Fame.

ISLANDS OF ADVENTURE
You'll find countless rides at this theme park, but the hottest attraction is the new Wizarding World of Harry Potter. The park dedicated to the bespectacled boy wizard brings the magic with rides like Harry Potter and the Forbidden Journey, which sends you through Hogwarts and then soaring above the castle grounds.

UNIVERSAL STUDIOS FLORIDA
You might catch some big-name stars shooting a flick at Universal Studios, the largest working film and TV studio outside of Hollywood. Even if you don't, you'll be too busy on blockbuster-themed rides like Back to the Future and Jaws to notice.

WET 'N WILD
Be prepared to get soaked and have your adrenalin pumping at the country's top water park. Shoot down a slide with a 250-foot vertical drop in Der Stuka or battle the cyclone-like ride The Storm. Kids have their own park with mini-sized versions of the adult rides.

The most well-known of all the cities in this region is Orlando, the theme-park capital of the world. Orlando is a favorite for a devoted colony of year-round visitors, not only for Disney, Universal and the more than 100 attractions found in the city, but because it is as close to an urban oasis as it gets. Live oaks edge picturesque brick-lined streets surrounding the central focal point of Lake Eola. The metro area has 300 lakes within its limits and retains an open, parklike atmosphere.

WHAT TO SEE

COCOA
BREVARD MUSEUM OF HISTORY AND NATURAL SCIENCE
2201 Michigan Ave., Cocoa, 321-632-1830; www.brevardmuseum.org
The exhibits at this small museum highlight what the mid-Florida region

---

HIGHLIGHT

WHAT IS SPEED WEEKS?

There's something about the energy, the noise, the excitement—every year, thousands flood into Daytona Beach for the Daytona 500 NASCAR stock-car racing. The big race takes place mid-February, but Speed Weeks kicks off the beginning of the month with the Rolex 24 sports-car race. If you want to stay close to the speedway, you'll need to make hotel reservations a year in advance. Accommodations are available within 10 minutes of the track, beachside, usually through December. Beginning the last week of December, the **Daytona Beach Area Convention and Visitors Bureau** *(800-854-1234)* posts a daily list of Speed Weeks' room availability. You can view it online *(www.daytonabeach. com)*. If you miss the big event, a film at the interactive attraction Daytona USA re-creates the thunder. You can also tour the track when races are not in session. To purchase Speed Weeks tickets, call **Daytona International Speedway** at 386-254-2700 or visit www.daytonaintlspeedway.com.

---

used to look like thousands of years ago through native artifacts, a hands-on Discovery Room, a mollusk collection, a nature center, an archaeological dig of the 7,000-plus-year-old Windover burial site, and 22 acres of nature preserves and trails through three diverse ecosystems. There's also a butterfly garden on the grounds.

Admission: adults $6, seniors $5.50, college students $5, children 5-16 $4.50, children 4 and under free. Tuesday-Saturday 10 a.m.-4 p.m.

COCOA VILLAGE

430 Delannoy Ave., Cocoa, 321-631-9075; www.cocoavillage.com

Take a self-guided tour of the restored, four-block historic downtown, which features Victorian-era buildings such as the Cocoa Village playhouse, Porcher House and the Gothic church, plus unique shops and restaurants. Visit the website for more information on the various craft fairs that happen at the village a few times a year.

Admission: free. Hours vary.

COCOA BEACH

COCOA BEACH

State Road A1A between 16th Street South and State Road 520, Cocoa Beach; www.cityofcocoabeach.com

Time it right, and you might be watching a space shuttle launch from the beach. Such is the appeal of Cocoa Beach, which is located near Cape Canaveral. Beyond blast-offs, otherworldly attractions here include surfing (pro surfer Kelly Slater hails from Cocoa Beach), white-sand shorelines, dunes (that you can look at, but not climb—it's a natural barrier protected by law) and wildlife. There are lifeguards on duty year-round at Shepard Park, Lori Wilson Park, Minutemen Causeway and Cocoa Beach Pier.

RON JON SURF SHOP

State Road A1A and State Road 520, Cocoa Beach; www.ronjons.com

Thanks to Cocoa Beach's reputation as prime surfing grounds, the local outpost of this national chain started in New Jersey and is one of the largest retailers in surfboards and surfing gear in the world. Housed in a blue-and-yellow art deco-style building on the beach, the store stocks boards, bathing suits, resort gear and more. Early-to-rise surfers will love that the shop is open 24 hours a day.

DAYTONA BEACH

DAYTONA 500 EXPERIENCE

1801 W. International Speedway Blvd., Daytona Beach, 386-947-6800; www.daytona500experience.com

Located just outside the speedway's Turn 4, this theme park is like a racing fan's Disney World—it features Speedway tours, loads of memorabilia, racing simulator rides, the car of the latest Daytona 500 winner and an IMAX Theatre, where you can watch NASCAR 3D: The IMAX Experience. In addition, the Daytona 500 Experience regularly hosts appearances by drivers and other celebrities.

Admission: adults $24, seniors and children $19. Daily 9 a.m.-7 p.m.

DAYTONA BEACH

State Road A1A between Granada Boulevard to Beach Street, 386-239-7873; www.daytonabeach.com

Daytona Beach boasts more than 20 miles of sparkling white beaches, so it's no surprise that it bills itself as the "World's Most Famous Beach." That claim rings true at least on one count: It's one of the few beaches where visitors can drive their cars right up on the sand, a perfect option for picnickers, surfers or people with disabilities. Drivers must obey the 10-mph speed limit and drive on the beach only during daylight. There's also a five-mile stretch where cars are not allowed on the sand, for beach-goers who'd rather tan than burn rubber.

DAYTONA INTERNATIONAL SPEEDWAY

1801 W. International Speedway Blvd., Daytona Beach, 386-254-2700; www.daytonaintlspeedway.com

This 2½-mile, high-speed, banked track with grandstand seating for 167,860 is a testing ground for car and accessory manufacturers, as well as the home of the Daytona 500 and other races and events. Tours—which include entry into the Daytona 500 Experience exhibit and a guided tour of the race track—are available year-round, except during races and special tests. Most racing events are held February, March, July, October and December.

Admission: varies by event. Daily 9 a.m.-7 p.m.

MARINE SCIENCE CENTER

100 Lighthouse Drive, Ponce Inlet, 386-304-5545; www.marinesciencecenter.com

The Marine Science Center is just around the corner from the Ponce de Leon Inlet Lighthouse. The facility may not be big, but inside you'll find small alligators, snakes, a moray eel, aquariums and environmental exhibits. Outside, stroll Turtle Terrace to observe the sea turtle rehabilitation area. The sea bird rehabilitation center is on the other end of the parking lot, and a nature trail is across the street.

Admission: adults $5, seniors $4, children 3-12 $2, children 3 and under free. Tuesday-Saturday 10 a.m.-4 p.m., Sunday noon-4 p.m.

MUSEUM OF ARTS AND SCIENCES

352 S. Nova Road, Daytona Beach, 386-255-0285; www.moas.org

This museum, situated in an 86,000-square-foot building, is home to more than 30,000 objects, including a vast permanent collection of American, Cuban and African-American art. It also has a formidable Chinese art collection, and exhibits run the gamut from photographs of jazz greats to a collection of Coca-Cola 2-D art and images.

Admission: adults $14, seniors and children $11, children 6-17 $7, children 5 and under free. Tuesday-Saturday 9 a.m.-5 p.m., Sunday 11 a.m-5 p.m.

OCEAN WALK SHOPPES AT OCEAN WALK VILLAGE

250 N. Atlantic Ave., Daytona Beach, 386-258-9544; www.oceanwalkshoppes.com

This dining, shopping and entertainment complex offers specialty shops and restaurants (including Johnny Rockets and Bubba Gump Shrimp Co.), a movie theater, live entertainment and more. To the east, find the historic oceanfront Bandshell. Built in 1937 of coquina shells, the Bandshell hosts concerts and events throughout the year. The Daytona Lagoon (www.daytonalagoon.com), complete with a water park, an arcade and go-karts, is across the street from the Shoppes.

PONCE DE LEON INLET LIGHTHOUSE AND MUSEUM

4931 S. Peninsula Drive, Ponce Inlet, 386-761-1821; www.ponceinlet.org

The scenic town of Ponce Inlet—about 14 miles southeast of Daytona Beach—features the country's second-tallest lighthouse, located at the southern tip of the Daytona area's barrier island. At the top is an incredible view of both the Intracoastal Waterway and the ocean. Once back on dry land, explore the original homes and buildings that surround the lighthouse. Each is filled with exhibits on lighthouse, maritime and area history, including a black-and-white video of 1940s beach races running on a loop.

Admission: adults $5, children 11 and under $1.50. Daily 10 a.m.-6 p.m.

KISSIMMEE

GATORLAND

14501 S. Orange Blossom Trail, 407-855-5496, 800-393-5297; www.gatorland.com

For the quintessential Florida experience, visit this 110-acre park and wildlife preserve with thousands of alligators and crocodiles. Shows include Jungle Crocs, the Up Close Encounters snake show, Gator Wrestlin' and the Gator Jumparoo, where large alligators jump out of the water to grab food from a trainer's hand.

Admission: adults $23, children $15. Daily 9 a.m.-6 p.m.

OLD TOWN

5770 W. U.S. Highway 192, Kissimmee, 407-396-4888; www.old-town.com

This replica turn-of-the-century Florida village features brick-lined streets, specialty shops and restaurants and a general store. Kids will keep busy at the Ferris wheel, the Windstorm roller coaster and Kids Town, an area with 10 rides.

Admission: prices vary by event. Daily noon-11 p.m., stores: daily 10 a.m.-11 p.m.

ORLANDO

AMWAY ARENA

600 W. Amelia St., Orlando, 407-849-2001; www.orlandocentroplex.com

Magic happens at the Amway Arena. That is, the Orlando Magic basketball team. It calls the 17,740-seat arena in downtown Orlando is home, as do the Orlando Seals hockey team and the Orlando Predators arena football team. Plenty of other events take place here, including top-name concerts, rodeos, the circus, ice shows and much more. The center opened in 1989 and is still affectionately called the Orena (Orlando Arena) by old-timers.

BOB CARR PERFORMING ARTS CENTRE

401 W. Livingston St., Orlando, 407-849-2577; www.orlandovenues.net

Home to the Orlando Opera, the Florida Theatrical Association and the Orlando Celebrity Concert Association, the 2,518-seat Bob Carr Performing Arts Centre hosts a multitude of performances. You'll see everything from opera and ballet to rock concerts to the symphony and the annual Broadway Series.

Ticket prices vary by event. See website for schedule.

GRAND CYPRESS GOLF CLUB

1 N. Jacaranda, Orlando, 800-835-7377; www.grandcypress.com

The Grand Cypress has 45 holes designed by Jack Nicklaus. The North, South and East courses have nine holes each and can be played in different combinations, while the New course has 18 holes. The New course is designed to look like St. Andrews in Scotland, with stone walls along the 15th and 17th holes and deep pot bunkers lining some of the fairways. There's little water and only a few trees, so golfers can enjoy hitting a driver off of many tees without dire consequences.

HARRY P. LEU GARDENS

1920 N. Forest Ave., Orlando, 407-246-2620; www.leugardens.org

Harry P. Leu Gardens is 50 acres of "Old Florida" filled with fragrant blooms from the South's largest camellia collection and formal rose garden. Oaks and giant camphor trees line the miles of pathways surrounding the late-19th-century restored farmhouse, now the Leu House Museum, which depicts turn-of-the-century Florida lifestyle. The Butterfly Garden keeps more than 100 different plants designed to attract the winged insects year-round.

Daily 9 a.m.-5 p.m.; Leu House Museum closed in July.

ISLANDS OF ADVENTURE

1000 Universal Studios Plaza, Orlando, 407-363-8000

This 110-acre theme park boasts some of the world's most innovative and technologically advanced rides, located on five uniquely themed islands situated around a lagoon. The hottest attraction by far is the new Wizarding World of Harry Potter, a theme park devoted to the boy wizard with roller coasters, a ride that takes you through Hogwarts and cute stores like Ollivander's wand shop. For those muggles who aren't Potter fans, Islands of Adventure offers other themed fun. The islands bring to life the Marvel Comics superheroes (Marvel Super Hero Island), hundreds of comic-strip heroes (Toon Lagoon), the dinosaurs of *Jurassic Park* (Jurassic Park), the greatest myths of all times (The Lost Continent) and the classic books of Dr. Seuss (Seuss Landing). Seasonal celebrations include Grinchmas, which takes place from Thanksgiving through New Year's Eve on Seuss Landing, and Halloween Horror Nights, which occur on selected nights in October.

Daily; hours vary by season.

ORANGE AVENUE
Orlando; www.orlandoonline.com

If you're into antiques and bargain hunting, you'll find plenty of antique and thrift stores punctuating the sections of Orange Avenue known as Antique and Ivanhoe Rows. Stop in at Rock-n-Roll Heaven (1814 N. Orange Ave., 407-896-1952; www.rock-n-rollheaven.com) for a huge selection of vinyl records at bargain prices (some are only $1). Then head to Flo's Attic Antiques (310 E. New Hampshire St., 407-894-5959; www.flosantiquesaccents.com) for a large selection of antiques and jewelry. Located just north of the city beyond main thoroughfare Colonial Drive, the antique district offers a tranquil alternative to the nonstop world of the theme parks.

Hours vary.

ORLANDO MUSEUM OF ART
2416 N. Mills Ave., Orlando, 407-896-4231; www.omart.org

Considered one of the best art museums in the South, the Orlando Museum of Art was founded in 1924 and presents 10 to 12 major exhibits throughout the year focusing on a broad range of artwork by both local and international artists. For example, past exhibits included Clyde Butcher: Big Cypress Swamp and the Western Everglades, which featured large black and white photographs taken at Big Cypress Swamp; and African Textiles, which included a Zulu wedding cape and tribal headdresses. The museum also houses impressive collections of American, ancient American and African art.

Tuesday-Friday 10 a.m.-5 p.m., Saturday-Sunday noon-4 p.m.

ORLANDO SCIENCE CENTER
777 E. Princeton St., Orlando, 407-514-2000, 888-672-4386; www.osc.org

Hands-on experiential exhibits abound in this 207,000-square-foot facility. Permanent exhibits include BodyZone, a tour inside the human body; ShowBiz Science, which highlights movie special effects; and NatureWorks, a large exhibit exploring Florida's vast ecosystem. The center also features the world's largest I-Works domed theater and planetarium shows, with combination tickets available.

Admission: adults $17, seniors $16, children 3-11 $12, children 2 and under free. Sunday-Tuesday, Thursday-Saturday 10 a.m.-5 p.m.

SEAWORLD ORLANDO
7007 SeaWorld Drive, Orlando, 407-351-3600, 800-327-2424; www.seaworld.com

Home to the famous killer whale, Shamu, Seaworld has rides, shows and entertaining exhibits featuring everything from thousands of penguins to turtles and dolphins to shark (see them swimming over your head in the shark tunnel). Directly across the street is its sister park, Discovery Cove, an exclusive resort that limits daily attendance to 1,000 people and provides guests the opportunity to swim with dolphins or enjoy beaching, snorkeling and swimming in a quiet and intimate setting. The Waterfront resembles a seaside village with restaurants, shops and a large oyster pool.

Daily; hours vary by season. Adult: 78.95, children $68.95. Combination tickets are available.

SKYVENTURE ORLANDO

6805 Visitors Circle, Orlando, 407-903-1150, 800-759-3861; www.skyventureorlando.com

If you've always wanted to try skydiving, but don't love the prospect of jumping out of an airplane thousands of feet in the sky, this vertical wind tunnel with 120-mph winds allows you to experience the same feeling of weightlessness. The experience lasts approximately one hour and includes use of a flight suit and helmet.

Monday-Friday 2-11:30 p.m., Saturday-Sunday noon-11:30 p.m.

THORNTON PARK HISTORIC DISTRICT

Thornton Park, Washington Street and Summerlin Avenue, Orlando

In this charming and eclectic neighborhood, historic homes peacefully coexist with new construction. Located directly east of downtown Orlando, the district encompasses a diverse collection of boutiques and retail shops alongside restaurants, bookstores, cafés, lofts and early Florida Craftsman-style homes on stately oak-lined brick streets. The area is also home to Dickson Azalea Park, 5 acres of lush Florida foliage.

UNIVERSAL ORLANDO RESORT

1000 Universal Studios Plaza, Orlando, 407-363-8000; www.universalorlando.com

Encompassing 840 acres, Universal Orlando combines the hip with the classic in its two theme parks, Universal Studios Florida and Islands of Adventure; three Loews hotels, Portofino Bay, Hard Rock and Royal Pacific Resort; and CityWalk, a dynamic dining, shopping and entertainment complex. Academy Award-winning director/producer Steven Spielberg serves as creative consultant to both theme parks, which feature state-of-the-art rides and attractions. Don't miss the new Wizarding World of Harry Potter, a theme park within Islands of Adventure. All the Universal Orlando resort hotels, theme parks and CityWalk are connected by waterways, and complimentary water taxis are available to take you around.

Daily; hours vary by season.

UNIVERSAL STUDIOS FLORIDA

1000 Universal Studios Plaza, Orlando, 407-363-8000; www.universalorlando.com

At 125 acres, Universal Studios Florida is the largest working film and television production studio outside Hollywood. Drawing on its movie heritage as inspiration for its blockbuster rides and attractions, this theme park brings movies to life. Fan favorites include Back to the Future: The Ride; Men in Black Alien Attack; Jaws; E.T. Adventure; and Terminator 2: 3-D Battle Across Time. Numerous movies, television shows, commercials and music video productions routinely utilize the theme park's street sets, so you might get a glimpse of live moviemaking and real stars at work. Past movies that have filmed here include *Ace Ventura*.

Daily; hours vary by season.

SPECIAL EVENTS

ARNOLD PALMER INVITATIONAL

Bay Hill Country Club, 9000 Bay Hill Blvd., Orlando, 407-876-2888, 866-764-4843; www.bayhill.com
As long as theme parks have dominated the central Florida landscape, this tournament, held at Arnold Palmer's spectacular Bay Hill Country Club, has been a top draw on golf's PGA Tour. The tournament attracts some of the top names on the tour.
Mid-March.

CAPITAL ONE BOWL

1 Citrus Bowl Place, Orlando, 407-839-3900; www.fcsports.com
Played annually and nationally televised on New Year's Day, the Capital One Bowl pits the Big Ten and SEC championship teams against each other. For this game, stadium capacity is increased from 65,538 to 70,000. If you go, take advantage of the city shuttles running from the downtown parking lot underneath I-4 at Central Boulevard beginning at 10 a.m. The cost is just $5 and is well worth the price of avoiding traffic.
January 1.

DAYTONA 500

Daytona International Speedway, 1801 W. International Speedway Blvd., Daytona Beach, 386-254-2700; www.daytonaintlspeedway.com
This 200-lap, 500-mile NASCAR Sprint Cup Series race is more than 50 years old. And after all these years, it remains an exciting event that draws thousands of spectators to the track, and millions of television viewers.
Mid-February.

HALLOWEEN HORROR NIGHTS AT ISLANDS OF ADVENTURE

1000 Universal Studios Plaza, Orlando, 407-363-8000; www.universalorlando.com
Halloween Horror Nights has become one of the world's best Halloween events. Originally held at Universal Studios, the event has moved to the Islands of Adventure theme park. Featuring the best in high-tech haunted houses and live shows, the park literally crawls with hundreds of costumed actors with one goal in mind: to scare the living daylights out of unsuspecting guests. The action takes place on select nights in October and early November and separate admission is required.

MARDI GRAS AT UNIVERSAL STUDIOS FLORIDA

1000 Universal Studios Plaza, Orlando, 407-363-8000; www.universalorlando.com
Universal Studios turns its back lot into the largest Mardi Gras celebration outside of the Big Easy during select nights in February, March and April. Millions of beads are tossed from 14 authentic floats during the 10-city-block-long parade. Dine on authentic New Orleans-style cuisine and enjoy real Mardi Gras-style beverages. Select Saturdays feature top acts in concert, while weekday celebrations feature the best in local music.
Dates vary, so call for information.

WET 'N WILD

6200 International Drive, Orlando, 407-351-1800, 800-992-9453; www.wetnwildorlando.com

The No. 1 water park in the world is adjacent to its owner, Universal Orlando. You can save money on entry with a combo ticket, such as the Orlando FlexTicket. Open year-round, the 25-acre facility features heated pools (when needed) with 12 major thrill rides, including Hydra Fighter, a swing ride that you control, and Der Stuka, a six-story speed slide. The Kids Park has a tiny wave pool, mini versions of the park's most popular rides and a life-size sand castle.

Daily; hours vary by season.

WONDERWORKS

9607 International Drive, Orlando, 407-351-8800; www.wonderworksonline.com

How could you not take the time to explore an upside-down building? Interactive fun abounds in this unusual museum brimming with more than 100 hands-on exhibits focusing on the unexplainable, the amazing and the downright weird. Scale a virtual cliff or design your own roller coaster and then ride it. WonderWorks also houses the world's largest extreme laser tag arena/arcade.

Daily 9 a.m.-midnight.

WHERE TO STAY

COCOA BEACH
★★★HILTON COCOA BEACH OCEANFRONT

1550 N. Atlantic Ave., Cocoa Beach, 321-799-0003, 800-445-8667; www.cocoabeachhilton.com

This oceanfront hotel is 10 minutes from Port Canaveral, home to luxury cruise liners and deep-sea fishing charters. The hotel claims to have the largest sun deck on the Florida space coast—it's 10,000 square feet and features the Sea Breeze Beach Bar (if you need refreshments). Rooms here are comfortable, with subdued, sand-colored decor, and some face the Atlantic Ocean. If you're itching to have fun in the sun, you can arrange for surfing lessons and kayak and boogie board rentals. Afterward, satisfy that voracious appetite at Atlantis Bar & Grill with gorgeous ocean views.

296 rooms. Restaurant, bar. Business center. Fitness center. Pool. Beach. $151-250

DAYTONA BEACH
★★★THE SHORES RESORT & SPA

2637 S. Atlantic Ave., Daytona Beach Shores, 386-767-7350, 866-396-2217; www.shoresresort.com

This oceanfront resort has a beach-cottage feel to it with its wicker-and-terra-cotta-filled lobby. Guest rooms are tastefully decorated in Florida-chic style, and feature plush bedding, pillow-topped beds, flat-screen televisions and Molton Brown bath products. The onsite restaurant, Azure, is lauded for its upscale seafood cuisine. End the evening with a nightcap while catching sea breezes from the oceanfront Tiki Bar.

212 rooms. Restaurant, bar. Business center. Fitness center. Pool. Spa. Pets accepted. Beach. $61-150

KISSIMMEE

★★★GAYLORD PALMS RESORT AND CONVENTION CENTER

6000 W. Osceola Parkway, Kissimmee, 407-586-0000; www.gaylordpalms.com

Located in Kissimmee, Gaylord Palms is also only a few miles away from Walt Disney World. The contemporary guest rooms reflect regions of Florida. Bold colors define the Key West wing; a breezy, natural style pervades the Everglades; European elegance dominates the St. Augustine rooms; and modern sophisticates will like the Emerald Bay area, which have a Spanish Renaissance architecture. Each room includes a flat-screen computer equipped with the "I-connect" program, allowing guests to send room-to-room emails, make dining reservations, request valet service and more.

1,406 rooms. Restaurant, bar. Business center. Fitness center. Pool. Spa. $151-250

★★★RADISSON RESORT ORLANDO-CELEBRATION

2900 Parkway Blvd., Kissimmee, 407-396-7000, 800-333-3333;
www.radisson.com/orlando-celebration

This beautifully designed resort is set on 20 acres. Meeting spaces are available, and families traveling here will enjoy the super-sized pool complete with a waterfall and a 40-foot water slide—not to mention complimentary shuttle service to Walt Disney World. Rooms are clean and comfortable, with double- or king-sized beds covered in European-style duvet covers and Italian-influenced furniture. The rooms also come with 25-inch televisions and complimentary high-speed Internet access. There are four restaurants and bars on the premises, plus a seasonal Thursday-night theater show.

718 rooms. Restaurant, bar. Business center. Fitness center. Pool. Tennis. $61-150

ORLANDO

★★★CROWNE PLAZA HOTEL UNIVERSAL

7800 Universal Blvd., Orlando, 407-355-0550, 866-864-8627; www.cporlando.com

If you're traveling to Orlando to visit its theme parks, this contemporary hotel is a great choice. Within a mile of Universal and Wet 'n Wild and within three miles of SeaWorld and Discovery Cove, the Crowne Plaza offers free transportation to all the local theme parks. In case you're worried that the nearby hubbub will keep you up at night, rooms feature plush beds and amenities such as night lights, sleep CDs, lavender eye masks and ear plugs to help you sleep soundly.

400 rooms. Restaurant, bar. Business center. Fitness center. Pool. $151-250

★★★FOUR POINTS BY SHERATON ORLANDO STUDIO CITY

5905 International Drive, Orlando, 407-351-2100, 800-327-1366; www.starwoodhotels.com

Conveniently located next to Universal Studios and near many theme parks, this circular tower hotel is a good home base for a family-oriented Orlando vacation. Hollywood is the theme here, with murals and pictures of movie stars adorning the walls of the lobby.

301 rooms. Restaurant, bar. Fitness center. Pool. $61-150

★★★GRAND BOHEMIAN, ORLANDO

325 S. Orange Ave., Orlando, 407-313-9000, 866-663-0024; www.grandbohemianhotel.com

Part of Marriot's new autograph collection hotels, the artistic interior design is the hallmark of this hotel, with rooms decorated in rich jewel tones, Java wood and velvet. Distinctive artwork is a Grand Bohemian signature, from the pieces decorating the hotel to the 19th- and 20th-century European artwork displayed in the private gallery. The artistic spirit continues in the restaurant and lounge, where blues, jazz and classical music are performed nightly.

250 rooms. Restaurant, bar. Business center. Fitness center. Pool. Pets accepted. $351 and up

★★★HARD ROCK HOTEL

5800 Universal Blvd., Orlando, 407-503-2000, 888-832-7155; www.hardrockhotelorlando.com

The Hard Rock Hotel at Universal Orlando sits on 14 landscaped acres and has a classic California Mission design. You'll find classic rock 'n' roll memorabilia throughout the hotel and hear music virtually everywhere, including underwater at the massive zero-entry pool with a 260-foot water slide. In-room CD sound systems keep the tunes going. Restaurants include the full-service Sunset Grill (featuring an open kitchen) and an Orlando outpost of the famous Palm restaurant.

650 rooms. Restaurant, bar. Business center. Fitness center. Pool. Pets accepted. $151-250

★★★HYATT REGENCY ORLANDO INTERNATIONAL AIRPORT

9300 Airport Blvd., Orlando, 407-825-1234, 800-228-9000; www.hyatt.com

Perfect for travelers with limited time in the Orlando area, the Hyatt Regency Orlando International Airport is located inside the airport's main terminal. A nice perk is that the hotel will arrange for your luggage to be delivered from the baggage claim to your room. There are more than 30 specialty stores within the Hyatt Atrium, as 113 well as an outdoor pool and spa.

445 rooms. Restaurant, bar. Business center. Fitness center. Pool. $151-250

★★★INTERNATIONAL PLAZA RESORT AND SPA

10100 International Drive, Orlando, 407-352-1100, 800-327-0363; www.intlplazaresort.com

Located next to SeaWorld and a short drive to both Disney and Universal Studios, this resort gives you a break from the touristy spots among its 28 acres of tropical landscaping. There's an onsite fitness club and spa, as well as free miniature golf. Caribbean flair sets the tone at the multilevel Blue Marlin Grille, or for a quick meal, try Max's Deli. Visiting the Disney parks is easy with free shuttle service there as well as to the nearby Florida Mall.

1,102 rooms. Restaurant, bar. Business center. Fitness center. Pool. Pets accepted. $151-250

★★★JW MARRIOTT ORLANDO GRANDE LAKES

4040 Central Florida Parkway, Orlando, 407-206-2300, 800-682-9956; www.grandelakes.com

Although this large hotel caters to business travelers, it's also a good bet for those who come to Orlando for rest and relaxation. Set on 500 landscaped acres, the hotel provides three lighted tennis courts, a heated outdoor lagoon-style pool and a 40,000-square-foot spa. Nearby is the Ritz-Carlton Golf Club, an 18-hole course designed by links legend Greg Norman, where JW Marriott guests enjoy preferred tee times and the hotel's personal golf caddie-concierge program. Guest rooms feature cozy duvets as well as laptop safes.

1,000 rooms. Restaurant, bar. Business center. Fitness center. Pool. Tennis. $151-250

★★★MARRIOTT ORLANDO LAKE MARY

1501 International Parkway, Lake Mary, 407-995-1100, 800-380-7724; www.marriott.com

This north Orlando hotel caters to business travelers with "Rooms That Work." If you're looking for a modern hotel that isn't overrun with children wearing Mickey Mouse ears, you've found a winner. Guest rooms feature Marriott's signature Revive bedding with 300-thread count linens, custom European furnishings and granite-and-marble baths. In case you need to continue business over drinks, Cobalt's lounge specializes in martinis. But if doing deals on the golf course is more your style, there are several courses in the area.

299 rooms. Restaurant, bar. Business center. Fitness center. Pool. $151-250

★★★ORLANDO WORLD CENTER MARRIOTT RESORT

8701 World Center Drive, Orlando, 407-239-4200, 800-380-7931; www.marriottworldcenter.com

More is more than the Orlando World Center Marriott Resort. The resort, set on 200 acres, has a spa, an 18-hole championship golf course, five outdoor pools, six whirlpools, two children's pools and a basketball court. Bar and restaurant options range from casual poolside dining to upscale Italian and Japanese restaurants. Guest rooms are also spacious and feature down comforters, comfortable desks and flat-screen televisions.

2,000 rooms. Restaurant, bar. Business center. Fitness center. Pool. Spa. Golf. Tennis. $151-250

★★★★THE PEABODY ORLANDO

9801 International Drive, Orlando, 407-352-4000; www.peabodyorlando.com

Famous for the flock of ducks that waddle through the hotel's lobby twice daily to perform a water ballet in the fountain, this hotel is located across from the Orange Convention Center and close to Orlando's theme parks and performing and visual arts. Spacious rooms have soothing neutral colors, plasma televisions and refrigerators, while the bathrooms come with soap in the shape of the famed resident ducks. The hotel recently added the 32-story Peabody Tower to its property as part of an expansion. The athletic club, pool and tennis courts lure guests away from their rooms, while top-rated golf is just a short drive away. The Peabody's restaurants have something for everyone, from the 1950s-style B-Line Diner—which has a pastry counter filled with drool-inducing desserts—to Capriccio Grill, a sophisticated steak house.

891 rooms. Restaurant, bar. Business center. Fitness center. Pool. Spa. Tennis. $251-350

★★★PORTOFINO BAY HOTEL

5601 Universal Blvd., Orlando, 407-503-1000, 888-430-4999; www.loewshotels.com

The Portofino Bay Hotel at Universal Orlando re-creates the famed Italian fishing village of the same name. Guest rooms feature fluffy white duvets and warm wood furnishings. The hotel has eight different eateries, including the romantic Delfino Riviera; the full-service Trattoria del Porto; and Mama Della's, a family-style Italian restaurant. For drinks, try the Bar American or for a more casual cocktail, head to the Thirsty Fish at the water's edge.

750 rooms. Restaurant, bar. Business center. Fitness center. Pool. Spa. Pets accepted. $251-350

★★★RADISSON HOTEL LAKE BUENA VISTA

12799 Apopka Vineland Road, Orlando, 407-597-3400, 800-395-7406; www.radisson.com

There's sun and a whole lot of fun at this family-friendly vacation spot, which is right in the middle of all the action. The hotel is only a short walk to Disney World and a few minutes from SeaWorld, Universal Studios and the city's best shopping, so you'll always be close to home when you just want to crash at the end of a very long day. Rooms are outfitted with HD flat-screen TVs and Sleep Number Beds.

196 rooms. Restaurant, bar. Fitness center. Pool. $61-150

★★★RENAISSANCE ORLANDO HOTEL AT SEAWORLD
6677 Sea Harbor Drive, Orlando, 407-351-5555, 800-327-6677; www.renaissancehotels.com

Conveniently located across the street from SeaWorld and one mile from the Orange County Convention Center, this resort has an atrium lobby reaching 10 stories high with a free-flowing waterfall, Japanese koi pond and a Venetian free-flight aviary. In case you need activities to keep you busy after visiting Shamu, the hotel offers ping-pong, basketball and volleyball, along with a playground and game room.

781 rooms. Restaurant, bar. Business center. Fitness center. Pool. Tennis. $251-350

★★★★THE RITZ-CARLTON ORLANDO, GRANDE LAKES
4012 Central Florida Parkway, Orlando, 407-206-2400, 800-241-3333; www.ritzcarlton.com

Architecturally, it's an homage to the Grand Palazzo of Italy. Spiritually, the Ritz-Carlton Orlando, Grande Lakes resort draws its Zen-like calm from the Far East. You'll achieve a blissful state in the excellent 40,000-square-foot spa, which features 40 treatment rooms. Golfers reach nirvana on the Greg Norman–designed 18-hole golf course. You'll also find a small oasis in the guest rooms, which have light woods, warm pastel colors, HD LCD televisions and, best of all, private balconies with views of the gardens, lakes and pool. The spacious marble bathrooms have two sinks and separate tubs and showers. Take a break from it all with a meal at one of the hotel's six onsite restaurants, including the elegant Norman's.

584 rooms. Restaurant, bar. Business center. Fitness center. Pool. Spa. Golf. Tennis. $251-350

★★★ROYAL PACIFIC RESORT
6300 Hollywood Way, Orlando, 407-503-3000, 800-235-6397; www.loewshotels.com

The 53-acre Royal Pacific Resort has a South Seas theme and features a towering bamboo forest and

WHAT ARE THE MOST LUXURIOUS HOTELS?

The Peabody Orlando: The hotel's probably best known for its resident ducks. But just as note-worthy are the marble halls, an atrium lobby with palm trees and a fountain, a new 32-story tower as well as spacious rooms with plasma TVs and refrigerators.

The Ritz-Carlton Orlando, Grande Lakes: This Italian-inspired hotel doles out rest in relaxation with its excellent spa and 18-hole golf course. The rooms also provide respite with private balconies overlooking gardens and lakes, and marble bathrooms with separate soaking tubs.

an authentic Balinese tower. Bamboo accents, dark woods and richly colored fabrics lend an air of the tropics to the guest rooms. For outdoor pursuits, the hotel provides a croquet lawn and sand volleyball courts. There are five restaurants and six lounges from which to choose. Perhaps the best amenity for guests is the free Universal Express ride access, which allows you to go to the head of the line at Universal Orlando attractions.

946 rooms. Restaurant, bar. Business center. Fitness center. Pool. Spa. $151-250

★★★ROYAL PLAZA IN THE WALT DISNEY WORLD RESORT

1905 Hotel Plaza Blvd., Lake Buena Vista, 407-828-2828; www.royalplaza.com

Those planning their vacations around Disney will want to consider staying at the Royal Plaza. This large hotel with spacious rooms offers continuous transportation to all of the Disney parks, plus priority seating to Disney restaurants and shows. Kids under 10 can eat for free for breakfast and dinner in the café.

394 rooms. Restaurant, bar. Business Center. Fitness center. Pool. $61-150

★★★WYNDHAM ORLANDO RESORT

8001 International Drive, Orlando, 407-351-2420, 800-421-8001; www.wyndham.com

Offering a taste of Old Florida on the bustling International Drive, the 42-acre Wyndham Orlando Resort is a tranquil retreat from the theme parks. Indoor or outdoor entrances are available for guest rooms, which are surrounded by tropical gardens and lagoons. Amenities include Herman Miller Aeron work chairs, pillow-top mattresses and play areas for the kids.

1,275 rooms. Restaurant, bar. Business center. Fitness center. Pool. Pets accepted. Tennis. $61-150

WHERE TO EAT

COCOA BEACH
★★★MANGO TREE

118 N. Atlantic Ave., Cocoa Beach, 321-799-0513; www.themangotreerestaurant.com

Take a moment to walk around the restaurant's tropical garden, because it's a lush wonderland with bright, striking flowers and a darling fish pond. The dining room inside is just as colorful, if not a bit outdated, and the kitchen serves contemporary American dishes such as scallops in puff pastry with lobster beurre blanc, roasted Long Island duckling, veal scallopini and Indian River crab cakes. The wine list features a nice variety available by the glass and bottle, as well as bottles of champagne, if it's that kind of occasion.

American. Dinner. Closed Monday. Bar. $36-85

ORLANDO
★★★BERGAMO'S

5250 International Drive, Orlando, 407-352-3805; www.bergamos.com

Best known for its singing waitstaff, who take the stage throughout the night to belt out everything from Broadway tunes to opera, this restaurant has definite tourist appeal yet draws a strong local following. Sea bass served in a truffle broth with handmade semolina gnocchi is a house specialty.

Italian. Dinner. Outdoor seating. Children's menu. Bar. $16-35

★★★CHRISTINI'S

7600 Drive Phillips Blvd., Orlando, 407-345-8770; www.christinis.com

A true Italian experience is in store for diners at this International Drive restaurant. The menu features dishes such as linguine with fresh little neck clams, chicken Marsala and veal scaloppini. Owner Chris Christini can often be seen greeting diners in the richly decorated dining room.

Italian. Dinner. Bar. $36-85

★★★DEL FRISCO'S PRIME STEAK AND LOBSTER

729 Lee Road, Orlando, 407-645-4443; www.delfriscosorlando.com

If you're in the mood for a good steak in a unique setting, this is the place for you. Dark wood décor creates the perfect clubby steak house atmosphere. Or take a seat in the more elegant piano lounge, where you'll dine to live music. Tender cuts of beef are accompanied by homemade breads, dressings and desserts (try the bread pudding with Jack Daniel's butter sauce). The wine cellar holds more than 6,500 bottles.

American. Dinner. Closed Sunday. Reservations recommended. Bar. $86 and up

★★★EMERIL'S TCHOUP CHOP

6300 Hollywood Way, Orlando, 407-503-2467; www.emerils.com

Celebrity chef Emeril Lagasse's Orlando restaurant is set in a cavernous, colorful space inside Universal Studio's Royal Pacific Resort. Though the name of the restaurant is a nod to New Orleans' Tchoupitoulas Street, the menu takes its cues from Polynesia, with Asian ingredients and preparations in most dishes. Starters include kim chee spiced shrimp and cucumber poke with Thai sticky rice, while main dishes may include tender sake braised beef short ribs on caramelized onion mashed potatoes with hoisin-honey infused veal jus. You'll also find sushi on the menu. Desserts include crowd-pleasers such as banana cream pie and coconut cake, as well as homemade ice creams and sorbets.

Asian, American. Dinner. Bar. $36-85

★★★★NORMAN'S

4012 Central Florida Parkway, Orlando, 407-393-4333; www.normans.com

The Ritz-Carlton Orlando, Grande Lakes Resort is home to the Orlando outpost of Norman's, owned by celebrity chef and fusion pioneer Norman Van Aken. Menu items change frequently to reflect whatever is fresh and in season, and may include items such as pecan-crusted Florida catfish with sweet potatoes and bacon-braised collard greens, or grilled pork with a smoky plantain crema. An excellent wine list accompanies the innovative menu.

American, Caribbean. Dinner. Closed Monday. Reservations recommended. Outdoor seating. Bar. $36-85

★★★VITO'S CHOP HOUSE

8633 International Drive, Orlando, 407-354-2467; www.vitoschophouse.com

Brick archways lead into the bar and dining areas at this classic steak house with an Italian twist, where the menu includes everything from fresh stone crab to massive steaks and lobsters and meatball marinara. Steaks are flame broiled in a custom-built fire pit. Completing the experience, specialty martinis are available in addition to a large wine list.

American. Dinner. Reservations recommended. Children's menu. Bar. $36-85

SPA

KISSIMMEE

★★★★RELACHE AT GAYLORD PALMS RESORT

6000 W. Osceola Parkway, Kissimmee, 407-586-2051, 800-742-9000; www.gaylordhotels.com

This European-style spa at the Gaylord Palms Resort is the perfect place to spend the day unwinding. Treatments have names like the Muscle Melt, Gaylord Glow and Sole Rejuvenation, and are both luxurious and effective. You can boost the relaxation factor of any treatment by adding an enhancement such as a scalp massage, hand or foot treatment or crystal exfoliation. Massages run the gamut from stone massage to deep tissue to Thai, while facials focus on anti-aging, deep cleansing and hydration. There are also a variety of body therapies and treatments for moms-to-be, as well as a plethora of hair, nail and other salon services.

ORLANDO

★★★★THE RITZ-CARLTON SPA ORLANDO, GRANDE LAKES

4012 Central Florida Parkway, Orlando, 407-206-2400, 800-241-3333; www.ritz-carlton.com

From citrus body polishes to orange-inspired manicures and pedicures, Florida's famous fruit is the basis for many of the treatments at this 40,000-square-foot facility, which also has a lap pool, meditation room, fitness center and salon. Bindi, Thai and shiatsu massage are offered along with Shirodhara and Javanese Lulur rituals. Kids and teens have their own menu, including treatments such as the Ritz Kids fizzing manicure and pedicure or kids massage. Fitness consultations and salon services are also available.

WALT DISNEY WORLD

While Disney World resides in Orlando, the theme park is such a global phenomenon that it deserves its own category. Since opening in 1971, Disney World has received millions of visitors, making it the most popular tourist attraction in the world. From its major theme parks to its resort hotels, everything is run with a bit of make-believe in mind.

While the Magic Kingdom may be the best-known area of the park, it takes up only a fraction of the 28,000-acre resort complex, which is almost twice the size of the island of Manhattan. Combined with Epcot, Disney's Hollywood Studios, Animal Kingdom and a variety of new attractions, Disney World offers loads of fun for days on end.

The Magic Kingdom, the first of the four major parks, has more than 46 attractions as well as shows, shops, exhibits and special theme areas divided into seven lands: Adventureland, Frontierland, Liberty Square, Fantasyland, Tomorrowland and Main Street, U.S.A.

Epcot takes visitors through two distinct worlds. Future World combines rides and attractions, technical innovations, discovery and scientific achievements, bringing to life a world of new ideas, adventures and entertainment. World Showcase unites 11 celebrated nations re-created in detail through architectural landmarks, shops, authentic food and entertainment.

Disney's Hollywood Studios explores the world of movies and television, both on-stage and off, and includes a working studio. Palm-lined, Art Deco-style Hollywood Boulevard offers adventure, entertainment, shopping and dining in true Hollywood style. The park offers a mix of cinema nostalgia, sensational stunt work, television magic and backstage wizardry.

Animal Kingdom incorporates a love for animals. The park contains forests, streams and waterfalls, tropical jungles and savannahs where many animals roam. A thousand birds and mammals representing more than 200 species call the Kingdom home.

In addition, Disney World offers many resorts, hotels, a campground facility with a water park, a 7,500-acre wilderness area, daily parades and fireworks displays, shopping and fine dining, and limitless activities for people of all ages.

WHAT TO SEE

DISNEY'S ANIMAL KINGDOM PARK
407-939-6244; disneyworld.disney.go.com

Part wildlife refuge, part theme park, part horticultural paradise, this place is home to 1,500 animals representing 250 different species. While thrill rides are featured here, the animal habitats take priority. After all, it is a nature conservancy with an active endangered-species-breeding program. More than just an entrance, the Oasis is filled with exotic flora and fauna. Don't miss the opportunity to smell the roses and tropical gardens here. Take the bridge from the Oasis to Discovery Island to begin your adventure. Discovery Island is the central spoke of Animal Kingdom, home to Safari Village, an African-inspired area with a number of shops. For a quick bird's-eye view of the park, ride Expedition Everest, a 200-foot high coaster that speeds forward and backward through the darkness.
Admission: adults $79, children 3-9 $68. Daily; hours vary.

DISNEY'S BLIZZARD BEACH AND TYPHOON LAGOON
407-939-6244; disneyworld.disney.go.com

Blizzard Beach is home to one of the world's tallest and fastest free-falling water-slides as well as raft rides, toboggan slides and a 1-acre wave pool. Typhoon Lagoon features nine water slides descending from a 95-foot summit, a surfing lagoon, saltwater snorkeling with actual sharks and inner tube rides. Both parks offer changing areas, lockers, showers and restaurants.
Daily 9 a.m-7 p.m.

CIRQUE DU SOLEIL LA NOUBA
407-939-7600; ww.cirquedusoleil.com

Its name means "to party" and that's exactly what you'll do at this 90-minute (no intermission) circus that's unlike any you've ever seen. The party is put on by the contortionists of Cirque du Soleil, so expect lots of amazing acrobatics and whimsical characters. Eclectic and colorful, the show appeals to all ages. Located at Downtown Disney's West Side, La Nouba is performed in a 1,671-seat theater designed for the production.
Shows at 6 p.m. and 9 p.m. Tuesday-Saturday.

EPCOT

407-939-6244; disneyworld.disney.go.com

At 300 acres, Epcot is nearly three times the size of the Magic Kingdom. Built around a central lake, Epcot is a figure-eight-shaped park with two distinct areas. Future World features eight pavilions, including Spaceship Earth, a 16-million-pound, 180-foot-tall geosphere; Mission: SPACE, a thrilling and realistic space flight simulator ride; and Journey into Your Imagination, a 14-minute ride that features one of Disney's best-loved characters, Figment, who escorts you through arts, literature and music. The World Showcase pavilions, surrounding a 40-acre lagoon, highlight the cuisine, customs and sundries of 11 nations of the world. Nightly fireworks fill the air over Epcot during Illuminations, a dramatic 15-minute laser, pyrotechnic and water show set to symphonic music, presented around the World Showcase Lagoon.

Daily 9 a.m-9 p.m

DISNEY'S HOLLYWOOD STUDIOS

407-939-6244; disneyworld.disney.go.com

Just southwest of Epcot off the main entrance road, this area houses three film and television soundstages of the Walt Disney Company. You can see the backlots, animation studios, and soundstages of famous films, and hear about how stunt work is done. There are also rides here; feel your stomach drop on a 13-story plunge from The Twilight Zone Tower of Terror or speed through the Rock 'n' Roller Coaster to the tunes of Aerosmith blaring in the background.

Daily 9 a.m-8 p.m.

DOWNTOWN DISNEY

disneyworld.disney.go.com

Located on 120 acres on the north shore of the Buena Vista Lagoon, Downtown Disney includes three sections: Downtown Disney Marketplace, Pleasure Island and Downtown Disney West Side. It's a great place to spend an afternoon away from the theme parks. There are plenty of restaurants, such as Bongos Cuban Cafe and Wolfgang Puck Café, as well as entertainment venues such as the House of Blues, the theater that houses Cirque du Soleil, and for kids, DisneyQuest, which features video games and virtual reality experiences to please all.

Daily.

MAGIC KINGDOM

407-939-6244; disneyworld.disney.go.com

The landscape of the Magic Kingdom is filled with some of the world's most photographed sites that draw millions of families to the park every year. The most notable is Cinderella's Castle, built in 1971. Upon entering the park, stroll down Main Street, U.S.A., the first of seven lands that make up the Magic Kingdom. Others include Adventureland, Frontierland, Liberty Square, Fantasyland and Tomorrowland. There are countless adventures to be had exploring each. Thrill-seekers will make a mad dash for Frontierland's Splash Mountain, a seemingly innocent flume ride through the South, culminating in a 52-foot drop. There's also "It's a Small World" at Fantasyland; Big Thunder Mountain Railroad at Frontierland; Cinderella's Castle at Fantasyland;

SPECIAL EVENTS

DISNEY MARATHON & HALF-MARATHON

407-939-6244; disneyworld.disney.go.com

For the past decade, the Disney Marathon has consistently drawn huge crowds, both runners and spectators alike. The 26.2-mile race begins at Epcot, continues through the Magic Kingdom, Animal Kingdom, the Wide World of Sports complex and Disney's Hollywood Studios, and ends where it began. The half-marathon also begins at Epcot, but after circling the World Showcase, it continues through to the Magic Kingdom and the finish line. Runners must be able to maintain a minimum pace of 16 minutes per mile. Register early for the half-marathon, as participation is capped at 8,000 runners.
Early January.

EPCOT INTERNATIONAL FOOD AND WINE FESTIVAL

Epcot, 407-939-6244; disneyworld.disney.go.com

For almost a decade, Epcot has expanded travelers' palates with its International Food and Wine Festival, showcasing incredible creations from around the world. Appetizers are available for between $1 and $4.50. This celebration of flavor also features more than 30 brewed beers and ales. Wine-tasting seminars are offered at an additional cost, as are dinner pairings. Daily Eat to the Beat concerts by top-name artists are included in the price of admission.
Call ahead for dining reservations. September- early-November.

Country Bear Jamboree at Frontierland; Jungle Cruise at Adventureland; Libery Square Riverboat at Liberty Square; Main Street Vehicles at Main St. Disney darling Jiminy Cricket narrates the nightly fireworks spectacle, Wishes, above Cinderella's Castle and visible throughout the park and surrounding property.
Daily 9 a.m-10 p.m

MAGNOLIA GOLF COURSE
407-938-4653; disneworld.disney.go.com

Magnolia is the longest of the courses at Disney World, but the wide fairways make up for its length and are more forgiving for big hitters whose shots aren't always as straight as they want them to be. More than 1,500 namesake trees dot the landscape, and there are several elevated tee boxes and greens. At the edges of the greens are some 97 bunkers, including one on the sixth hole shaped like the head of the resort's famous mouse mascot.
Admission: $59-180.

OAK TRAIL GOLF COURSE
407-938-4653; disneworld.disney.go.com

Located near the Magnolia Golf Course, Oak Trail is a family-friendly and economical option, both for playing and for simply enjoying the scenic oak-lined trails adjoining the walking course. At 2,913 yards, this Ron Garl-designed course provides a fun yet challenging quick 9 (par 36) with 15 sand bunkers and water on four holes.

OSPREY RIDGE GOLF COURSE
407-938-4653; disneyworld.disney.go.com

Laid out by Tom Fazio, this course features rolling fairways and high mounds that guard medium- to large-sized greens. Known as the most challenging course in the area, it's also the priciest. Though, there is also a cheaper twilight rate. Nearby is the Callaway Golf Performance Center at Bonnet Creek, which allows players to test out new clubs and have their swings evaluated via computer simulation.

PALM GOLF COURSE
407-938-4653; disneyworld.disney.go.com

Up-and-coming course designer Joe Lee laid out the Palm, which has 94 bunkers, 10 holes with water and several holes where sections of the fairway are separated by lengths of water. The 18th hole is a long par-four to an island green that consistently ranks among the toughest 10 holes played by golfers on the PGA Tour. Big hitters may be disappointed because they are forced to lay up to many greens due to water or elevation that makes the approach shot considerably more difficult. Still, it's a challenging and rewarding course to play.

RICHARD PETTY DRIVING EXPERIENCE
Walt Disney World Speedway, Lake Buena Vista, 407-939-0130, 800-237-3889; www.1800bepetty.com

Sports fans can feel the power and speed of stock car racing at this race-track attraction. Different programs include Ride-Along (for those 16 and older), where you ride shotgun with a professional driver. The Rookie Experience, for the true stock car beginner (18 and older), is a three-hour session that goes eight laps around the track with you in charge. The more experienced can try the Kings Experience, where you race around the track for 18 laps, run in one eight-lap and one 10-lap session. And finally, for the true stock car junkie, there is the Experience of a Lifetime (18 and older): 30 white-knuckle laps driven in 10-lap increments.
See website for scheduling details.

DISNEY'S WIDE WORLD OF SPORTS COMPLEX
407-939-6244; disneyworld.disney.go.com

The complex features 200 acres of spectator sports facilities, including a baseball stadium, a cross-country course, a track and field complex, a martial arts venue and various sports fields. Spring training for baseball's Atlanta Braves is held here.

WHERE TO STAY

★★★BOHEMIAN HOTEL CELEBRATION
700 Bloom St., Celebration, 407-566-6000, 888-499-3800; www.celebrationhotel.com

Part of Marriot's new autograph collection hotels, this intimate boutique hotel offers a decidedly adult experience compared to other hotels in the Disney

World area. Rooms are luxurious with four-poster beds in some. Golf here is top notch, and Plantation restaurant is a great spot for a relaxing dinner.

115 rooms. Restaurant. Business center. Fitness center. Pool. $151-250

★★★CARIBE ROYALE

8101 World Center Drive, Lake Buena Vista, 407-238-8000, 800-823-8300; www.cariberoyale.com

This hotel is a smart choice for families wanting close proximity to the theme parks. But you needn't leave the hotel grounds to find recreational fun. You can play basketball on the lighted full-size court, or you can cool off in the free-form pool with cascading waterfalls and a 75-foot water slide. Suites are spacious and include separate bedrooms with queen or king beds, and pull-out sofa beds in the living rooms. Lakeside villas have kitchens and either screened lanais or balconies.

1,218 rooms. Restaurant. Complimentary breakfast. Business center. Fitness center. Pool. Tennis. $151-250

★★★DISNEY'S ANIMAL KINGDOM LODGE

2901 Osceola Parkway, Lake Buena Vista, 407-939-6244; disneyworld.disney.go.com

Disney offers the next best thing to a safari at the 75-acre Animal Kingdom Lodge, located in the middle of a lush 33-acre savannah that's home to more than 200 exotic animals. African influences permeate the property, from the handcrafted furnishings to the native cuisine served in two of the onsite restaurants. This resort isn't as close to Downtown Disney and the Magic Kingdom as other resorts, but transportation is free and frequent.

1,293 rooms. Restaurant, bar. Fitness center. Pool. Spa. $251-350

★★★DISNEY'S BOARDWALK INN

2101 N. Epcot Resorts Blvd., Lake Buena Vista, 407-939-6244; disneyworld.disney.go.com

With the feel of the Atlantic City Boardwalk in the 1940s—complete with vintage roller coasters and period furnishings—the main hotel is a bit more luxurious than its time-share villa counterpart on the same waterfront Boardwalk. The Boardwalk that the hotel overlooks is chock-full of midway attractions and nightlife, and is home to some of Disney's best restaurants.

372 rooms. Restaurant, bar. Business center. Fitness center. Pool. Spa. Tennis. $351 and up

★★★DISNEY'S BEACH CLUB RESORT

1800 Epcot Resorts Blvd., Lake Buena Vista, 407-939-6244; disneyworld.disney.go.com

Architect Robert A.M. Stern has re-created a New England village with a nautical, turn-of-the-century theme. Built to look like a real seaside resort, it has waterslides and the sandy-bottomed Stormalong Bay, which holds 750,000 gallons of water. Rent boats at the marina, play a game of sand volleyball or ride bikes around the grounds.

854 rooms. Restaurant, bar. Business center. Fitness center. Pool. Spa. Beach. Tennis. $351 and up

★★★DISNEY'S CONTEMPORARY RESORT

4600 N. World Drive, Lake Buena Vista, 407-939-6244; disneyworld.disney.go.com

One of Walt Disney World's original resorts, this 14-story A-frame contemporary hotel is one of the most unusual Disney icons. Inside there's a cavernous atrium and on the fourth floor, you can catch a monorail that travels directly through the hotel's center to attractions like Magic Kingdom and Epcot. The "futuristic" property, which opened with the Magic Kingdom in 1971, features modern textures and designs, as well as vibrant colors. Go to the rooftop California Grill for great views of the Magic Kingdom fireworks.

655 rooms. Restaurant, bar. Fitness center. Pool. Spa. $251-350

★★★DISNEY'S CORONADO SPRINGS RESORT

1000 W. Buena Vista Drive, Lake Buena Vista, 407-939-6244; disneyworld.disney.go.com

Located near Epcot, Disney's Hollywood Studios and Animal Kingdom, the boardwalk at Disney's Coronado Springs Resort draws its inspiration from Francisco de Coronado's travels from Mexico to the American Southwest. The hacienda-style resort is accented by mosaics, arched windows and doorways, clay-tile roofs, and even has a five-story Mayan pyramid waterfall at the family pool.

1,917 rooms. Restaurant, bar. Business center. Fitness center. Pool. Spa. Beach. $151-250

★★★DISNEY'S GRAND FLORIDIAN RESORT & SPA

4401 Floridian Way, Lake Buena Vista, 407-939-6244; disneyworld.disney.go.com

Resembling a fairy-tale castle with white towers and a red-tiled roof, Disney's Grand Floridian Resort & Spa offers a lakefront location right in the center of Walt Disney World. The Victorian lobby has an 85-foot-tall ceiling, crystal chandeliers and an aviary. Cooking-themed events, Alice in Wonderland tea parties and even pirate-ship cruises are just a few of the kids programs offered here. Dining options are plentiful as well.

867 rooms. Restaurant, bar. Business center. Fitness center. Pool. Spa. Beach. Tennis. $351 and up

★★★DISNEY'S POLYNESIAN RESORT

1600 Seven Seas Drive, Lake Buena Vista, 407-939-6244; disneyworld.disney.go.com

One of the original resorts at Walt Disney World, the Polynesian opened alongside the Magic Kingdom in 1971. Its tropical-themed rooms, decorated with upscale furnishings, are nestled along the shores of the Seven Seas Lagoon. The marina offers an assortment of boats to rent, and there is a large waterslide in one of the pool areas. The hotel affords incredible views of the Magic Kingdom's nightly fireworks show. The popular Polynesian Luau Dinner Show at the Great Ceremonial House is presented twice nightly (depending on the weather).

847 rooms. Restaurant, bar. Fitness center. Pool. Spa. Beach. $351 and up

★★★DISNEY'S PORT ORLEANS RIVERSIDE RESORT

1251 Riverside Drive, Lake Buena Vista, 407-939-6244; disneyworld.disney.go.com

The banks of Disney's re-created Sassagoula River provide a Deep South setting for the moderately priced Port Orleans Riverside Resort, reminiscent of a bayou mansion. The guest rooms are rustic with birch furniture and stone accents in the bathrooms. The resort features seven pools and a 3-acre Ol' Man Island that's great for fishing for catfish, bass and bluegill and swimming.

2,048 rooms. Restaurant, bar. Pool. $151-250

★★★DISNEY'S WILDERNESS LODGE

901 Timberline Drive, Lake Buena Vista, 407-939-6244; disneyworld.disney.go.com

The Pacific Northwest and all the glory of the country's national parks are recalled in the beauty of the rustic Wilderness Lodge. Located on the south shore of the 340-acre Bay Lake, the lobby boasts a massive 82-foot-tall, three-sided quarried stone fireplace and décor inspired by Native American designs. Adding to the ambience are bubbling springs and a 12-story geyser that erupts every hour. Boat and bicycle rentals are available, as is an onsite health club and biking and jogging trails.

727 rooms. Restaurant, bar. Fitness center. Pool. Spa. Beach. $251-350

★★★DISNEY'S YACHT CLUB RESORT

1700 Epcot Resort Blvd., Orlando, 407-939-6244; disneyworld.disney.go.com

Designed by architect Robert A.M. Stern, this waterside hotel feels like a coastal New England inn, complete with a working lighthouse. Just a short walk from Disney's Boardwalk and convenient to all of the parks, the wrap-around porch and sandy-bottomed pool make it feel like a retreat. Rent a bicycle for two to ride around the grounds or take a short cruise around the man-made lake.

630 rooms. Restaurant, bar. Business center. Fitness center. Pool. Spa. Beach. Tennis. $351 and up

★★★HILTON IN THE WALT DISNEY WORLD RESORT

1751 Hotel Plaza Blvd., Lake Buena Vista, 407-827-4000, 800-445-8667; www.hilton-wdwv.com

Located inside the Walt Disney World Resort, this pink and blue hotel is set on 23 private acres, complete with sparkling fountains, two outdoor pools and nine restaurant and lounge options. The hotel offers complimentary transportation to the parks and also has a program that allows guests extended hours in the park. Guest rooms were recently renovated and feature soft colors and LCD televisions.

814 rooms. Restaurant, bar. Business center. Fitness center. Pool. $151-250

★★★HYATT REGENCY GRAND CYPRESS

1 Grand Cypress Blvd., Orlando, 407-239-1234, 800-554-9288; www.hyattgrandcypress.com

The amenities abound at this large hotel. You'll find a private lake, miles of tropical nature trails that are great for hiking, a pool with cascading waterfalls, 12 tennis courts, a game room for the kids, an equestrian center and plenty of golf, played on 45 magnificent holes designed by Jack Nicklaus. The resort recently underwent a $45 million renovation, making guest rooms more modern and energy-efficient.

750 rooms. Restaurant, bar. Business center. Fitness center. Pool. Golf. Tennis. $251-350

★★★VILLAS OF GRAND CYPRESS

1 N. Jacaranda, Orlando, 407-239-4700, 877-330-7377; www.grandcypress.com

Tucked away behind a private gate, these villas within the 1,500-acre Hyatt resort are spacious and elegantly appointed with traditional furnishings. Each villa has its own private terrace with a view of the water or the fairways of the North Course. The Golf Academy is renowned, while the resort's equestrian center, approved by the British Horse Society, offers instruction for all levels. You'll also find two pools, a rock climbing wall, jogging trails and lots more,

plus you're still connected to Disney, so you'll never run out of things to do.
146 rooms. Restaurant, bar. Fitness center. Pool. Golf. Tennis. $251-350

★★★WALT DISNEY WORLD DOLPHIN
1500 Epcot Resorts Blvd., Lake Buena Vista, 407-934-4000, 888-828-8850;
www.swandolphin.com

Designed by renowned architect Michael Graves, this hotel features a waterfall
cascading down the front of the building into a pool supported by two towering
dolphin statues. A great place for conventioneers and vacationers alike, the
Dolphin has many dining options, great access to the theme parks and a view
of Epcot's fireworks over the lake. Guests receive free transportation to Walt
Disney World by both land and water.

2,265 rooms. Restaurant, bar. Business center. Fitness center. Pool. Spa. Tennis. $251-350

★★★WALT DISNEY WORLD SWAN
1200 Epcot Resort Blvd., Lake Buena Vista, 407-934-3000, 888-828-8850;
www.swandolphin.com

You're not likely to miss this hotel. Designed by architect Michael Graves, it
features two nearly five-story-tall swans that nest regally above the hotel, with
multicolored waves fanning the building's outer walls. The resort has four
onsite pools and a beach surrounded by lush, tranquil gardens. An impressive
17 restaurants and lounges are available between the Swan and the adjoining
Dolphin hotel. Rooms at the Swan include Westin's Heavenly Beds, designer
headboards and carpeting and picture-wash lighting.

1,500 rooms. Restaurant, bar. Business center. Fitness center. Pool. Spa. Tennis. $251-350

WHERE TO EAT

★★★ARTIST POINT
901 W. Timberline Drive, Lake Buena Vista, 407-824-1081; disneyworld.disney.go.com

Enjoy Pacific Northwest cuisine at this restaurant in Disney's Wilderness
Lodge and Resort, where salmon and wild game are the specialties. The seven-
story fireplace in the lobby and the man-made geyser that erupts several times
an hour make for a dramatic backdrop.

Pacific Northwest. Dinner. Reservations recommended. Children's menu. $36-85

★★★JIKO—THE COOKING PLACE
2901 Osceola Parkway, Lake Buena Vista, 407-939-3463; disneyworld.disney.go.com

Jiko takes a unique approach to Disney dining with its African-inspired
seasonal menu. Twin wood-burning ovens turn out a variety of meat dishes,
like barbecue beef short ribs, alongside vegan and vegetarian fare, like seared
maize pudding with chakalaka and basil beurre blanc.

African. Dinner. Reservations recommended. Children's menu. $36-85

★★★★VICTORIA AND ALBERT'S
Grand Floridian Resort and Spa, 4401 Floridian Way, Lake Buena Vista, 407-939-3463;
disneyworld.disney.go.com

Victoria and Albert's is tailor-made for those craving sophistication. Thick
drapes, plush carpeting and elegant table settings help give it a Victorian feel. To
match the regal ambience, the kitchen provides an equally impressive six-course

prix fixe menu. Dinner begins with an assortment of amuse bouche and ends with petit fours and a large selection of Madeira, ports and cognacs. The wine list is diverse and extensive, and wine pairings are offered. Personalized menus and complimentary long-stem roses for the ladies are just a few of the special touches you can expect while dining at this elegant establishment.

French, International. Dinner. Reservations recommended. Bar. $86 and up

★★★YACHTSMAN STEAKHOUSE

1700 Epcot Resort Blvd., Lake Buena Vista, 407-939-3463; disneyworld.disney.go.com

The feel of casual New England pervades this American steak house with a blue-and-khaki nautical décor. The display of aged meats as you walk in clues you in to what's on the menu—juicy steaks and chops. There is also a variety of seafood as well as chicken and lamb dishes. Sides include a decadent truffle mac and cheese and creamed spinach, while desserts feature mango cheesecake and sundaes. Kids can order chicken strips and pasta.

Steak. Dinner. Reservations recommended. Children's menu. Bar. $36-85

RECOMMENDED

CALIFORNIA GRILL

Disney's Contemporary Resort, 4600 N. World Drive, Lake Buena Vista, 407-939-3463; www.disneyworld.disney.go.com

You can reach this restaurant via a private express elevator that will take you up to the 15th floor at Disney's Contemporary Resort, where this restaurant is located. As the name suggests, the focus is on fresh California cuisine, with everything from sushi to steak to vegetarian fare on the menu. The menu changes regularly to reflect what's in season and may include Sonoma goat cheese ravioli or crispy chicken with leek and manchego fondue. The California-focused wine list pairs perfectly. Depending on where you sit, you may get a view of the Seven Seas Lagoon below, Magic Kingdom or the fireworks above Cinderella Castle.

American. Dinner. Reservations recommended. Children's menu. Bar. $36-85

CITRICOS

Grand Floridian, 4401 Floridian Way, Lake Buena Vista, 407-939-3463; www.disneyworld.disney.go.com

Wine lovers should book a table at this casually upscale restaurant within the Grand Floridian resort. Servers are well versed on just the right wine pairing to accompany your selections from the Mediterranean menu, which may include braised short ribs with creamy polenta or Berkshire pork prepared as pork tenderloin and braised pork belly. (Helpful wine pairings are also listed on the menu.) Desserts are also paired with wine for the perfect finish.

Mediterranean. Dinner. Reservations recommended. Bar. $36-86

FLYING FISH CAFÉ

2101 N. Epcot Resorts Blvd., Lake Buena Vista, 407-939-2359; www.disneyworld.disney.go.com

If you're looking for fresh seafood and a lively atmosphere, you'll be very happy with the Flying Fish Café. The décor takes its cue from the Atlantic Boardwalk—decorative roller coaster tracks, fun house mirrors and a backlit Ferris wheel are used to set a fun and laid-back tone. Try the signature potato-wrapped red

snapper with a leek fondue, and a side of the truffle and herb-laced fries served with a garlic aioli. The after-dinner flights are a nice way to end the evening.
Seafood. Dinner. Bar. $16-35

OHANA

Disney's Polynesian Resort, 1600 Osceola Parkway, Lake Buena Vista, 407-939-2359; www.disneyworld.disney.go.com

Family-style dining is the name of the game here (Ohana means family in Hawaiian culture). Skewers of pork loin, shrimp, steak, and turkey, which are roasted over an open fire pit, are served tableside. Feast on these alongside a variety of noodle dishes, fried dumplings and stir-fried vegetables.
Pan-Asian. Breakfast, dinner. Reservations recommended. Children's menu. $16-35

PORTOBELLO

1650 Buena Vista Drive, Lake Buena Vista, 407-934-8888; www.levyrestaurants.com

Portobello's offers a taste of Italy with its antipasti platters, bubbling-hot pizza and fresh seafood. Signature pizzas made in a wood-burning oven are topped with ingredients such as salumi and sun-dried tomatoes. Sandwiches are also made in the wood-burning oven. Hearty pasta dishes include a penne bolgnese with slow booked beef and a pork ragu, or a black linguine with Florida rock shrimp. A value menu includes soup or salad, penne bolognese or chicken farfalle and gelato, for only $24.95. A children's menu features tasty and healthy choices, including whole wheat cheese pizzas, spaghetti and build-your-own sundaes made with non-fat ice cream.
Italian. Lunch, dinner. Outdoor seating. Children's menu. $16-35

SOUTHWEST FLORIDA

Its location along the Gulf of Mexico makes Southwest Florida a beachy retreat. Fort Myers Beach, located beside the seven-mile sliver of Estero Island, has the Gulf on one side and Estero Bay, never more than three blocks away, on the other. The 18th-century pirates who frequented the area might be gone, but tourists love to poke in the sand for treasures—most likely they will just find seashells, starfish and sea horses. The beach stretches the length of the island and is considered one of the safest in the state.

If you are a beachcomber looking for shells by the seashore, try Sanibel Island. Linked to the mainland by a causeway, Sanibel Island is considered the third-best shelling site in the Western Hemisphere, with deposits on both bay and Gulf beaches. North of Sanibel, only a bridge away, is Captiva. Legend has it that the pirate Jose Gaspar used the island to harbor his women captives. Together the islands comprise the Sanibel National Wildlife Refuge, a haven for more than 200 varieties of birds. The islands are a popular tourist destination.

Wedged between Fort Myers to the north and Naples to the south, Bonita Springs boasts its own distinct Gulf vibe. The town is known for its golfing, fishing and boating, since the Imperial River flows through the city.

Named after the Italian city and complete with a "Bay of Naples," Naples has 10 miles of beach and a 1,000-foot fishing pier, both of which are visitor favorites. Naples is also home to more than 60 golf courses and is a stop on the Senior PGA Tour.

Other sun-and-sand spots can be found just off the coast of the region. Marco Island is the largest and northernmost of the Ten Thousand Islands. The island is noted for its luxurious hotels, restaurants and golf courses. Siesta Key has been hailed as a top island destination, and Crescent Beach has been rated as one of the top three beaches in the world. Shell hunters, snorkelers and anglers usually have great success here. With close proximity to Sarasota and its attractions, Siesta Key is a good base from which to take in the sights.

WHAT TO SEE

BONITA SPRINGS
EVERGLADES WONDER GARDENS
27180 Old U.S. Highway 41, Bonita Springs, 239-992-2591

Opened in 1936, this small zoological garden is one of the oldest in Florida and features reptiles, birds and animals native to the Everglades. There's also a charming, if slightly outdated, natural history museum on the site. Guided tours are available throughout the day; call for details.
Admission: $15. Daily 9 a.m.-5 p.m.

MIROMAR OUTLETS
Corkscrew Road at Interstate 75, Estero, 239-948-3766;
www.miromaroutlets.com

Outlet malls are a fixture in South Florida, and this one contains more than 140 factory stores for you to shop till you drop. Stores include Adidas, Aldo, Coach, Michael Kors, BCBG Max Azria and Neiman Marcus Last Call.
Monday-Saturday 10 a.m.-9 p.m., Sunday 11 a.m.-6 p.m.

FORT MYERS
CALUSA NATURE CENTER & PLANETARIUM
3450 Ortiz Ave., Fort Myers, 239-275-3435;
www.calusanature.com

This nature center has more than 100 acres of pine flatwoods and bald cypress swamp. There's also a butterfly aviary with more than 30 different species. The Planetarium portion features star shows, and laser light and music shows. Other draws for tourists include nature exhibits, a natural history shop, two miles of nature trails and guided walks.
Admission: adults $9, children 3-12 $6, children 2 and under free. Monday-Saturday 9 a.m.-5 p.m., Sunday 11 a.m-5 p.m.

EDISON WINTER HOUSE & BOTANICAL GARDENS
2350 McGregor Blvd., Fort Myers, 239-334-7419; www.efwefla.org

In 1885, inventor Thomas Edison, ailing at the age of 38, built this 14-acre riverfront estate, where he wintered for the next half century. The house and guesthouse, designed by Edison, were brought by ship from Maine. The complex includes a museum with inventions, mementos and a chemical labo-ratory; the first modern swimming pool in the state; and an extraordinary botanical garden with mature specimens from around the world.

Admission: adults $20, children 6-12 $11 (for both Edison Winter House and Henry Ford Winter House). Daily 9 a.m.-5:30 p.m.

HENRY FORD WINTER HOUSE

2350 McGregor Blvd., Fort Myers, 239-334-7419; www.efwefla.org

Mangoes, the winter residence of Henry Ford, one of the world's first billionaires, is next door to the house of Ford's good friend, Thomas Edison. The house reflects the home-grown Midwestern values of Ford and his wife, Clara, as well as the impact extraordinary wealth had on their lives.

Admission: adults $20, children 6-12 $11 (for both Edison Winter House and Henry Ford Winter House). Daily 9 a.m.-5:30 p.m.

SOUTH FLORIDA MUSEUM OF HISTORY

2300 Peck St., Fort Myers, 239 321-7430; www.swflmuseumofhistory.com

In this museum, visitors will learn about the area's early Native American inhabitants, including the Paleo Indians, the Calusa and Seminoles, and Spanish explorers.

Admission: adults $9.50, seniors $8.50, students and children 3-12 $5. Tuesday-Saturday 10 a.m.-5 p.m.

MARCO ISLAND

TIGERTAIL BEACH

490 Hernando Court, Marco Island, 239-389-5000; www.cityofmarcoisland.com

This public beach, operated by the City of Marco Island, is a great location for shelling and bird-watching along the soft white sand. Facilities include restrooms, a concession stand—which offers equipment rentals and food—parking spaces and five boardwalks.

Admission: free, $4 parking fee. Daily dawn-dusk.

NAPLES

DELNOR-WIGGINS PASS STATE RECREATION AREA

11100 Gulfshore Drive, Naples, 239-597-6196; www.floridastateparks.org

This beachfront island park is known for fishing, shelling and swimming. Visitors can also enjoy picnicking and views from an observation tower.

Admission: $3-5 per car. Daily 8 a.m.-dusk.

NAPLES ZOO AT CARIBBEAN GARDENS

1590 Goodlette-Frank Road, Naples, 239-262-5409; www.caribbeangardens.com

This 52-acre botanical garden features animals, birds

and plants from around the world. There are also boat tours, wild animal shows, tropical bird circus and lectures, plus a picnic area, snack bar, petting zoo and gift shop.

Admission: adults $20, seniors $19, children 3-12 $12, children 2 and under free. Daily 9:30 a.m.-5:30 p.m.

ROOKERY BAY NATIONAL ESTUARINE RESEARCH RESERVE

300 Tower Road, Naples, 239-417-6310; www.rookerybay.org

This 9,400-acre reserve encompasses a variety of habitats, including extensive mangrove forests, sea grasses, salt marshes and upland pine flatwoods. You can also observe various wildlife and bird species. Ask about slide shows, interpretive displays, boat and canoe trips (in winter) and guided boardwalk tours.

Admission: $5. Daily 8 a.m.-5 p.m.

SANIBEL AND CAPTIVA ISLANDS
BAILEY-MATTHEWS SHELL MUSEUM

3075 Sanibel-Captiva Road, Sanibel Island, 239-395-2233, 888-679-6450; www.shellmuseum.org

This is the only museum in the United States devoted entirely to the shells of the world. Major exhibits include "Shells in Architecture," "Mollusks and Medicine and Man," and "Kingdom of the Land Shells."

Daily 10 a.m.-5 p.m.

ISLAND HISTORICAL MUSEUM

950 Dunlop Road, Sanibel Island, 239-472-4648; www.sanibelmuseum.org

This former Cracker-style homestead was restored and furnished to depict the lifestyle of early settlers. The village includes a grocery store, tea room and post office.

Wednesday-Saturday 10 a.m.-4 p.m.

WHERE TO STAY

BONITA SPRINGS
★★★HYATT REGENCY COCONUT POINT RESORT & SPA

5001 Coconut Road, Bonita Springs, 239-444-1234, 800-233-1234; www.hyatt.com

Keep the whole family entertained at this 26-acre tropical resort on Estero Bay. You can relax on the secluded beach, glide down the 140-foot waterslide into the lagoon-style pool or get pampered at the Stillwater Spa. Beach lovers can tan to their heart's content at the resort's private beach, and outdoorsy types can check with the concierge about kayaking though the area's lush mangroves. Comfortable guest rooms feature Floridian décor in shades of peach and sage, marble-topped vanities and balconies with views.

454 rooms. Restaurant, bar. Business center. Fitness center. Pool. Spa. Beach. Golf. Tennis. $251-350

FORT MYERS
★★★SANIBEL HARBOUR RESORT & SPA

17260 Harbour Point Drive, Fort Myers, 239-466-4000, 800-767-7777; www.sanibel-resort.com

Dubbed a fishing paradise in the late 1800s, this 80-acre resort was rebuilt on the original site of the Tarpon House Inn. A Victorian-inspired getaway on the private Punta Rassa peninsula, the resort offers a spa and fitness center. A large, free-form pool is a waterfront oasis surrounded by palm trees and lounge chairs.

240 rooms. Restaurant, bar. Business center. Fitness center. Pool. Spa. Beach. Tennis. $251-350

FORT MYERS BEACH

★★★PINK SHELL BEACH RESORT & SPA

275 Estero Blvd., Fort Myers Beach, 239-463-6181, 888-222-7465; www.pinkshell.com

With 1,500 feet of beach, this resort is located on 12 acres at the northern end of Estero Island. The whimsical pool, with infinity edges and sculptures of shells and sea horses, is popular with kids. Adults love the onsite Aquagëne Spa for its stress-relieving aromatherapy treatments, massages and body wraps, and Bongo's Bar and Grill, the poolside-serving restaurant and bar. The villas and suites at Pink Shell offer all the conveniences of home, such as a refrigerator, stove and microwave, plus the great perks of a hotel, such as daily housekeeping and amazing ocean views.

225 rooms. Restaurant, bar. Pool. Spa. Beach. Tennis. $251-350

LONGBOAT KEY

★★★HILTON LONGBOAT KEY BEACH RESORT

4711 Gulf of Mexico Drive, Longboat Key, 941-383-2451, 800-445-8667; www.hilton.com

This resort has a 400-foot private beach on the Gulf of Mexico, and is convenient to exclusive shopping and restaurants. Guest rooms are spacious and comfortable, drenched in serene colors punctuated by bright touches, such as one brick-red wall or navy ottomans. Some rooms overlook the beach and the pool. Latitude's Beach Cafe offers indoor or alfresco dining on a beachside deck. For guests who can't get enough of the Gulf, other activities available include fishing, jet-skiing and sailing.

102 rooms. Restaurant, bar. Fitness center. Pool. Beach. $151-250

★★★LONGBOAT KEY CLUB AND RESORT

301 Gulf of Mexico Drive, Longboat Key, 941-383-8821, 888-237-5545; www.longboatkeyclub.com

This property sits on the barrier island of Longboat Key off the Sarasota coast. Located here are 45 holes of golf, 38 Har-Tru tennis courts, a comprehensive fitness center, a spa and a private beach with water sports. Dining options are also as diverse, from a poolside bar to an elegant restaurant with a view of the marina. The resort's rooms and suites are comfortable, with calming natural-toned bedding and furniture. All include flat-screen televisions and beds with crisp linens. If it takes more than a good night's sleep to relax, then head to the 9,000-square-foot Island House Spa, which offers everything from massages and body treatments to salon services.

218 rooms. Restaurant, bar. Fitness center. Pool. Spa. Beach. Golf. Tennis. $151-250

MARCO ISLAND
★★★HILTON MARCO ISLAND BEACH RESORT
560 S. Collier Blvd., Marco Island, 239-394-5000, 800-445-8667; www.hilton.com

At this resort, you can enjoy a variety of water sports, including sailing, parasailing and jet skiing, or choose to stay dry while playing tennis or volleyball. The large, free-form heated pool, surrounded by comfy lounge chairs, is also a huge draw for those looking to kick back. However, the 11,000 square feet of meeting space makes this place a popular choice for business gatherings as well. Guest rooms are well-maintained—with large beds and complimentary HBO on the flat-screen TVs—and many afford expansive views of the sparkling beach.

300 rooms. Restaurant, bar. Complimentary breakfast. Business center. Fitness center. Pool. Spa. Beach. Tennis. $151-250

★★★MARCO BEACH OCEAN RESORT
480 S. Collier Blvd., Marco Island, 239-393-1400, 800-715-8517; www.marcoresort.com

This hotel is on Marco Island's white-sand Crescent Beach. Each suite is elegantly furnished and amenities include marble showers and vanity tops, fully equipped kitchens and floor-to-ceiling sliding glass doors through which to catch that vibrant Gulf sunset, plus they all have balconies or garden patios. Sale e Pepe, the fine Italian restaurant on the premises, offers delicious seasonal fare in a regal setting. The resort's spa boasts eight treatment rooms—for a bevy of massages and facials—saunas and steam rooms.

98 rooms. Restaurant, bar. Business center. Fitness center. Pool. Spa. Beach. Golf. Tennis. $251-350

★★★MARCO ISLAND MARRIOTT BEACH RESORT
400 S. Collier Blvd., Marco Island, 239-394-2511, 800-438-4373; www.marcoislandmarriott.com

This recently renovated Gulf-front hotel sits along a long stretch of white sand, meaning that most rooms and suites have great views of the water and from

WHICH HOTEL IS BEST FOR FAMILIES?

The Ritz-Carlton, Naples:
In addition to the pool and beach, kids will love the high-tech entertainment lounge, which hosts Wii bowling tournaments. If you can pry them away, there's also a wonderful nature program, which includes a sanctuary with eleven aquariums, a small lab filled with all the tools that a budding biologist needs, a theater where National Geographic, Discovery programs and Disney movies are shown, and daily activities that include nature walks and boat rides.

a private balcony, no less. If you can tear yourself away from the vistas, you'll appreciate the Bali-inspired room decor, flat-screen television and 300-count sheets on the bed. Golfers can visit the onsite golf club, and everyone can relax at the pool or try one of the six restaurants.

727 rooms. Restaurant, bar. Business center. Fitness center. Pool. Spa. Beach. Golf. Tennis. $151-250

NAPLES

★★★BAYFRONT INN 5TH AVENUE
1221 Fifth Ave. S., Naples, 239-649-5800, 800-382-7941; www.bayfrontinnnaples.com
One mile from the beach, this hotel is on the bay and within walking distance to Tin City, Bayfront Marketplace and other shops. Guest rooms feature contemporary décor with rich, dark wood, flat-screen TVs, comfortable beds and large bathrooms. The restaurant and bar offer a relaxing place to sit and enjoy the view of the bay.

98 rooms. Restaurant, bar. Complimentary breakfast. Business center. Pool. $151-250

★★★EDGEWATER BEACH HOTEL & CLUB
1901 Gulf Shore Blvd. N., Naples, 888-325-7711;
www.edgewaternaples.com
This contemporary beachfront hotel offers suites with a crisp, clean design and plenty of amenities, like flat-screen TVs in the bedroom and living room; a kitchen with a refrigerator, toaster and microwave; and a sleeper sofa. It also offers a long stretch of sandy beach, which is best enjoyed if you book a Gulf-view room.

126 rooms. Restaurant, bar. Fitness center. Pool. Spa. Beach. Golf. Tennis. $251-350

★★★HILTON NAPLES AND TOWERS
5111 Tamiami Trail N., Naples, 239-430-4900, 800-445-8667;
www.hiltonnaples.com
This convenient hotel is located in Naples' business and shopping districts and near the beach. Contemporary guest rooms and the impressive lobby area are tastefully decorated, and verdant grounds surround the pool area. Onsite activities include basketball, ping-pong and bicycling. The ever popular Shula's Steakhouse serves lunch and dinner.

199 rooms. Restaurant, bar. Business center. Fitness center. Pool. $151-250

★★★INN ON FIFTH
699 Fifth Ave. S., Naples, 239-403-8777, 888-403-8778;
www.innonfifth.com
Formerly a bank built in the 1950s, this elegant inn is done up in Mediterranean décor and features marble flooring, elaborate chandeliers and wrought-iron balconies. Guest rooms are spacious and have pillow-top beds, fluffy robes and complimentary newspapers. Suites feature sliding French doors that open up to balconies outfitted with rattan rocking chairs—perfect for sunning yourself. Situated in the heart of downtown Naples, this hotel is surrounded by boutiques and restaurants.

87 rooms. Restaurant, bar. Complimentary breakfast. Fitness center. Pool. $251-350

★★★LAPLAYA BEACH & GOLF RESORT
9891 Gulf Shore Drive, Naples, 239-597-3123, 800-237-6883;
www.laplayaresort.com

With the Gulf of Mexico on one side and the bay on the other, LaPlaya has beautiful views from every direction. Waterfalls and lush plants surround the pool area, and a large covered porch awaits guests who want to relax in one of the rocking chairs. Shuffleboard, bike rentals, jet skis and parasailing are among the activities offered onsite.

189 rooms. Restaurant, bar. Fitness center. Pool. Spa. Pets accepted. Beach. Golf. $251-350

★★★THE NAPLES BEACH HOTEL & GOLF CLUB
851 Gulf Shore Blvd. N., Naples, 239-261-2222, 800-455-1546; www.naplesbeachhotel.com

Orchids are the theme here, with various colors and sizes displayed throughout the hotel. Rooms have plantation shutters and balconies, and are decorated in pastel greens and blues. For guests who need extra space to spread out, one- and two-bedroom suites are also available—they come complete with a kitchenette, microwave and refrigerator.

318 rooms. Restaurant, bar. Pool. Spa. Golf. Tennis. $251-350

★★★NAPLES GRANDE BEACH RESORT
475 Seagate Drive, Naples, 239-597-3232, 888-422-6177; www.naplesgranderesort.com

The Naples Grande Beach Resort captures the elegance of this western Florida resort town. Spacious guest rooms are richly decorated and well-equipped. Contemporary bungalows awash in serene colors and streamlined, Asian-inspired furnishings are also available. Three miles of beach fronting the Gulf of Mexico are accessed by a tram that winds its way through some of the resort's 300 acres of mangrove forest. Of course, if you're an avid golfer, you probably won't leave the green—the resort boasts an 18-hole, par-72 course.

474 rooms. Restaurant, bar. Complimentary breakfast. Business center. Fitness center. Pool. Spa. Beach. Golf. Tennis. $251-350

★★★★THE RITZ-CARLTON GOLF RESORT, NAPLES
2600 Tiburon Drive, Naples, 239-593-2000, 800-241-3333; www.ritzcarlton.com

Greg Norman's award-winning Tiburón golf course is the focal point at the Ritz-Carlton Golf Resort, Naples. Just three miles down the road from its beachfront sister property, the Ritz-Carlton, Naples, the course is legendary for its beauty and difficulty. The onsite Rick Smith Golf Academy offers its innovative instructional techniques. The resort's architecture presents a fresh take on the Mediterranean villa, with vibrant colors, red-tiled roof and striped awnings.

295 rooms. Restaurant, bar. Business center. Fitness center. Pool. Pets accepted. Golf. Tennis. $251-350

★★★★★THE RITZ-CARLTON, NAPLES
280 Vanderbilt Beach Road, Naples, 239-598-3300, 800-241-3333; www.ritzcarlton.com

Three miles of white-sand beaches attract visitors to this Mediterranean-inspired resort. Take part in water sports, sample the menu at the full-service spa or hop the shuttle to the Ritz-Carlton Golf Resort just down the road to hit the links. Kids can choose to hunker down with video games in the high-tech entertainment lounge or check out the Nature's Wonder center, an interactive environmental program. Meanwhile, you can hang out in the poolside cabanas and get personal concierge service or use one of the complimentary beach chairs and umbrellas and relax on the beach. Guest rooms are beautifully appointed with European-style décor and have 32-inch flat-screen LCD televisions with DVD players. They also boast breathtaking views of the Gulf of Mexico and its impeccable beaches. Several restaurant options run the gamut from casual to formal and the world-class spa features saunas, steam rooms, and an alfresco mineral pool. The Grill steakhouse offers aged prime meats and fresh seafood paired with an excellent wine list and classically crafted cocktails in a richly decorated and cozy setting.

463 rooms. Restaurant, bar. Business center. Fitness center. Pool. Spa. Beach. Golf. Tennis. $351 and up

WHERE TO EAT

FORT MYERS

★★★VERANDA

2122 Second St., Fort Myers, 239-334-8634; www.verandarestaurant.com

This restaurant—housed in two turn-of-the-century homes—creates a charming, classic-Florida atmosphere in Fort Myers' historic downtown. Try the garden courtyard for a romantic dinner under the stars. The menu features traditional American dishes, such as herb-crusted and grilled Atlantic salmon, pan-seared yellowtail snapper, chateaubriand and veal piccata.

American. Lunch, dinner. Closed Sunday (except Easter, Mother's Day). Reservations recommended. Outdoor seating. Bar. $16-35

LONGBOAT KEY

★★★THE COLONY DINING ROOM

The Colony Beach & Tennis Resort, 1620 Gulf of Mexico Drive, Longboat Key, 941-383-6464, 800-282-1138; www.colonybeachresort.com

Views of the ocean provide the backdrop for dinner at this longtime restaurant inside the Colony Beach resort. The restaurant, which opened more than 40 years ago, is a local favorite for its seasonal Floribbean-fusion favorites, such as roasted Colorado rack of lamb, madras curry lobster risotto and skillet-seared snapper. Take in gorgeous views of the Gulf of Mexico from the dining room or the alfresco seating area.

Caribbean, continental. Breakfast, lunch, dinner, late-night, Sunday brunch. Reservations recommended. Outdoor seating. Children's menu. Bar. $36-85

★★★EUPHEMIA HAYE

5540 Gulf of Mexico Drive, Longboat Key, 941-383-3633; www.euphemiahaye.com

Located in a lush, tropical garden, this restaurant serves hearty dishes such as roast duckling with bread stuffing, flambéed prime pepper steak and crisp roasted duck with seasonal-fruit sauce. The Haye Loft—the restaurant's second floor, converted from three apartments—is a dessert and gourmet coffee room, and a great spot for sampling one of the many ports on the dessert wine menu. Desserts, of course, are not to be missed; think delicious sweets such as apple-walnut crumble pie and silky chocolate mousse.

International. Dinner. Closed three weeks in September. Reservations recommended. Bar. $36-85

NAPLES
★★★BLEU PROVENCE
1234 Eighth St. S., Naples, 239-261-8239; www.bleuprovencenaples.com

Perfect for special occasions, this downtown Old Naples restaurant features whitewashed floors and tables topped with candles and fresh flowers. Located in an upscale neighborhood, the restaurant enhances its outdoor garden with Italian lights for a warm ambience that will go well with your crispy duck confit with potato gratin and mango fries. A wine selection of 12,000 bottles and 1,000 varieties is available.

French, Mediterranean. Dinner. Reservations recommended. Outdoor seating. Bar. $36-85

★★★THE GRILL
The Ritz-Carlton, Naples, 280 Vanderbilt Beach Road, Naples, 239-598-3300, 800-241-3333; www.ritzcarlton.com

Situated right off the lobby of the Ritz-Carlton, Naples, The Grill feels like an exclusive club with its warm, wood paneling, sophisticated artwork, lovely fireplace and live music. Chef de cuisine Mark Vuckovich's menu focuses on all-American cuisine, specifically grilled meats. You can order everything from dry filet mignon, rib-eye, New York strip to Colorado rack of lamb, veal and pork chops. These go along with classic sides like creamed spinach and hand-cut French fries. You'll also find contemporary meat dishes such as beef short ribs with root vegetable-sweet potato hash, and there's a nice seafood selection, such as Dover sole with brown butter or whole Maine lobster.

Steak. Dinner. Closed August-early September. Reservations recommended. Children's menu. Bar. $86 and up

★★★LEMONIA
The Ritz-Carlton Golf Resort, Naples, 2600 Tiburon Drive, Naples, 239-593-2000, 800-241-3333; www.ritzcarlton.com

Lemonia serves contemporary Tuscan fare, like marinated salmon tartare with basil, tarragon and citrus fruit dressing, or crispy Mediterranean sea bass with tomato compote and saffron sauce. Dine inside the casual Mediterranean-style restaurant or have your meal outside on the terrace overlooking the Tiburón golf course.

Italian. Breakfast, lunch, dinner, Sunday brunch. Reservations recommended. Outdoor seating. Children's menu. Bar. $36-85

SIESTA KEY
★★★OPHELIA'S ON THE BAY
Turtle Beach Resort Hotel & Marina, 9105 Midnight Pass Road, Siesta Key, 941-349-2212, 877-229-9601; www.opheliasonthebay.net

You'll find flavorful American offerings in an understated, tasteful atmosphere at this Sarasota Bayfront destination in the Turtle Beach Resort. Choose from two glass-walled dining rooms or the dockside patio to enjoy the pleasant view. The menu changes nightly, but it's always composed of fresh seafood, meats and Florida-grown produce.

Continental. Dinner. Outdoor seating. Children's menu. Bar. $36-85

RECOMMENDED

NAPLES
CAMPIELLO
1177 Third St. S., Naples, 239-435-1166; www.campiello.damico.com

This Italian restaurant is very popular so don't be surprised if you feel like you've been transported to South Beach upon entry. Dishes are prepared in the Tuscan tradition with a selection of pizza, pasta, steak and seafood, and there's a large wine list to choose from. The elegant restaurant is in the heart of downtown Old Naples, just a few blocks from the Gulf.

Italian. Lunch, dinner. Reservations recommended. Outdoor seating. Bar. $36-85

SPA

NAPLES
★★★★THE RITZ-CARLTON SPA, NAPLES
280 Vanderbilt Beach Road, Naples, 239-598-3300, 800-241-3333; www.ritzcarlton.com

In addition to an extensive menu of massages, facials, wraps and scrubs, The Ritz-Carlton Spa, Naples features rejuvenating and healing steam rooms, saunas, aqua lounges and an outdoor mineral pool to complete the spa experience. Therapies run the gamut from the signature body wrap, a detoxifying and slimming treatment that utilizes a rich coffee oil to tone the body, to the Gulf Stone massage, which uses warm mineral-rich, basalt stones to melt away stress. The onsite fitness center offers personal training, group exercise classes and nutrition consultation, as well as a one-on-one equipment orientation session designed to acclimate guests to the gym.

FORT LAUDERDALE

Spring break is back in Fort Lauderdale—and it brought the fun with it. Once a sleepy little sister to Miami, the town became the "spring break capital of the world" in the 1950s and '60s before a citywide crackdown paved the way to restoring its squeaky-clean family-friendly reputation in the '90s. Now the pendulum has landed firmly in the middle. The city of 23 miles of beach dishes out luxury and economy hotels, casual and destination dining, shopping, nightlife and kids attractions. Come any time of year and expect to see families frolicking on the beach, newlyweds lounging by a hotel pool, college kids hitting the bars and snowbirds dining along Las Olas. There are 33,000 hotel rooms, 60 golf courses and more than 4,000 restaurants standing by to greet tourists with open arms.

Roughly 10 million people come each year to visit the "Venice of America," so named for the city's winding canal system and close ties to aquatics. Water is definitively top priority in this town with 42,000 resident yachts, 100 marinas, hundreds of waterfront cafes, shops and bars, 69 miles of live coral reef and 300 miles of inland waterways. Visitors tend to spend the day at the beach or on the water—whether it be for fishing, snorkeling or diving—then hit downtown Las Olas or the Riverwalk for drinks, shopping and dinner. Come to relax, come to shop, come to eat, come to party—just come.

HIGHLIGHTS

WHAT ARE THE TOP THINGS TO DO?

WHILE AWAY THE DAY ON LAS OLAS BOULEVARD

Spend the afternoon on Las Olas, Miami's version of Rodeo Drive. Grab lunch at one of the numerous restaurants and reserve the rest of your time for window-shopping and people-watching.

CATCH A SHOW AT THE BROWARD CENTER FOR PERFORMING ARTS

Touring Broadway hits like Avenue Q stop off at this theater. But you can also see performances from the city's best arts groups, including the Florida Grand Opera and the Miami City Ballet.

HIT THE BEACH

Fort Lauderdale's beaches catapulted to spring-break fame in the '60s movie *Where the Boys Are.* Find out why spring breakers continue to plant their towels on these sandy shores today.

BRING THE KIDS TO THE MUSEUM OF DISCOVERY AND SCIENCE

Children and their parents will geek out over the Manned Maneuvering Unit space ride and walk-through simulated Florida habitats like the Everglades in this hands-on science museum.

HUNT FOR BARGAINS AT SAWGRASS MILLS

Sawgrass Mills is the largest outlet mall in the state. Shop for discounted goods from high-end stores like Barneys New York and Burberry.

WHAT TO SEE

BILLIE SWAMP SAFARI AT BIG CYPRESS NATIONAL PRESERVE

Interstate 75 (Alligator Alley) to exit 49; 19 miles north of exit 49, 863-983-6101, 800-949-6101; www.seminoletribe.com/safari

This Everglades tour covers 2,200 acres of the Big Cypress preserve. The daily

SPECIAL EVENT

FORT LAUDERDALE INTERNATIONAL BOAT SHOW

Billed as the world's largest boat show, this annual tradition has been attracting domestic and international vendors and visitors for more than a half a century. The 2010 fair featured more than $3 billion worth of boats, yachts, super yachts, electronics, engines and accessories. (www.showmanagement.com) *October-November.*

tours—on swamp buggy or airboat, and some of which can be taken at night—showcase the natural beauty of this Seminole reservation's wetlands, including flora and fauna, such as deer, wild hogs, alligators and, occasionally, the rare Florida panther. The Ah-Tha-Thi-Ki Museum, which preserves the Seminole culture, is also nearby.

Admission: tours: adults $15-30, seniors $15-28, children $15-20. Daily 9:30 a.m.-6 p.m.

BONNET HOUSE
900 N. Birch Road, Fort Lauderdale, 954-563-5393; www.bonnethouse.org

This historic home was constructed by Chicago artist Frederic Clay Bartlett in 1919. His third wife, Evelyn, donated it to the Florida Trust for Historic Preservation in 1983. The Caribbean-style home contains the couple's furnishings as well as an extensive collection of art. The 35-acre property also boasts beautiful gardens, including a very large orchid collection.

Admission: adults $20, seniors $18, children 6-12 $16, children under 6 free. Tuesday-Saturday 10 a.m.-4 p.m., Sunday 11 a.m.-4 p.m.

BROWARD CENTER FOR THE PERFORMING ARTS
201 S.W. Fifth Ave., Fort Lauderdale, 954-462-0222; www.browardcenter.org

If you're in the mood for big theater productions, you've happened upon the right place—Broadway staples such as *Stomp, Avenue Q* and *Mamma Mia!* have all made pit stops at the 2,700-seat theater. The center also hosts dance performances, classical music shows, films and lectures.

BUTTERFLY WORLD
3600 W. Sample Road, Coconut Creek, 954-977-4400; www.butterflyworld.com

Spend an afternoon outside and browse 10 acres of aviaries, botanical gardens, a butterfly farm and a research facility.

Admission: adults and seniors $24.95, children 3-11 $19.95, children under 3 free. Monday-Saturday 9 a.m.-5 p.m., Sunday 11 a.m.-5 p.m.

INTERNATIONAL SWIMMING HALL OF FAME AND AQUATIC COMPLEX
1 Hall of Fame Drive, Fort Lauderdale, 954-462-6536; www.ishof.org

The Swimming Hall of Fame is a leading repository for aquatic displays, photos, sculpture, art and memorabilia. You'll also find computerized exhibits, film and video presentations and an aquatic library. There are two Olympic-size swimming pools, in which you can do some laps (for $4 extra) when there are no live events or competitions.

Admission: museum: adults $8, seniors $6, students $4, military and children 6 and under free. Daily 9 a.m.-5 p.m.

MUSEUM OF ART

1 E. Las Olas Blvd., Fort Lauderdale, 954-525-5500; www.moafl.org

The MoA's collection of more than 6,000 pieces has an international scope, though it emphasizes Florida and Caribbean cultural expression. The museum showcases permanent and changing exhibits of works by artists such as Salvador Dalí, Andy Warhol, Pablo Picasso and Normal Rockwell.

Admission: adults $10, seniors and children 6-17 $7, students and children 5 and under free. Tuesday, Wednesday, Friday and Saturday 11 a.m.-5 p.m.; Thursday 11 a.m.-8 p.m.; Sunday noon-5 p.m.

MUSEUM OF DISCOVERY AND SCIENCE AND AUTONATION IMAX 3-D THEATER

401 S.W. Second St., Fort Lauderdale, 954-467-6637; www.mods.org

This hands-on science museum has seven permanent exhibit areas, including KidScience, Space Base, Choose Health and Florida Ecoscapes. The museum features a Manned Maneuvering Unit space ride and walk-through simulated Florida habitats as well as rotating/traveling exhibitions. The IMAX 3-D Theater shows large-format films on a five-story screen.

Admission: museum: adults $11, seniors $10, children 2-12 $9, children 1 and under free; IMAX: adults $9, seniors $8, children 2-12 $7, children 1 and under free. Monday-Saturday 10 a.m.-5 p.m., Sunday noon-6 p.m.

RIVERWALK ARTS & ENTERTAINMENT DISTRICT

N. New River Drive E. between S.W. Second and S.E. Eighth avenues, Fort Lauderdale, 954-468-1541; www.riverwalkartsandentertainment.com

This waterfront park and walkway connects Las Olas Boulevard to many of the city's other attractions and venues, such as the Broward Center for the Performing Arts, Museum of Discovery and Science, Museum of Art and Stranahan House.

STRANAHAN HOUSE

335 S.E. Sixth Ave., Fort Lauderdale, 954-524-4736; www.stranahanhouse.org

This house, built in 1901, is Fort Lauderdale's oldest home. It was once used as an Native American trading post, town hall and post office. It was renovated many times but currently represents its 1913 configuration and is an excellent example of Florida vernacular architecture. House tours are available.

Admission: adults $12, seniors $11, children $7. Daily 1-4 p.m.

WHERE TO STAY

★★★HILTON FORT LAUDERDALE AIRPORT

1870 Griffin Road, Fort Lauderdale, 954-920-3300, 800-445-8667; www.hilton.com

Abundant fruit-bearing trees dot the landscape of this secluded hotel located adjacent to the Fort Lauderdale airport. Soundproof guest rooms are decorated in soft, tranquil tones and punctuated with dark-wood furnishings, and the lobby is bright and spacious, with cream-colored marble floors. The dining room, Ocean Blu, features a seafood-heavy menu as well as a good selection of steaks. Cap the evening off at Liquid Lounge, the onsite bar. The pool is a good place to unwind before catching that flight.

388 rooms. Restaurant, bar. Business center. Fitness center. Pool. Pets accepted. $61-150

★★★HYATT REGENCY BONAVENTURE

250 Racquet Club Road, Weston, 954-389-3300, 800-238-1234; www.bonaventure.hyatt.com

This resort near Fort Lauderdale has rooms with luxury bedding, flat-screen televisions and marble baths. Sporty types will get access to nearby tennis and golf. An onsite Elizabeth Arden Red Door spa offers a full menu of treatments, while lounging around one of the pools is a nice way to spend a sunny afternoon. The hotel is also a short drive away from Sawgrass Mills Mall, Port Everglades, the airport and Sun Life Stadium, for those in town for Dolphins games.

496 rooms. Restaurant, bar. Business center. Fitness center. Pool. Spa. Pets accepted. $151-250

★★★HYATT REGENCY PIER SIXTY-SIX

2301 S.E. 17th St., Fort Lauderdale, 954-525-6666, 800-233-1234; www.pier66.hyatt.com

Situated on the Intracoastal Waterway, this hotel offers a 127-slip marina, a spa, shops, an aquatic club and tennis courts. You won't have to use a car when staying here—in addition to the many onsite activities, a water taxi is available to take you to the beach, restaurants and nightclubs. Rooms themselves are modern with a touch of retro, all done in whites and beiges to create a relaxing atmosphere. There are also three pools and Spa 66, which features a myriad of massage and body treatments.

384 rooms. Restaurant, bar. Business center. Fitness center. Pool. Spa. Tennis. $251-350

★★★LAGO MAR RESORT AND CLUB

1700 S. Ocean Lane, Fort Lauderdale, 954-523-6511, 800-524-6627; www.lagomar.com

Five hundred feet of private beach await at this lively resort between Lake Mayan and the ocean. The beach is dotted with hammocks, cabanas and umbrellas while the pool area, with two beachside pools and a poolside bar, is a tropical oasis. The lobby features a large-scale mosaic built into the floor, lovely architecture and antiques. Guest rooms are decorated in a cool mint, warm coral and pale yellow palette. There's plenty to do here: A putting green, shuffleboard, a giant outdoor chess set and table tennis are among the onsite activities. Kayak and hammock rentals are also available.

204 rooms. Restaurant, bar. Business center. Fitness center. Pool. Spa. Beach. Tennis. $151-250

★★★MARRIOTT HARBOR BEACH RESORT AND SPA

3030 Holiday Drive, Fort Lauderdale, 954-525-4000, 800-222-6543; www.marriottharborbeach.com

This sprawling resort rests along the ocean, convenient to cruise ships, shopping and dining. The casual and elegant décor includes fabrics and colors evoking the water and the sun. A bubbling fountain is a fitting soundtrack to the picturesque ocean views. Guest rooms are sunny, and most have balconies. Activities include basketball, bike rentals, beach volleyball, scuba and snorkeling, golf, fishing, yachting, boating and water sports. Those who just want to sit back and relax should sign up for one of the beach hammocks and let the sound of the ocean carry them away to deep relaxation.

637 rooms. Restaurant, bar. Business center. Fitness center. Pool. Spa. Beach. Tennis. $151-350

★★★RENAISSANCE FORT LAUDERDALE HOTEL

1617 S.E. 17th St., Fort Lauderdale, 954-626-1700, 800-627-7468; www.marriott.com

This Caribbean-inspired hotel has sleek, luxurious guest rooms outfitted with pillow-top beds, luxury bedding, down duvets and down pillows for a comfortable night's sleep. A sparkling pool tempts guests too tired to go to make the short drive east to the beach.

233 rooms. Restaurant, bar. Business center. Fitness center. Pool. Spa. $151-250

★★★★THE RITZ-CARLTON, FORT LAUDERDALE

1 N. Fort Lauderdale Beach Blvd., Fort Lauderdale; 954-465-2300; www.ritz-carlton.com

Opened in the summer of 2008, the Ritz-Carlton, Fort Lauderdale is the city's premier luxury resort. Which means it's alarmingly easy to idle away the day without leaving the oceanfront property. Start the day with a personal training session at the 8,000-square-foot fitness center, grab lunch and a passion fruit cocktail at the pool, indulge in a sea spray massage and close out the day with dinner under the stars. Then retire to your room, a blend of old and new with black-and-white family snapshots from the 1940s paired with flat-panel LCD TVs.

192 rooms. Restaurant, bar. Business center. Fitness center. Pool. Spa. Pets accepted. Beach. $351 and up

★★★RIVERSIDE HOTEL

620 E. Las Olas Blvd., Fort Lauderdale, 954-467-0671, 800-325-3280; www.riversidehotel.com

Experience Old Florida as you walk through the pillared entryway and into the wicker-filled lobby of this Las Olas Boulevard landmark on the New River— the hotel opened in the 1930s, and the decor remains an updated ode to the era. Guest rooms are big and comfortable, and they have marble bathrooms.

217 rooms. Restaurant, bar. Business center. Pool. $151-250

★★★SHERATON FORT LAUDERDALE BEACH HOTEL

1140 Seabreeze Blvd., Fort Lauderdale, 954-524-5551; www.starwoodhotels.com

Formerly the Yankee Clipper, the oceanfront Sheraton Fort Lauderdale Beach Hotel is the recipient of a multimillion renovation that ushered the oceanfront property into the 21st century. Think complimentary Wi-Fi, flat-screen TVs, an infinity pool and a well-stocked fitness center. The décor skews beach chic with an aquamarine and canary-yellow color palette, polished wood accents and expansive ocean views. Families will feel particularly at home with a colorful 1950s-themed diner and ice cream parlor, the Sheraton Adventure Club and two inviting pools.

486 rooms. Restaurant, bar. Business center. Fitness center. Pool. Pets accepted. Beach. $151-250

★★★THE WESTIN FORT LAUDERDALE

400 Corporate Drive, Fort Lauderdale, 954-772-1331, 800-937-8461; www.westin.com

This large hotel is located near the Palm Aire golf course and numerous corporate offices (such as Citibank and Motorola), yet it's also close to the beach. Because the hotel caters to business travelers and conferences, rooms are loaded with technological amenities, from high-speed Internet access to ergonomic desk chairs. However, the geometrical pool and cushioned poolside lounges come in handy for people who need to unwind. Rooms are elegant, with dark-wood furniture and headboards, and all-white bedding.

293 rooms. Restaurant, bar. Business center. Fitness center. Pool. Pets accepted. $151-250

RECOMMENDED

THE W FORT LAUDERDALE

401 N. Fort Lauderdale Beach Blvd., Fort Lauderdale, 954-414-8200; www.starwoodhotels.com

Starwood opened W Fort Lauderdale, its first W property in Florida, in the spring of 2009. The property spans 4.5 acres and features most of the traditional W amenities: Bliss Spa, Whiskey Blue lounge and a big-name restaurant, in this case, Steak 954 by Philadelphia restaurateur Stephen Starr. The hotel's aesthetic skews beach chic, with bold, bright turquoise curtains paired with sleek slate walls and a rooftop fire pit. Book a "Fabulous Room" and enjoy 510 square feet and a private balcony overlooking the Atlantic. After admiring the view, slide open your glass doors, snuggle into your signature W bed, select a pillow from the menu and flip on your 32-inch TV, or opt for a Bliss Spa-inspired soak in your tub.

486 rooms. Restaurant, bar. Business center. Fitness center. Pool. Spa. Pets accepted. Beach. $151-250

WHERE TO EAT

★★★BLUE MOON FISH CO.

4405 W. Tradewinds Ave., Lauderdale-by-the-Sea, 954-267-9888; www.bluemoonfishco.com

This seafood lover's paradise is set right on the Intracoastal Waterway on the east side of the bridge. The creative menu is peppered with Caribbean accents, and the elegant, Art Deco-tinged interior and waterside patio are usually packed with a crowd of locals celebrating special occasions or enjoying delectable seafood dishes such as the peppercorn-crusted big-eye tuna and soy Chilean sea bass served with Asian stir fry. Show up hungry for the all-you-can-eat Sunday brunch—it brims with shrimp, shucked oysters, steamed mussels, pancakes, omelets and more.

Seafood. Lunch, dinner, Sunday brunch. Outdoor seating. Children's menu. Bar. $36-85

★★★CASA D'ANGELO

1201 N. Federal Highway, Fort Lauderdale, 954-564-1234; www.casa-d-angelo.com

This is one of the most talked-about Italian restaurants in South Florida, so don't even try to show up on a weekend night without reservations. The restaurant has Corinthian columns and creamy stucco walls, but as nice as the décor is, your focus should be on the menu. Entrées include a delicious array of pastas—such as lasagna with housemade mozzarella and Parmigiano-Reggiano cheese, or porcini-mushroom risotto—and a selection of fish, chops and steaks, all prepared with fresh, seasonal ingredients. The 500-bottle Italian and Californian wine list includes many gems under $50.

Italian. Dinner. Reservations recommended. Outdoor seating. $36-85

★★★CHARLEY'S CRAB

3000 N.E. 32nd Ave., Fort Lauderdale, 954-561-4800, 800-589-6837; www.muer.com

This seafood chain, located on the Intracoastal Waterway, serves volumes of fish and shellfish each day. The 600-seat venue attracts a varied crowd of locals and tourists with its lovely covered terrace and fresh seafood selection, which ranges from raw bar items to entrée specialties like salmon Rockefeller and

Parmesan-crusted snapper "Hemingway." Call ahead to reserve a table, ideally on the deck for the best views.

Seafood. Lunch, dinner. Reservations recommended. Outdoor seating. Bar. $36-85

★★★RUTH'S CHRIS STEAK HOUSE

2525 N. Federal Highway, Fort Lauderdale, 954-565-2338; www.ruthschris.com

Founded by the late Ruth Fertel, this branch of the national chain serves melt-in-your-mouth steaks and chops on sizzling plates in a dimly lit, masculine atmosphere. The wine list is comprehensive, with a hefty selection of reds to go with that tender filet mignon or porterhouse. Desserts are decadent affairs, so save room for the chocolate cake. The service is attentive without being cloying.

Steak. Dinner. Reservations recommended. Children's menu. Bar. $36-85

★★★SAGE FRENCH CAFÉ

2378 N. Federal Highway, Fort Lauderdale, 954-565-2299; www.sagecafe.net

Despite its humble location in a strip mall, this café offers French country cuisine that is worth the trip. Chef Laurent Tasic's menu is elegantly prepared and reasonably priced, with traditional French dishes like coq au vin, daube de boeuf and crêpes. The restaurant also features an oyster bar.

French. Lunch, dinner, Sunday brunch. Outdoor seating. Children's menu. Bar. $16-35

★★★SHULA'S ON THE BEACH

321 N. Fort Lauderdale Beach Blvd., Fort Lauderdale, 954-355-4000; www.donshula.com

Miami Dolphins coach-turned-restaurateur Don Shula delivers a high-quality steak house with matching service in a memorabilia-packed setting. The restaurant offers striking views of the ocean, which diners appreciate while noshing on dishes like filet mignon, "cowboy" steak, French-cut chicken breast and seared ahi tuna.

Steak. Breakfast, lunch, dinner. Reservations recommended. Outdoor seating. Children's menu. Bar. $36-85

★★★VIA LUNA

The Ritz-Carlton, Fort Lauderdale, 1 N. Fort Lauderdale Beach Blvd., Fort Lauderdale, 954-302-6460; www.ritzcarlton.com

Casual Italian meets midcentury modern and South Florida chic at the recently opened Via Luna, "moon path" in Italian. The indoor/outdoor venue boasts oceanfront views and a friendly, accessible menu. House specialties include the spaghetti and meatball, an 8-ouncer made of pork, beef and veal; locally caught yellowtail snapper Livornese and an 18-ounce bone-in rib-eye Florentina. Save room for dessert and indulge in Nutella beignets and pizzetta de mala layered with apples and topped with housemade mascarpone gelato.

Italian. Breakfast, lunch, dinner. Outdoor seating. Bar. $36-85

RECOMMENDED

DA CAMPO OSTERIA

Il Lugano Suite Hotel, 3333 N.E. 32nd Ave., Fort Lauderdale, 954-226-5002, www.dacampoosteria.com

Celebrity chef Todd English brings his Boston-based empire to Fort Lauderdale through Da Campo Osteria in the Il Lugano Suite Hotel. The menu focuses on regional Italian fare, with favorites such as fresh mozzarella pulled tableside and the jumbo meatball blending veal, beef and pork. English draws locals and tourists to the casual, earth-toned space for breakfast, lunch and dinner. Italian influences transform all three meals into something unexpected: eggs da Campo come with prosciutto, basil hollandaise and prosciutto home fries; a tomato mozzarella panini is slathered with black olive tapenade; and wild local snapper is doused in a marsala sauce.

Italian. Breakfast, lunch, dinner. Reservations recommended. Outdoor seating. Bar. $16-35

STEAK 954

401 N. Fort Lauderdale Beach Blvd., Fort Lauderdale, 954-414-8333; www.steak954.com

Philadelphia restaurateur Stephen Starr (Buddakan, Morimoto) mans this chic temple of beef at the W Hotel Fort Lauderdale. The oceanfront steak house features dry-aged beef and locally sourced seafood, with menu highlights including Kobe cheesesteak and miso-glazed black cod. The cavernous space, which seats 200 plus, is adorned with bold lime-green banquettes, royal-blue window accents, polished wood tables and a 15-foot jellyfish tank. Come for dinner and expect a scene—cocktails flow from the stainless steel bar while foie gras tacos and tempura onion rings sate chicly dressed diners.

Steak. Breakfast, brunch, lunch, dinner. Reservations recommended. Outdoor seating. Bar. $36-85

SPA

★★★★THE RITZ-CARLTON SPA, FORT LAUDERDALE

The Ritz-Carlton, Fort Lauderdale, 1 N. Fort Lauderdale Beach Blvd., Fort Lauderdale, 954-465-2300; www.ritzcarlton.com

Guests at the Ritz-Carlton can get their bodies bikini-ready with a day at the hotel's spa and fitness center. First, stop in for a yoga class or a run on a treadmill that overlooks the ocean. Then, it's time to relax those tired limbs with a De-Stress Muscle Release or a dip in the pool deck Jacuzzi. The 8,500-square-foot spa features 11 treatment rooms, including a private couple's suite where you can get his (Balance Men's) and hers (Renew Rose Radiance) facials.

WHERE TO SHOP

THE FORT LAUDERDALE SWAP SHOP

3291 W. Sunrise Blvd., Fort Lauderdale, 954-791-7927; www.floridaswapshop.com

Grab some kitsch with your culture at the Swap Shop. Opened in 1963 as a drive-in movie theater, the indoor/outdoor flea market bills itself as South Florida's second-largest attraction. It's open seven days a week, 365 days a year, and features a rotating display of about 2,000 vendors, a 14-screen drive-in movie theater, an arcade, carnival rides and a roster of live entertainment. Willy Nelson and KC and the Sunshine Band each have graced the Swap Shop stage.

Monday-Wednesday 9 a.m.-5 p.m., Thursday, Saturday and Sunday 7:30 a.m.-6 p.m., Friday 9 a.m.-6 p.m.

TOUR

WHAT'S THE BEST WAY TO TOUR LAS OLAS BOULEVARD?

Las Olas Boulevard is Fort Lauderdale's most fashionable street—it begins at the beach and connects to Riverwalk, a linear park that follows New River to many of the city's best cultural sights. Start out at the famous beach that was the backdrop of the iconic '60s spring-break flick *Where the Boys Are* with the International Swimming Hall of Fame nearby to the south. In recent years, though, spring breakers have been replaced by trendsetters. Then pass by the shops and cafés and discover the **Stranahan House** *(335 S.E. Sixth Ave.)* off to your left. Take a tour of Fort Lauderdale's oldest home, built at the turn of the last century, and learn about the days of Indian trading posts and the frontier.

Continue on to the Riverwalk, a paved sidewalk for strollers, cyclists and in-line skaters that features educational stations, including one that lets you fiddle around with marine navigational instruments. It passes by charter boats, including the Water Taxi, which will take you anywhere along Fort Lauderdale's extensive system of canals. On Sundays, jazz artists entertain visitors along the Riverwalk, and there are plenty of park benches where people sit and listen. Toward the end of the walk, you will come to a cluster of cultural attractions. **At the Museum of Art** *(1 E. Las Olas Blvd.)*, you'll find impressive visiting exhibits, as well as the museum's own collection.

Las Olas Riverfront, a shopping and entertainment complex, is a good place to stop for lunch on the patio overlooking the river. After a quick bite, check out the **Museum of Discovery and Science** *(401 S.W. Second St.)*, which explores physics, space flight, health, fitness and nature. It also has a 3-D IMAX theater that shows science-oriented films. Down the street is the **Broward Center for the Performing Arts** *(201 S.W. 5th Ave.)*. If you have the evening free, you can catch a performance from the Florida Grand Opera, the Florida Philharmonic, the Miami City Ballet, or even a touring Broadway show.

www.lasolasboulevard.com

THE GALLERIA

2414 E. Sunrise Blvd., Fort Lauderdale, 954-564-1015; www.galleriamall-fl.com

Opened in 1980, the Galleria features a bevy of name-brand shops and department stores, like Neiman Marcus, Cole Haan, J. Crew, Abercrombie & Fitch, and Kate Spade. The hub is also home to various restaurants, such as P.F. Chang's and The Capital Grille.

Monday-Saturday 10 a.m.-9 p.m., Sunday noon-6 p.m.

LAS OLAS BOULEVARD

www.lasolasboulevard.com

Fort Lauderdale's answer to South Beach's Lincoln Road, Las Olas is an expansive pedestrian-only walkway stocked with inviting shops, galleries and restaurants. Window shopping is a primary sport, but locals and visitors regularly open their wallets for designer denim and accessories at Shop 603

(603 E. Las Olas Blvd.), day-to-night T-shirts, skirts and sandals at hip shop Blue (617 E Las Olas Blvd.), sexy but high-end American and European intimates at Under Wraps (610 E. Las Olas Blvd.) and diamond-studded necklaces and earrings at family owned Carroll's Jewelers (915 E. Las Olas Blvd.). Lounge over lunch at one of the 30 eateries along the strip then wander the street.

SAWGRASS MILLS

12801 W. Sunrise Blvd., Sunrise, 954-846-2350; www.sawgrassmills.com

With more than 350 discount designer stores from which to choose, Sawgrass Mills is the largest outlet center in Florida. Don't miss the Colonnade shops—this wing houses the outlets for Barneys New York, Max Mara, Burberry, Theory and many other stores, all of which offer deep discounts. Scattered throughout the rest of the mall are other high-end favorites like Lacoste and Le Creuset, along with chains like Gap and American Apparel.

Monday-Saturday 10 a.m.-9:30 p.m., Sunday 11 a.m.-8 p.m.

THE VILLAGE AT GULFSTREAM PARK

501 S. Federal Highway, Hallandale, 954-426-2991; www.thevillageatgulfstreampark.com

Equal parts retail outlet, open space and dining destination, the Village at Gulfstream Park is the 21st-century version of a strip mall. About 13 miles from Fort Lauderdale, the Village woos locals and tourists with live music, horse-drawn carriage rides and other seasonal programming. The retail focus is on home furnishings, with spacious outposts of West Elm, Pottery Barn, Crate and Barrel, Liapela Modern Baby, Williams-Sonoma and The Container Store. There's also a racetrack and casino in the Village, in case you tire of shopping.

MIAMI AND MIAMI BEACH

To most visitors, Miami includes both the city of Miami and its across-the-bay twin, Miami Beach. Each is a separate community, and each is vibrantly different in personality. Miami is older, more settled and sophisticated. Miami Beach is youth on a fling. The city of Miami (i.e., downtown) has the bustle of business, rush-hour traffic and skyscrapers. It's also a popular place for cruise-goers; the Port of Miami is the largest embarkation point for cruise ships in the world.

Contrary to popular belief, Miami Beach is not the same thing as South Beach. South Beach is a tiny portion of the expansive whole of Miami Beach—South Beach runs from First Street to around Dade Boulevard (a few blocks north of Lincoln Road). Small it may be, but this area has enough flash to make even Vegas blush. Skimpily dressed, taut-and-tanned locals mix it up with the rich and famous inside trendy clubs, swanky boutique hotels and shops along Collins Avenue.

South Beach is also home to the thickest concentration of Miami's acclaimed Art Deco buildings. A walk down Ocean Drive between Fifth and 16th streets is like taking a trip to the 1930s. And at the enclave's northern tip, you can find Lincoln Road, a pedestrianized street with shops and restaurants galore. It's exactly what you thought of Miami, only brasher, brighter, and in real-time.

When it comes to what to see in Miami, many people think of only two things:

sand and the sea. But there's a lot more on offer in this sunny southern city than beaches and swimming. With oodles of history, culture, arts and fashion around town, you'll be spending more time off the sand than you might think. Stroll the Art Deco district and learn how this magic city developed such a unique architectural style. Escape the midday sun and visit the Miami Art Museum to see a fine collection of contemporary works by local artists. Or head back in time to St. Bernard de Clairvaux Church, an ancient Spanish monastery dating back to the 12th century. Whatever your interest or curiosity, you're sure to find something to quell it.

WHAT TO SEE

MIAMI

FLORIDA GRAND OPERA

Ziff Ballet Opera House, Adrienne Arsht Center for the Performing Arts, 1300 Biscayne Blvd., Miami, 305-854-1643; www.fgo.org

Opera is a big deal in South Florida, at least in size: Formed in 1994, Florida Grand Opera was the result of a merger of The Opera Guild Inc. of Fort Lauderdale and Greater Miami Opera (The latter started in 1941 and was one of the oldest performing arts organizations in the state.) Collectively, the FGO has more than 65 productions under its belt and is the largest opera company in the region. The FGO, which has presented Florida premieres of productions like Richard Strauss' *Salome*, Britten's *The Turn of the Screw* and Handel's *Julius Caesar*, puts on five mainstage productions a year at the Ziff Opera House.

Admission prices and performance dates vary.

THE FREEDOM TOWER

600 Biscayne Blvd., Miami

What Ellis Island is to New York City, the Freedom Tower is to Miami. Though the Magic City is young compared to cities like Boston and New York, it has nevertheless encountered its fair share of cultural struggles. It was here where hundreds of thousands of Cuban exiles fleeing the Communist Revolution were processed for entry into the United States. The tower now stands as a memorial dedicated to those refugees who have helped make Miami the beautiful, diverse metropolis it is today. Unfortunately the interior is now home to various private businesses, so you can only walk around the exterior.

JUNGLE ISLAND

1111 Parrot Jungle Trail, Miami, 305-400-7000; www.jungleisland.com

Although originally founded as Parrot Jungle in 1936, this small but well-designed zoo-like park is no longer just for the birds—the facility also holds 3,000 exotic animals, including hippos and even rare albino alligators. For a closer look at the fair-feathered friends, head for the open-air aviary or for the daily flamingo feedings. And if you can't make it to the real swamp, check out the Everglades Habitat and Walk—a true replica of the Glades—which demonstrates what life there is like for wildlife, complete with alligator feeding habitats. If the gators make you or the kids nervous, head to the Hippo Slide. Set on a private beach, this plastic waterslide stands three stories tall and features a 40-degree drop. You'll

WHAT ARE MIAMI'S BEST FESTIVALS?

SPRING

WINTER MUSIC CONFERENCE

Miami Beach Resort & Spa, 4833 Collins Ave., Miami Beach, 954-563-4444; www.wintermusicconference.com

Now in its 24th year, the Winter Music Conference attracts dance-music professionals from more than 70 countries to network on the dance floor. You'll find artists and DJs competing with each other in spin-offs and looking to get their music picked up by retailers and radio and video programmers, while nightclubs around the city take advantage of the influx of party people to schedule some of the best entertainers in the world.

Last week of March

FALL

MIAMI BOOK FAIR INTERNATIONAL

Miami Dade College, Wolfson Campus, 300 N.E. Second Ave., Downtown, 305-237-3258; www.miamibookfair.com

Bibliophiles of all stripes flock to Miami in November for the nation's largest literary gathering. More than 300 authors from around the world provide back-to-back presentations all weekend, with reading and panel discussions that have featured Caroline Kennedy, Chris Matthews and Richard Russo. If all the book talk makes you feel stuffy, there's also an entire set of programs on graphic novels and comics as well as a festival showcasing South Florida's emerging arts groups with film, dance and music programs.

Second week of November

WHITE PARTY WEEK

Various locations, 305-576-1234; www.whiteparty.org

White Party began in 1985 as a way to generate funds to help those affected by the AIDS epidemic spreading through Miami's gay community, and it has since become the city's hottest benefit. Though it is now part of an entire week of fundraising festivities, the White Party itself is still the biggest highlight, bringing out thousands of people dressed in white for a night of dancing with live music and DJs, with food and drinks provided by more than a dozen of the city's best restaurants.

Last week of November-first week of December

WINTER

ART BASEL MIAMI BEACH

Miami Beach Convention Center, 1901 Convention Center Drive, Miami Beach;
www.artbaselmiamibeach.com

Art Basel proclaims to be most important art show in the United States, and that's not an exaggeration. Sister to the 40-year-old Switzerland event of the same name, the Miami Beach version is a four-day celebration of the arts that includes parties, film, music and exhibitions by more than 2,000 artists representing 220 galleries around the world. Just be mindful of wearing yourself out—the show is yet another excuse to party, and some of Miami's hottest soirees take place that weekend.
First week of December

CALLE OCHO

S.W. Eighth Street between Fourth and 27th avenues, Little Havana, 305-644-8888;
www.carnavalmiami.com

This celebration of South Florida's thriving Latino community floods Little Havana with more than 1.5 million people from all over the world who drop by to revel in its massive street party. Spread over 23 blocks, you'll see strolling musicians and street performers along with top Latino entertainers at every intersection. (Past performers include the revered queen of salsa, Celia Cruz, plus contemporary Latin dance musicians like Gloria Estefan, Willy Chirino and Olga Tañon.) Not only that, but hundreds of kiosks will tempt you with international food. Once you've filled up on plantains and empanadas, work it off on the dance floor to the tune of salsa, merengue, bachata and more.
Late-February-early-March

DESIGN MIAMI

N.E. 39th Street and First Court, Design District, 305-572-0866; www.designmiami.com

In the last four years, this four-day festival has become the place to check out the best in local and international architecture and design. You can gawk at the newest trends and take bets on how long they'll last, or pick up a limited-edition piece to take home with you.
First week of December

WINTER PARTY WEEK

Various locations; www.winterparty.com

Winter Party was just supposed to be a one-time charity dance on South Beach when it started in 1994. Now it's a weeklong festival to benefit the local and national gay, lesbian, bisexual and transgender community, and draws 10,000 guests from all over the world for a week of dance, fashion, art and dining events. The focal point is still dancing the night away on the sands of South Beach.
End of February-early March

HIGHLIGHT

WHAT ARE THE BEST MIAMI NEIGHBORHOODS TO VISIT?

ART DECO DISTRICT, MIAMI BEACH

You won't find anything like this square mile of Art Deco, streamline moderne and Spanish Mediterranean Revival architecture anywhere in the world. Take a guided tour of the designated national historic district.

LINCOLN ROAD, MIAMI BEACH

Hoof it over to the pedestrians-only Lincoln Road for some shopping. The legendary strip is likened to New York's Fifth Avenue because of its busy mix of nightclubs bars, restaurants and boutiques.

LITTLE HAVANA, MIAMI

Head to Calle Ocho, or Eighth Street, to be at the epicenter of Miami's Cuban culture. It's a hot destination for everything Cuban, including food, coffee, music and hand-rolled cigars.

SOUTH BEACH, MIAMI BEACH

Of course, the beautiful beach itself is a big attraction. But people also flock to this trendy neighborhood to experience frequent celeb sightings, the unique Art Deco architecture and the most bumping nightclubs.

especially enjoy gliding down the slide during the Miami heat from mid-March to September. So, don't forget your bathing suit.

Admission: adults $29.95, seniors $27.95, children ages 3-10 $23.95, children under 3 free. Daily 10 a.m.-6 p.m.

MIAMI ART MUSEUM

101 W. Flagler St., Miami, 305-375-3000; www.miamiartmuseum.org

Sure, the art collections are impressive. But what really sets MAM apart from other museums in South Florida is JAM at MAM, an event held the third Thursday of every month, where you can enjoy art with a twist: cocktails, hors d'oeuvres, DJs and live music—as well as extended museum hours. It's a hit with young professionals and art aficionados, as they get to add a little mingling to their art appreciation. Exhibits tend to lean toward a Miami theme—with local artists or local topics being at the forefront—and there's international art from the perspective of the Americas.

Admission: adults $8, seniors $4, students and children under 12 free. Tuesday-Friday 10 a.m.-5 p.m. Saturday-Sunday noon-5 p.m. JAM at MAM: third Thursday of every month 5-9 p.m. (admission $10).

MIAMI CITY BALLET

Ziff Opera Ballet House, Adrienne Arsht Center for the Performing Arts, 1300 Biscayne Blvd., Miami, 305-532-7713; www.miamicityballet.org

It's hard to think of ballet in Miami without Miami City Ballet coming to mind first. The company held its debut season in 1986 and has since grown to be one of the largest in the U.S., currently comprised of 55 dancers from all over the world. Under founder and artistic director Edward Villella, MCB's performances follow the neoclassical 20th-century style established by choreographer George Balanchine. The company performs its repertory series throughout various South Florida cities, but in their hometown, they perform their full season and an annual production of *The Nutcracker* at Ziff. The theater—part of the Arsht Center, which opened in 2006—is the second-largest performing arts center in the U.S., after the Lincoln Center in New York City, with 2,400, seats.

Admission price varies by performance and date.

OLYMPIA THEATER

Gusman Center for the Performing Arts, 174 E. Flagler St., Miami, 305-374-2444; www.gusmancenter.org

The enchantment at the Gusman starts way before the first act begins. The venue itself is a work of art—the theater was built in 1926 as an elaborate movie theater in an ornate Mediterranean style, so expect stars to shine overhead on the ceiling mural, arches along the walls showcasing ancient statues and busts, and intricately carved golden balconies towering over the stage. The theater is the main venue for Ballet Gamonet, one of Miami's younger contemporary ballet companies, though it also plays host to various events, from the FAMA Awards (for Spanish-language soap operas) to piano concerts by the likes of Horacio Gutiérrez. Often times, though, the main star of the show is the theater itself.

Admission: $25-$50. Friday-Saturday 8 p.m.

MIAMI BEACH

ARTCENTER SOUTH FLORIDA

800 Lincoln Road, Miami Beach, 305-674-8278; www.artcentersf.org

Despite being on the corner of Lincoln Road and Eighth Street wedged between clothing boutiques, trendy restaurants and high-fashion modeling agencies, ArtCenter South Florida is as low-key as art gets. This non-profit gallery is free and open to the public, and is always experimenting with new works by lesser-known artists such as painter Jenny Brillhart (www.jbrillhart.com) and mixed media artist Luis Garcia-Nerey (www.luisgarcianerey.com), so don't be deterred by outward appearances. (The gallery displays abstract paintings and sculptures behind a glass case.) Once you step inside, you'll get a taste of the rawness the ArtCenter goes for—high ceilings with exposed rods and air ducts, and rooms partitioned by white walls that don't reach the top.

Monday-Wednesday 11 a.m.-10 p.m., Thursday-Sunday 11 a.m.-11 p.m.

BASS MUSEUM OF ART

2121 Park Ave., South Beach, 305-673-7530; www.bassmuseum.org

Museums in South Florida have their work cut out for them; they need to compete with the paradise-worthy beaches, so any attempt to educate usually comes sweetened with some sort of entertainment. The Bass Museum of Art excels at this, featuring activities that step outside the box, such as theater play readings, wine tastings, concerts and films—all somehow relating to art or the museum. Inside the box (and we mean this literally—the main building is a simple structure built in 1930 as a Miami Beach public library), you'll find a permanent collection that varies from European tapestries to Japanese woodblock prints. Temporary exhibits have ranged from architectural renderings and music, and more classic media like photography, printing and painting (Picasso and Miro had works in a recent exhibit).

Admission: adults $8, seniors and students $6, children under 6 free. Tuesday-Saturday 10 a.m.-5 p.m., Sunday 11 a.m.-5 p.m.

CASA CASUARINA

1116 Ocean Drive, South Beach, 305-576-8003; www.thevillabybartong.com

Casa Casuarina was built in 1930 in homage to the oldest existing house in the Western Hemisphere, the Alcazar de Colon in the Dominican Republic (which also served as home to Christopher Columbus' son Diego in 1510). One of Casa's cornerstones even contains original bricks from the Alcazar. The building's three stories and 22 apartments have been home to artists and visionaries, among them the brother of celebrated dancer Isadora Duncan. But its most notable inhabitant was fashion designer Gianni Versace, who purchased the mansion in 1992. Unfortunately, in 1997, Casa Casuarina was again made famous with the murder of Versace on its front steps as he returned from a morning stroll. In 2010, the building underwent its latest transformation, opening as a boutique hotel and restaurant under the direction of local event planner and restauranteur, Barton G.

THE COLONY THEATER

1040 Lincoln Road, Miami Beach, 305-674-1040

There's no mistaking this iconic building: Originally opened in 1934 as a Paramount Pictures' movie theater chain, the Colony Theater was moved to the corner of Lenox Avenue and Lincoln Road when development for the Lincoln Road Mall began in 1960. The Art Deco building's marquee—with old-school neon letters—stretches overhead as you walk by the box office, and its angular exterior and black-and-white awnings pay tribute to the architecture-style's geometric shapes. The theater, which is listed on the National Register of Historic Places, is owned by the City of Miami Beach. Gawking and posing with the theater's gorgeous exterior is free, but to get a glimpse at the intimate, 440-seat interior, you'll have to buy a ticket—the theater is now used as a performing arts venue for productions by the Miami Contemporary Dance Company, New World Dance Theater and Momentum Dance Company.

Admission prices and hours of operation vary.

THE JEWISH MUSEUM OF FLORIDA

301 Washington Ave., South Beach, 305-672-5044; www.jewishmuseum.com

They say you need to know where you came from in order to know where you're going. And whether you're Jewish or not, this museum gives a good glimpse of a people's past and is an excellent educational resource. The museum developed out of a statewide grassroots project, set to educate and preserve the Florida Jewish experience—nowadays, the institution holds more than 100,000 items

HIGHLIGHT

WHAT IS THE MIAMI DESIGN DISTRICT?

Run-down buildings and a large homeless population were a common sight of downtown Miami covering the blocks between N.E. 2nd to North Miami avenues and N.E. 36th to 41st streets in the late '80s. But in recent years, the area has begun its slow transformation into the **Miami Design District** (*www.miamidesigndistrict.net*), as it's now known.

Real estate developers began rejuvenating the region in the mid-90s. These developers purchased several rundown Art Deco buildings in the area—known in the 1920s as Decorators' Row, a hub for home-design shops—and slowly began the process of urban renewal. By 1998, 50-plus showrooms were calling the neighborhood home, including **Kartell** (*155 N.E. 40th St., 305-573-4010; www.kartell.com*) and **Holly Hunt** (*3833 N.E. 2nd Ave., 305-571-2012; www.hollyhunt.com*).

Today, even though it is still undergoing renovations in some parts (and do keep in mind that the area sees petty crime very occasionally), the District is by and large a gentrified neighborhood in which to live, shop and play. Some artists and restaurateurs have been doing business in the district for years, while some are newcomers, such as **En Avance** (*161 N.E. 40th St., 305-576-0056; www.enavance.net*), a sparse, industrial-chic boutique that sells edgy but functional women's and children's clothing (think ostrich-feather dresses and organic cotton onesies). A **Poltrona Frau** showroom (*10 N.E. 39th St., 305-576-3636; www.frauatlantica.net*), an Italian furniture company known for setting the standard in upholstered leather furniture since 1912, also moved into the District in 2001. The eco-friendly jewelry by Theresa and Tommy Turchin at **Turchin Love and Light Collection** (*130 N.E. 40th St., 305-573-7117; www.loveandlightjewelry.com*) is worth a look; celebrities like Jennifer Aniston are fans.

Make sure to stop by the **Enea Garden Lounge** (*N.E. 40th Street and 2nd Avenue*), a rigorously landscaped oasis with sky-high bamboo and copper walls, and the **Moore Building** (*4040 N.E. 2nd Ave.*) a historic building which hosts the **Moore Space** (*www.themoorespace.org*), a gallery known for its cutting-edge installation and video art. Wrap it up by grabbing a bite at one of the many restaurants that dot the enclave. Have some fresh fish at **Domo Japones** (*4000 N.E. 2nd Ave., 305-573-5474; www.domojapones.com*), or settle somewhere more low-key but equally exotic, like Ethiopian restaurant **Sheba** (*4029 N. Miami Ave., 305-573-1819; www.shebamiami.com*).

It's entirely possible to get overwhelmed by the District's heady collision of art, design and fashion, so if you want just a tiny taste of how it all comes together, visit during the Art + Design Night, which takes place the second Saturday of every month from 7-10 p.m. On the other hand, if you live to be in the scene, book tickets now for **Art Basel Miami Beach** (*www.artbaselmiamibeach.com*), which takes place the first weekend in December and hosts a ton of events and parties in the District.

of interest of the Jewish faith. Collections are divided into categories, which include immigration, community relations and contributions—all spanning from 1763 onward. (Jews first settled in sunny South Florida that year.) The core exhibit, "MOSAIC: Jewish Life in Florida," includes more than 500 photos and artifacts that portray the Jewish experiences, along with three films and a Timeline Wall of Jewish History. Other activities in the museum include book reviews, concerts, dance and theater performances, community street festivals and children's puppet shows.

Admission: adults $6, seniors and students $5, children under 6 free. Free Saturday. Tuesday-Sunday 10 a.m.-5 p.m.

NEW WORLD SYMPHONY

Lincoln Theatre, 541 Lincoln Road, Miami Beach, 305-673-3330; www.nws.edu

Composed of top graduates of music programs worldwide, the New World Symphony's fellows hold classical concerts and chamber programs at their home base on Lincoln Road, and abroad. The intensive, three-year fellowship is meant to prepare emerging musicians for leadership positions in ensembles around the world. Graduates include Emmy Award-winning composer Anthony DiLorenzo and Edward Atkatz, principal percussionist for the Chicago Symphony Orchestra. But the fellows aren't the only ones who benefit; NWS patrons get to see the world's best talent before they get big. From October to May, the NWS presents a full season of concerts at the Lincoln Theatre, a treasure in and of itself. The Art Deco-style theater originally opened in 1936, and though it closed in the early '80s, it was purchased by the Symphony in 1990 and renovated. Though the NWS restored the outside to its original condition, inside, the theater was transformed into a 713-seat auditorium and remodeled for near-perfect acoustics.

Admission prices and performance dates vary.

ST. BERNARD DE CLAIRVAUX CHURCH: THE ANCIENT SPANISH MONASTERY

16711 W. Dixie Highway, North Miami Beach, 305-945-1461; www.spanishmonastery.com

The story of the Ancient Spanish Monastery is a long one, but here's a bite-sized recap: The stone structure was built between 1133 and 1141 in Segovia, Spain, where it stood until William Randolph Hearst purchased the cloisters and the monastery's outbuildings in 1925. The buildings were carefully dismantled and then packed in about 11,000 crates to be shipped to the U.S. But hoof-and-mouth disease upset the travel plans and the crates arrived to a quarantine in a New York facility. After switching ownership a few times, the stones made their way to North Miami Beach and were rebuilt into what is now the oldest building in South Florida. And although the stones are no longer in beautiful Segovia, the land that surrounds this great monument is equally breathtaking. It's the go-to spot for memorable wedding photos and receptions, so be prepared to dodge a bride or two if you head here for the peace and quiet to be found amidst its lovely, ancient corridors and lush gardens.

Admission: adults $5, seniors and students $2.50, children under 12 $2. Monday-Saturday 9 a.m.-4:30 p.m., Sunday noon-4:30 p.m.

THE WOLFSONIAN-FIU

1001 Washington Ave., South Beach, 305-531-1001; www.wolfsonian.org

Despite its moniker, the Wolfsonian-FIU isn't on the Florida International University campus. Instead, it's appropriately in the heart of the museum-like Art Deco district in a wonderfully restored 1927 storage facility. Underscoring the impact that design has on our day-to-day lives, this modern museum explores a wide range of themes from the late 19th and 20th centuries, among them industrialization and consumerism. But what sets it apart from other institutions is the education component it offers. The Wolfsonian organizes trips to major museums, private collections and architectural landmarks around the globe. It also provides popular children's programs to encourage an interest in science and design. If you're just stopping by for the afternoon, be sure to catch the Transportation and Travel collection that includes perfectly intact models of ocean liners, early airplanes and zeppelins.

Admission: adults $7, seniors, students and children 6-12 $5, children under 6 free. Monday-Tuesday, Saturday-Sunday noon-6 p.m., Thursday-Friday noon-9 p.m.

SURROUNDING AREAS

CORAL CASTLE

28655 S. Dixie Highway, Homestead, 305-248-6345; www.coralcastle.com

The Coral Castle has often been compared to Stonehenge and the pyramids. It was built by a man with his bare hands—it should be noted that he was just over five feet tall and weighed only 100 pounds. The story goes that Ed Leedskalnin was engaged to be married only to have his fiancée call off the wedding the day before the ceremony. Erecting a monument as a tribute to that lost love became Leedskalnin's mission in life and he spent 28 years building it, completing the task in 1951. Though the castle is visually impressive in its own right, it becomes exceedingly more so when you realize it was built without any outside help or heavy machinery, and that Leedskalnin carved and sculpted more than 1,100 tons of coral rock using only hand tools. Talk about a labor of love.

Admission: adults $9.75, seniors $6.50, children 7-12 $5, children under 6 free. Sunday-Thursday 8 a.m.-6 p.m. Friday-Saturday 8 a.m.-9 p.m.

THE DEERING ESTATE AT CUTLER

16701 S.W. 72 Ave., Cutler, 305-235-1668; www.deeringestate.com

Listed on the National Register of Historic Places, the Deering Estate was once the home of businessman, artist and philanthropist Charles Deering (half brother to James). The estate's more than 440 acres include houses that date back to 1896, hiking areas teeming with butterflies, canoe rides and guided tours. A tour of the estate homes is a virtual history lesson, with some houses (like the Stone House) displaying what remains of the 4,000 pieces of art he collected throughout his lifetime—one of the largest art collections in the world that included the Old Masters like Rembrandts and was appraised at $60 million in 1922. As if hiking, canoes and tours weren't enough, the estate's memory is kept alive by hosting a seafood festival, a summer cabaret series, jazz concerts and arts festivals.

Admission: adults $10, children ages 4-14 $5. Daily 10 a.m.-5 p.m.

HOMESTEAD MIAMI SPEEDWAY

One Speedway Blvd., Homestead, 305-230-5000; www.homesteadmiamispeedway.com

It's a bit of a drive to the Homestead Miami Speedway, but auto-racing fans don't seem to mind. About thirty minutes by turnpike from Miami, the Speedway hosts the Ford Championship Weekend, parts of the NASCAR Sprint Cup Series, Nationwide Series and the Craftsman Truck Series. Built in 1993 to help revive the city of Homestead after its devastation by Hurricane Andrew a year prior, the track's architecture pays homage to the Art Deco style popular in Miami. It's heavy on bright colors like aqua, silver and violet, which somewhat contrasts with the red-blooded American sport it hosts.

MIAMI METROZOO

12400 S.W. 152 St., South Miami, 305-255-5551; www.miamimetrozoo.com

In 1992 Metrozoo was devastated by Hurricane Andrew, but the rebuilt zoo is better than ever. South Florida's major zoo now boasts larger exhibits and wildlife shows, an ever-growing menagerie of exotic animals. More than 80 exhibits pack the park's 740 acres, and over 1,000 animals representing more than 400 different species call the zoo home. Metrozoo unveiled Amazon & Beyond in late 2008; the exhibit showcases 600 new animals from Central and South American species, such as black howler monkeys and anacondas. On top of the traditional zoo fare, educational animal meet-and-greets, supervised pelican feedings, rides atop dromedary camels and tram tours are all popular activities. But perhaps one of the coolest activities at the zoo are the "overnights": these sleepovers allow visitors to get a behind-the-scenes look at many of the exhibits without demanding that they live like animals (guests sleep in air-conditioned buildings, on beds).

Admission: adults $15.95, children 3-12 $11.95, children under 3 free. Daily 9:30 a.m.-5:30 p.m.

MUSEUM OF CONTEMPORARY ART (MOCA)

770 N.E. 125 St., North Miami, 305-893-6211; www.mocanomi.org

True to form for a contemporary art museum, MOCA's exhibits are well known in Miami for being a bit off-kilter and thought-provoking. But MOCA's commitment to stirring minds takes a populist approach with exhibits that involve museum-goers, such as the interactive 2008 show "Sympathy for the Devil: Art and Rock & Roll Since 1967," which revealed the relationship between visual arts and rock 'n' roll culture—and also came with a full instrument set that visitors were encouraged to jam with while in the museum. MOCA attracts a hip group with its new, updated weekly shows, and ongoing events, which include Contemporary Art Boot Camp (one-hour, bite-sized lectures on art-related topics), Jazz at MOCA, film screenings and art classes for kids and families. Who said art needed to be unattainably abstract?

Admission: adults $5, seniors and students $3, children under 12 free. Tuesday-Saturday 11 a.m.-5 p.m., Sunday noon-5 p.m. Jazz at MOCA: last Friday of each month 7-10 p.m.

MIAMI SCIENCE MUSEUM

3280 S. Miami Ave., Miami 305-646-4200; www.miamisci.org

This museum is a refresher course for everything that you forgot from high school. Situated near Vizcaya, the Miami Science Museum contains hands-on exhibits that run a spectrum of topics from Newton's laws to national flags to the impact of Latinos on the music industry. The outdoor wildlife center includes snakes, reptiles, turtles and even birds of prey—among them an owl, a hawk and a bald eagle. Aspiring astronomers will swoon in the planetarium and Weintraub Observatory upon seeing the two Meade telescopes powerful enough to make out the rings of Saturn and the four moons of Jupiter. Be sure to attend the planetarium laser show if you're in town on the first Friday of every month to see the stars set to music—which often includes the Beatles and Pink Floyd. Who knew science could be this cool?

Admission: adults $10, seniors and students $9, children 3-12 $6.50, children under 3 free. Daily 10 a.m.-6 p.m.

VIZCAYA MUSEUM AND GARDENS
3251 S. Miami Ave., Miami, 305-250-9133; www.vizcayamuseum.com

Even if you're not mad for 17th century antiques, there's little doubt you'll be able to appreciate the majestic surroundings of Vizcaya. A National Historic Landmark, the Vizcaya Museum and Gardens was once home to American industrialist James Deering (his half brother lived across town in an equally impressive abode). Built to look like an Italian villa, it has 34 decorated rooms (and 70 in total) with 15th- to 19th-century antique furnishings and a massive collection of original artwork. Did we mention the property also sits directly along Biscayne Bay, earning some of the best views in the city? Dignitaries from around the world have visited, such as Queen Elizabeth II, Pope John Paul II, President Ronald Reagan and King Juan Carlos I and Queen Sofia of Spain. Try to plan your visit around lunchtime as Vizcaya's 1917 pipe organ serenades visitors inside the mansion from noon to 12:30 p.m. on weekdays. Among the 50 acres, 10 are composed of the breathtaking botanic gardens, which include mazes and a view overlooking Biscayne Bay.

Admission: adults $15, seniors and students $10, children 6-12 $6, children under 6 free. Daily 9:30 a.m.-4:30 p.m.

WHERE TO STAY

MIAMI
★★★CONRAD MIAMI
1395 Brickell Ave., Miami, 305-503-6500; www.conradmiami.com

A business hotel in Miami's financial district, the Conrad Miami is a Hilton outpost that even Paris and Nicky would find suitable. You'll feel like the rich and famous at the sophisticated Conrad as you peer out of the 36-story glass tower with a concave curve and see amazing views of Miami's Biscayne Bay. The décor is also very Miami-nice—white-and-cream everything, except for furnishing touches in dark-chocolate browns. Perks include little details like complimentary slippers, nightly turndown service, dry cleaning and a shoeshine service. Spa Chakra is a haven for relaxation and indulging in high-end Guerlain Paris products. But if you plan on wandering the huge hotel, you better bring a map. A few key places to plot: The 25th floor is home to The Wine Attic and The Bar, which pair vintage wines and specialty cocktails with panoramic Bay views. The rooftop pool is another, but to get there, you'll have to go to an adjacent building and head to the 14th floor.

203 rooms. Restaurant, bar. Pool. Spa. $251-350

★★★DORAL GOLF RESORT & SPA, A MARRIOTT RESORT

4400 N.W. 87th Ave., Miami, 305-592-2000, 800-713-6725; www.doralresort.com

This place is not just a golfer's paradise (although it delivers on that front)—it's just paradise in general. The 650 tropical acres—which includes five championship golf courses (namely the famous Blue Monster course) and a family-friendly Blue Lagoon pool with a giant waterslide—are impeccably maintained. The Doral has become a top-notch place in Miami to host an event not only because of its vast accommodations, but because of its reputation of a staff that can handle anything from a modest wedding to the convergence of international media for the PGA. (It has pulled off the latter seamlessly for the past 45 years.) Okay, so you're not a duffer, and this doesn't sound like Utopia yet. Then book an appointment at The Spa at Doral. With more than 100 treatments to choose from, experiences are custom-made depending on the remedy you seek. There's even a nutritionist onsite who works with you to get your eating on track. Put the advice to practice at the spa's Atrium Restaurant, which serves low-calorie breakfasts and lunches, and encourages you to dine while wearing the comfy spa robe. Whether it's the links or the massage that's relaxed you, your guest room will be the icing on the cake. Elegantly appointed with rich golden and soft brown hues, the beds are comfortable and the bathrooms sparkling.

693 rooms. Restaurant, bar. Fitness center. Pool. Golf. $351 and up

★★★FISHER ISLAND HOTEL AND RESORT

1 Fisher Island Drive, Fisher Island, 305-535-6076, 800-537-3708; www.fisherisland.com

If you want to get a feel for how the Vanderbilts lived, book a stay at this resort which was once the splendid winter estate of William K. Vanderbilt in Fisher Island, which to this day is an exclusive private community and home to some of the world's most wealthy. Security is at a top level here; the only way you can get access to the island is if you live there, or if you can prove you are a guest at the resort. Once you prove it, though, you get a complimentary golf cart to use for the duration of your stay, just to get around the massive property. If you truly want to feel like part of the family, rent Rosemary's Cottage, which was once the home of the Vanderbilt's daughter: three bedrooms, three bathrooms and a formal living room with a fireplace.

62 rooms. Restaurant, bar. Pool. Spa. Golf. Tennis. $351 and up

★★★★FOUR SEASONS HOTEL MIAMI

1435 Brickell Ave., Miami, 305-819-5053, 800-332-3442;
www.fourseasons.com

This luxury resort really rolls out the red carpet for the kids. They get complimentary amenities upon arrival, including child-sized bathrobes, and free baby and children's toiletries. Everything, it seems, but easy access to water. The hotel is in Miami's downtown financial district (about a 15-minute drive from the beach), so it's better suited for business travelers. But it compensates for its lack of beach access with a lively pool scene. The Grand Pool Terrace covers two acres on the seventh floor. Three heated pools—a main pool, shade pool and whirlpool—plus an ample supply of chaise lounges offer plenty of room in which to sunbathe. Guest rooms feature the typical Four Seasons contemporary furnishings with blond wood, and dark green granite in the bedroom and bathroom. Plus, many of the rooms provide some of the best views of Miami's Biscayne Bay and the city. If you're visiting for work and want to do some networking, get the inside scoop on Miami's business climate on the fourth floor at the Sports Club/LA, which is free to hotel guests, and where suits are known to take their lunch breaks.

305 rooms. Restaurant. Business center. Fitness center. Pool. Spa. $251-350

★★★THE GROVE ISLE HOTEL & SPA

4 Grove Isle Drive, Miami, 305-858-8300, 800-884-7683;
www.groveisle.com

Need a place to park the yacht during your hotel stay? This hotel is sequestered on a small island in the middle of Biscayne Bay and offers guests the use of a 111-slip marina. In the lobby, majestic gold columns crowned with green-metal palm leaves point you to the reception area. Room interiors differ, but many are decorated in classic South Florida style, with rattan furnishings and terra-cotta floors in plantation greens and light browns. King canopy beds are elegant with large metal frames and draped in butterfly netting. The bayfront rooms offer multiple vistas of Biscayne Bay. The resort charges a "daily benefit fee" of 10 percent for housekeeping, newspaper delivery and the like. Whatever you do, don't leave without visiting SpaTerre and getting a Watsu pool massage, one of only eight locations in the Eastern United States to offer this unusual water therapy.

49 rooms. Restaurant, bar. Fitness center. Pool. Business center. $251-350

★★★HILTON MIAMI AIRPORT AND TOWERS

5101 Blue Lagoon Drive, Miami, 305-262-1000, 800-445-8667; www.hilton.com

Perfect for cruisers or those who need to be by the airport, the Hilton Miami Airport hotel gets the job done. A complimentary shuttle picks you up at Miami International Airport and 10 minutes later, you're at the check-in counter. The hotel is on a lagoon, where a half-mile jogging trail and walking path curves along the water's edge. The beige and periwinkle rooms aren't as exciting, with plain white walls and light wood furniture. Try to upgrade to the Executive Level guest room, where you make use of lounge's light breakfast and snacks throughout the day. The rooms on this level are a bit nicer, too.

500 rooms. Restaurant, bar. Business center. Fitness center. Pool. Tennis. $151-250

★★★HYATT MIAMI AT THE BLUE

5300 N.W. 87 Ave., Miami, 305-597-5970; www.theblue.com

Known by die-hard duffers just as "The Blue," this posh villa resort opened in April 2008 next to the famed Blue Monster at the Doral Golf Course. You'll feel at home in the streamlined (if a little boring) taupe and cappuccino suites, which feature fully equipped kitchens with full-size refrigerators, stoves, micro-waves and dishwashers, a rarity for lodging. When you're not putting around (on the green or in the kitchen), you'll probably be soaking your sore swinging arms in the bathroom's Jacuzzi and watching the plasma TV. If you're traveling with a gaggle of golf buddies, the three-bedroom suite is ultra luxurious, complete with four full baths. With so much golf to go around, the only thing that'll be blue is the resort's name.

215 suites. Restaurant, bar. Fitness center. Pool. Spa. Pets accepted. $151-250

★★★INTERCONTINENTAL HOTEL MIAMI AT MIAMI CENTER

100 Chopin Plaza, Miami, 305-577-1000, 800-327-3005; www.icmiamihotel.com

Famous for its yearly Big Orange drop countdown on New Year's Eve, Miami's version of Times Square's ball drop, the InterContinental is in a prime spot if your plans require that you stay downtown. Close to American Airlines Arena and minutes away from Miami's Brickell financial district, the hotel offers rooms with great views of Biscayne Bay. Walk outside of your door to the festi-val-like experience of Bayside shopping and beautiful Bayfront Park. If you're looking to live the high life, the concierge can book a special Art Deco-style golf experience at the Miami Beach Golf Club.

641 rooms. Restaurant, bar. Business center. Fitness center. Pool. Spa. $151-250

★★★JW MARRIOTT HOTEL MIAMI

1109 Brickell Ave., Miami, 305-329-3500, 800-228-9290; www.marriott.com

Strategically placed in the heart of the city's Brickell financial district, this JW Marriott caters to the business traveler. In fact, the interior has the feel of a cherry-wood-lined corporate boardroom. But what it lacks for in atmosphere, it makes up for in business-minded conveniences. Three executive floors feature a concierge lounge with continental breakfast and snacks served all day. Leave your laptop at home—this hotel installed PCs in the rooms for easy access to Internet and e-mail. And even though there isn't much nightlife in the financial district after 5:30 p.m., a cab ride can whisk you across the MacArthur Causeway to South Beach. There are restaurants in the hotel, and you can take a short walk to Capital Grille or Morton's Steakhouse, or grab a homemade brew and a burger at Gordon Biersch Brewery. Because sometimes, business-man habits die hard.

296 rooms. Restaurant, bar. Fitness center. Pool. $251-350

★★★★MANDARIN ORIENTAL, MIAMI

500 Brickell Key Drive, Miami, 305-913-8288, 866-526-6567; www.mandarinoriental.com

Without a doubt, this is one of the finest hotels in Miami, from the valets who remember your name to the impeccable customer service to the lobby area (a Zen den replete with dainty flowers on vases on the tables and satin pillows on the red-hued couches) that invites relaxation with its sky-high windows that look out onto the water. We could go on, and we will. The rooms are also pristine, and exude a calming vibe with their Asian-inspired flair and their color palette of pear-green, light yellow and tan. Balcony rooms have picture-perfect views of Biscayne Bay and the colorful city lights at night. The view is enough to inspire you to spend the day a bamboo bed on the hotel's private beach. Once the sun has zapped you of energy (in that good way), head for the Mandarin's spa, where you can get an exclusively local treatment such as the Kudalini Journey. The mix of oils, massage and yoga stretches will have you counting down the days until you return to this hotel.

327 rooms. Restaurant. Business center. Fitness center. Pool. Spa. Pets accepted. Beach. $351 and up

★★★MARRIOTT MIAMI BISCAYNE BAY
1633 N. Bayshore Drive, Miami, 305-374-3900, 800-228-9290; www.marriott.com

We'd rather be in Miami for pleasure instead of business, too, but this hotel is convenient consolation if you're in this tropical paradise for profes-sional reasons. Vacationers about to embark on a cruise also find this hotel's downtown location accommodating. Some of the rooms provide great views of the marina from the 31-story tower, and city-view rooms have balconies with chairs. The interiors have typical chain-hotel furnishings, as do the bathrooms, with their regulation tub/shower. Likewise, the hotel feels a bit routine as the staff shuttles people in and out under the assumption that mostly everyone staying at the property is there for a 12-hour stopover on a cruise. Still, breezy service is a small price to pay for accessibility and nearness to downtown office buildings and a host of Miami attractions (in case you're in need of a break).

610 rooms. Restaurant, bar. Fitness center. Pool. $151-250

★★★MAYFAIR HOTEL & SPA
3000 Florida Ave., Miami, 305-441-0000, 800-433-4555; www.mayfairhotelandspa.com

The Mayfair is a quirky-chic hotel with Japanese hot tubs and rattan couches on each balcony, carved wooden mahogany doors and a motel layout (though not, heaven forbid, any of the vibe—it's just that the doors open out into an airy outdoor hallway rather than an interior). Beautiful courtyards give the place a tropical, secluded vibe (not unlike a Southeast Asian getaway), despite the commotion of its busy Coconut Grove neighbor, CocoWalk, which leads to one of the major sources of dissatisfaction for most guests—the abundant weekend noise from the street. So if you're an early-to-bed type, bring the earplugs. The Asian-fusion cuisine of Ginger Grove, on the second floor, is popular with locals, as is the highly praised Jurlique Spa. There's also a rooftop infinity pool, sky bar and private cabanas.

179 rooms. Restaurant. Business center. Fitness center. Spa. $351 and up

★★★THE MUTINY HOTEL
2951 S. Bayshore Drive, Miami, 305-441-2100, 888-868-8469; www.mutinyhotel.com

This condo-hotel towers over Sailboat Bay and features individually owned suites, each with a full kitchen. Most have private balconies with excellent views. The units are managed as hotel rentals by a property management company, so the furnishings differ from room to room, but most maintain that tropical-British-colonial/Caribbean motif. One- and two-bedroom deluxe suites boast a king-size bed in the master bedroom, and any with second bedrooms have twin beds or a pull-out sofa, so you can really bring the whole clan here and spread out. The kitchen and separate dining area is ideal for big groups or those who don't feel like eating out every day. Room service, however, is limited, so stock up at the grocery store (there's a Publix Supermarket nearby) and make use of that kitchen.

120 rooms. Restaurant, bar. Fitness center. Pool. $151-250

★★★★THE RITZ-CARLTON, COCONUT GROVE

3300 S.W. 27th Ave., Miami, 305-644-4680, 800-241-3333; www.ritzcarlton.com

If you're looking for top-of-the-line service and amenities, but want to avoid the crushing hordes of tourists, you've come to the right place. This is quite possibly the most intimate hotel in The Ritz-Carlton family. That it lives inside the artsy enclave of Coconut Grove makes it even cozier. Relaxed and casual, the boutique hotel offers a more personal level of service because there are just over 100 rooms. The interior exudes European charm, with the marble columns and floors in the lobby, and mahogany furniture and overstuffed chairs in each room. Guest rooms also boast private balconies and floor-to-ceiling windows, and bathrooms with a separate shower and bathtub. The best part is that you can enjoy the off-the-beaten-path while still knowing there are places to go nearby: The hotel is a half mile away from CocoWalk, an alfresco shopping and entertainment center with solid restaurants.

115 rooms. Restaurant, bar. Business center. Fitness center. Pool. Spa. $251-350

★★★SHULA'S HOTEL & GOLF CLUB

6842 Main St., Miami Lakes, 305-821-1150, 800-247-4852; www.donshulahotel.com

Former Miami Dolphins coach Don Shula opened his golf resort in 1992 and has been getting rave reviews ever since. The coach ran his team with precision, and so it's no surprise that he runs the staff likewise. The staff is amenable and if you ask for an upgrade, often you'll get it. The location is a bit off the beaten path, in a Miami suburb, but it's just a 20-minute drive to South Beach. Shula's Senator Golf Course was originally designed by Bill Watts, and frequent green machines say that the 18-hole, par-72 course lends itself to a challenging round on the links. As for the rooms, get all thoughts of Dolphins cozies, football blankets and other sports paraphernalia out of your head, as they're outfitted in light creams and beiges, with black-and-tan-striped bedspreads. Several rooms are even designed in soft pinks and equipped with Aveda products for with female business travelers.

301 rooms. Restaurant, bar. Fitness center. Spa. Golf. Tennis. $61-150

★★★SOFITEL MIAMI

5800 Blue Lagoon Drive, Miami, 305-264-4888; www.sofitel.com

Many times hotels near the airport are merely adequate for quick overnight stays for business travelers or vacationers looking for a docking spot between cruise destinations. But the Sofitel goes above and beyond. The French hotel chain offers Miami guests comfortable, large rooms; a helpful staff; a reliable restaurant; and a good outdoor pool. The rooms are luxe thanks to a warm color scheme of tawny beige, gold, platinum and red. Contemporary art on the wall above the bed adds a burst of color as well. A French loveseat is a comfy place for reading the morning paper before catching your flight. Rooms also offer a Miami skyline or lagoon view. Speaking of Miami's skyline, don't think that because you're close to the airport you're not near the other city sights—they're just a short cab ride away.

281 rooms. Restaurant, bar. Fitness center. Pool. Tennis. $151-250

RECOMMENDED

FORTUNE HOUSE
185 S.E. 14th Terrace, Miami, 305-349-5200; www.fortunehousehotel.com

If you love Miami so much you could move there, this is the place to take a trial run. The high-rise condominium hotel near the Four Seasons is good for longer stays, and most of the building consists of condo owners or renters. The drawbacks are the lack of full-scale hotel amenities, including an in-building restaurant, in-room Internet and consistent housekeeping, but the security staff members are on their toes, and valet parking is available for a daily charge in a secure garage. The rooms are furnished with interiors ranging from sparsely modern to colonial-kitsch. This place is best for business travelers who require the condo lifestyle, so you vacationers should probably seek other arrangements.

296 suites. Fitness center. Pool. Business center. $151-250

VICEROY MIAMI
485 Brickell Ave., Miami, 305-503-4400; www.viceroymiami.com

Kelly Wearstler, Philippe Starck and local firm Arquitectonica joined up to create the provocative Viceroy Miami. The result is a thoroughly modern throwback with its vivid color palette of seafoam green, pink and turquoise, mod furnishings everywhere, and onyx, wood and glass accents. The hotel straddles downtown Miami and Brickell Avenue, making it a good choice for business travelers looking for something new (unfortunately, the hotel is not near the beach). Guests are greeted by a massive valet area lined with imposing artistic pillars evocative of Easter Island, immediately setting the scene for a dramatic experience. The drama extends to the 15th floor, where there are sweeping Biscayne Bay views and three inviting pools, one of which is billed as the largest infinity pool in Miami. Oversized lounging chairs easily fit three people, and there's a large fireplace and life-size chess set. The 28,000-square-foot Starck-designed spa includes a water lounge flanked by bookshelves set off by a huge yellow chandelier. Rooms are equally dramatic with their large poster beds "framed" by oversized artwork of a Florida bird. Kitchens are nicely tucked behind pocket doors and stocked with beautiful tableware, super-soft linens, coffee bars and organic mini bars. Dining at the Viceroy revolves around celeb-chef Michael Psilakis, who mans Eos at night and bistro e (in the same space) during the day.

168 rooms. Restaurant, bar. Business center. Fitness center. Pool. Spa. Pets accepted. $251-350.

MIAMI BEACH

★★★ALBION SOUTH BEACH
1650 James Ave., Miami Beach, 305-913-1000, 800-782-3557; www.rubellhotels.com

The neon sign atop the Albion screams Art Deco. But the building—designed by Igor Polevitzky, the originator of nautical Art Deco architecture—looks like a cruise liner from 1939, the year the hotel was built. You'll also feel like you're on a boat as you pass by three portholes along the side of the 60-foot-long above-ground pool, where you can scope out swimmers underwater. The hotel made national headlines in the 1970s as the headquarters of Abbie Hoffman and Students for a Democratic Society during the 1972 Democratic National Convention in Miami. It's also home to the Petite rooms, the economical, 180-square-foot guest room (there are 15 of these on the premises). The upside of a Petite room is you can usually secure it for pretty cheap, considering the sky-high South Beach rates. The downsides are obvious (nothing but a full-size bed and bathroom). Then again, you're within walking distance to Lincoln Road and South Beach nightlife.

100 rooms. Restaurant, bar. Pool. Business center. $150-251

★★★THE ALEXANDER
5225 Collins Ave., Miami Beach, 305-865-6500, 800-327-6121; www.alexanderhotel.com

This all-suite hotel may be one of the best choices for families visiting South Beach, since there's enough space in these rooms for mom, dad, the kids, and even grandma and grandpa. The room interiors have the air of old Miami Beach before it was known as South Beach (picture Nana's condo furnishings, wicker coffee tables and faux antique chairs). But bear in mind that The Alexander recently under went a $10 million renovation to update much of its interior and exterior, though it kept its stately décor, including the dark oak walls and the grand staircase in the lobby. Each suite comes with a full kitchen, so say goodbye to fast-food breakfasts. For dinner, head to Shula's Steakhouse, located inside the hotel. The restaurant, named for the legendary former Miami Dolphins coach, serves up juicy porterhouses and steak tartare in a classic clubby atmosphere.

150 rooms. Restaurant, bar. Fitness center. Pool. Spa. $251-350

★★★BLUE MOON HOTEL
944 Collins Ave., Miami Beach, 305-673-2262, 800-553-7739; www.bluemoonhotel.com

The rooms here are awash in tropical colors, and the quaint touches, such as the little seashell centerpieces on the tables, make this place feel more like a friendly bed and breakfast than a hotel. Blue Moon is actually two former hotels—the Art Deco-style Lafayette and the Mediterranean-style Les Suites—now connected by an arched breezeway. Both architectural styles remain intact, thanks to the stringent standards the hotel must adhere to since it's listed on the National Register of Historic Places. But significant architecture or not, the reason to pick this place from the may others on the beach is the staff. Miami has a reputation for unfriendly hotel workers (watch out, NYC), but here, they abide by their mission of guest-centered service. Whether you want an in-room massage or to switch your less-than-perfect room location, the staff makes it happen. There are things they can't help with, however, such as the size of the tiny pool, the loud air conditioning in the room and the $7 daily resort fee. (Of course, the latter goes toward the continental breakfast, an evening snack, a $5 coupon for a drink at the bar and free Wi-Fi, so we'll let it go.) Expect to find yourself humming the popular Rodgers and Hart song at least a few times during your visit: "Blue Moon, you saw me standing alone..."—a charming little ditty that somehow ends up in your memory, just like this hotel.

75 rooms. Bar. Complimentary breakfast. Pool. $251-350

★★★DELANO HOTEL

1685 Collins Ave., Miami Beach, 305-672-2000, 800-697-1791; www.delano-hotel.com

Many still visit the Delano just to brag that they've been here, but celebrity spotting isn't what it used to be at the peak of the hotel's heyday in the mid-90s. Still, the intimidating poseurs and model types will have you looking for a quick lipo treatment before you hit the pool. And you'll want to make repeat visits to the pool, as it and the Delano's bar scene are the reasons to empty your wallet to stay at this hotel—not the rooms. Interiors are minimalist and stark with shocks of color here and there, the handiwork of designer Philippe Starck, but rooms are tiny, which is typical among the South Beach boutique hotels. If the cramped quarters of your all-white room are making you a bit restless, head to the renowned rooftop Agua Spa instead. Don't miss Blue Door restaurant, either—still popular after all these years.

194 rooms. Restaurant, bar. Pool. Spa. $351 and up

★★★EDEN ROC RENAISSANCE MIAMI BEACH

4525 Collins Ave., Miami Beach, 786-276-0526, 800-319-5354; www.edenrocresort.com

This midcentury Miami Beach classic recently underwent a $200 million renovation and now boasts updated amenities in guest rooms such as flat-screen TVs, iPod stations, and floating staircases and balconies in the new Ocean Tower bungalow suites. The oceanfront bar Cabana Beach Club is a boardwalk hot spot, but don't miss drinks in the contemporary lobby lounge, faithfully outfitted with midcentury modern sofas and chairs. The new ELLE Spa is expected to open in late 2010 but for now, get a relaxing massage in your room.

631 rooms. Restaurant, bar. Business center. Fitness center. Pool. Spa. Pets accepted. Beach. $151-250

★★★FONTAINEBLEAU MIAMI BEACH RESORT

4441 Collins Ave., Miami Beach, 305-538-2000, 800-548-8886; www.fbresorts.com

Grand hotels of the past have a hard enough time competing with newer, hipper options as it is. So you have to give the Fontainebleau credit for not riding on its name alone—the spectacular veteran Morris Lapidus-designed landmark keeps it current. Although the hotel pays respect to the grandeur of a bygone era by rehabbing things here and there—such as the lobby's bow-tie floors, designed by Lapidus—its

---

WHICH HOTELS HAVE THE MOST UNIQUE DECOR?

The Tides:
Probably the best part about staying at The Tides, which was redone in May 2008, are the customized rooms by star interior designer Kelly Wearstler. Internationally known for her signature, Wearstler fuses Hollywood glamour with laid-back beach-chic at The Tides.

The Hotel:
This being a Todd Oldham-designed hotel, the rooms have utterly precious window seats and shelves with small vases and other darling decorative touches. The loft-style rooms are on the smallish side, and the bathroom is especially tight, but throw on your Oldham tie-dyed bathrobe and toss care to the wind.

Viceroy Miami:
All of the details at this hotel get a dose of design: Views from the spa's three-story water lounge are rivaled by a gigantic yellow chandelier, gaggles of painted nine-foot-tall cranes adorn the lobby's walls, and in the rooms, bird artwork is used as headboards.

suites now range from modest 550-square-footers to 4,300-square-foot Goliaths, and each has its own iMac and oversized Jacuzzi. Larger suites even have their own in-room washer and dryer. Outside, you can have your pick of a free-form pool or a European-style one. The massive complex also houses a bi-level center of serenity, the Lapis Spa. Book your signature resculpting facial now, or we guarantee you'll be waiting longer than it took the Fountainbleau to finally reopen.

1,504 rooms. Restaurant, bar. Pool. Spa. $351 and up

★★GANSEVOORT SOUTH

2377 Collins Ave., Miami Beach, 305-604-1000;
www.gansevoortsouth.com

Gansevoort South is the first extension of the Gansevoort brand (which includes the Hotel Gansevoort in Manhattan's Meatpacking District). Stylishly sleek, this hotel combines contemporary style with avant-garde design. In the lobby, a 50-foot-long shark tank features 27 varieties of fish. Hot pinks and dusty violets abound in the room interiors, but get those Barbie nightmares out of your head—guest rooms are tastefully done, with only splashes of these strident hues amidst white, tan and gray. Despite the girlish color scheme, the hotel is geared to adults on vacation—it's tailor-made for girlfriends' retreats with its adults-only plunge pool, 18-story views of the ocean below and a 110-foot swimming pool with cabanas equipped out with flat-screen televisions. Down below, at beach level, the private Gansevoort Beach Club shares the sultry Stephane Dupoux design of the chic Nikki Beach, which is just 20 blocks south of this beach club. You'll feel like you died and went to heaven as you relax on oversized beds amid palm trees and fire pits. Fitness icon David Barton also put in a massive gym and spa in the hotel.

334 rooms. Restaurant, bar. Fitness center. Pool. Spa. $351 and up

★★★THE HOTEL

801 Collins Ave., Miami Beach, 305-531-2222;
www.thehotelofsouthbeach.com

This being a Todd Oldham-designed hotel, the rooms have utterly precious window seats and shelves with small vases and other darling decorative touches. The loft-style rooms are on the smallish side, and the bathroom is especially tight, but throw on your Oldham tie-dyed bathrobe and toss care to the wind. You're in South Beach, darn it, and you'll feel it when you sashay up to the rooftop pool. A bit of trivia to share with friends after your stay: The Hotel used to be called The Tiffany when it opened in 1939, but the Fifth Avenue jewelers challenged developer Tony Goldman with a lawsuit to change the name when he reopened in 1998. Hence, in a bit of a protest of sorts, he reduced the moniker to its current ultra-generic form. Word on the street is that Goldman still refers to his hotel as The Tiffany. The jeweler, however, couldn't touch the Art Deco spire, which still stands strong atop the building and proudly reads "Tiffany" in neon blue and white—best seen at night while sipping a drink from the Spire Bar & Lounge, located on the alfresco pool deck.

53 rooms. Restaurant, bar. Fitness center. Pool. $151-250

★★★HOTEL NASH

1120 Collins Ave., Miami Beach, 305-674-7800, 800-403-6274; www.hotelnash.com

Perhaps it's the aromatic courtyard garden—home to three individual spa pools, each filled with either fresh, mineral or salt water—that lends this boutique hotel a therapeutic atmosphere. Or maybe it's the soothing sage-and-ivory color palette. Either way, you'll feel an instant calm settle over you when you step into this hotel. The rooms are hyper-chic and sparse, with breathtaking flora photos by Miami photographer Iran Issa-Khan and unusual, shield-shaped blond-wood armoires for spice here and there. But you may be too busy trying to sneak a peek at the famous Gianni Versace mansion, Casa Casuarina; the hotel is a block behind it and many of the rooms have a view of the mansion observatory. Dreamily unpretentious, this is one of the few true oases on the beach.

52 rooms. Restaurant, bar. Pool. $351 and up

★★★HOTEL OCEAN

1230 Ocean Drive, Miami Beach, 305-672-2579, 800-783-1725; www.hotelocean.com

Hotel Ocean trades swank for a great location, larger-than-usual rooms atypical of South Beach boutique hotels, and a cheaper asking price. Though the rooms aren't as chic as those in neighboring hotels, the Spanish-tiled, oval-shaped shower entrance in each room adds an interesting element. Also typical—the $9 daily fee, which goes toward the use of free beach chairs (grab them early because they go fast), towels and a thin breakfast. Unlike its neighbors, Ocean doesn't have a pool—but true to its name, the Atlantic is just across the street, so it's not like it needs one.

27 rooms. Restaurant, bar. Fitness center. Pets accepted. $251-350

★★★★LOEWS MIAMI BEACH HOTEL

1601 Collins Ave., Miami Beach, 305-604-1601, 800-235-6397; www.loewshotels.com

The expansive Loews Miami Beach sits amidst the sea of small Art Deco hotels that pepper South Beach. And although it's still done up in Art Deco style, the ornate façade and winding driveway give away the fact that it's a newcomer to Miami Beach (its main building was erected from the ground up in 1998). The advantage of building from scratch is that Loews could create a custom experience for each guest: Those looking for a classic Loews experience can stay in the main building, while those who prefer a South Beach boutique experience can book at the adjoining St. Moritz, also owned by the hotelier. Both feature the same top-drawer service, including obliging concierges who'll even send faxes from poolside. Pets get welcome gifts, including a bowl and treats; kids receive Fisher-Price welcome presents. You deserve a gift, too, so treat yourself to power-boosting facial at the Elemis Spa. Afterward, retreat to your island getaway of a room—the mostly cream décor pops with ocean-blue armchairs and wicker chairs, while a flat-screen television and iPod docking station give you those can't-live-without extras you won't find out on the sand.

790 rooms. Restaurant, bar. Fitness center. Pool. Spa. $251-350

★★★THE MERCURY SOUTH BEACH

100 Collins Ave., Miami Beach, 305-398-3000; www.mercuryresort.com

While it's tucked away at the very southern end of Collins Avenue, the Mercury is near plenty of hot spots, including Nikki Beach. The Mercury is all-suite hotel, and it does offer space in which to sprawl out—the living room couch turns into a pull-out bed. Unfortunately, the furniture is college dorm all the way, with blond wood entertainment shelving units and coffee tables on wheels. (Saving grace: there's a Jacuzzi in the bathroom, not a pony keg, which means you're totally not in college.) Once you catch a glimpse of your fellow clientele, though, it's right back to senior year—the hotel generally attracts a younger crowd who loves the nightlife at the ultra-chic Prive, just a few doors down.

44 rooms. Restaurant. Business center. Fitness center. Pool. $251-350

★★★MIAMI BEACH RESORT & SPA
4833 Collins Ave., Miami Beach, 305-532-3600, 866-767-6060;
www.miamibeachresortandspa.com

This space was formerly a Wydham Hotel, and it still looks like one, despite new owners. Located on the stretch of Collins Avenue near the famed Fontainebleau, the recent renovation of that hotel could be either a boom or a bust for this resort-style hotel. The Baroque-inspired lobby features a gargantuan chandelier and marble walls that take you back to the days of Old (as in, Spanish colonial-looking) Miami, though that's where ornateness ends. Guest rooms are bright and cheerful, outfitted in sunny yellows, blues and whites. The hotel continues to fill the niche created by the Wyndham before it of catering to meetings and convention types, so if you're here on vacation, you may feel a bit out of place but just head to the expansive pool with plenty of chairs—finally, a place where you don't have to fight for your place in the sun. Golfers, take note: Privileges extended to hotel guests include entrance to the tony Miami Beach Golf Club.

424 rooms. Restaurant, bar. Business center. Fitness center. Pool. Spa. $251-350

★★★THE NATIONAL HOTEL
1677 Collins Ave., Miami Beach, 305-532-2311, 800-327-8370; www.nationalhotel.com

If you want a real flavor of Art Deco South Beach, check into The National. The lobby maintains its original 1930s glamour with its high-style Hollywood mirrors and period-appropriate lamp sconces. The light beige color palette and blond furniture seem sedate in these Deco confines, as do the brown-carpeted hallways. You'll perk up, however, when you visit the hotel's famous aquamarine beauty of a pool. It's Miami's longest pool at 205 feet of pure blue bliss. On certain days, you may have to work your swim around a film crew shooting on location, since The National is frequently the backdrop for fashion shoots for magazines and television shoots Ready for your close-up?

151 rooms. Restaurant, bar. Fitness center. Pool. $251-350

★★★THE PALMS SOUTH BEACH
3025 Collins Ave., Miami Beach, 305-851-7748; www.thepalmshotel.com

True to its name, The Palms offers every variety of its namesake tree imaginable at the tropical oasis, including Alexander, areca, bamboo, coconut, fishtail, kentia, lady, robellini, silver, triangle and Washington varieties. Wild and domestic parrots flock to the greenery like bees to honey. They call the lush garden their home, as do exotic flowers such as wild orchids and bright-orange birds of paradise. Not only that, but the hotel is located on the north side of South Beach, about 13 blocks from the heart of the action. It's as if The Palms is trying its darndest to get you away from it all, and if that's the type of vacation you're looking for, then you're in the right place. Inside, the hotel is a mix of South Beach chic and Southern charm with old-fashioned, stirring ceiling fans and terra-cotta floors throughout the common areas. The guest rooms aren't quite as charming, thanks to standard furnishings and plain tan-and-white interiors. Still, that's no big deal, since you'll want to spend as much time on the hotel's quiet, private beach (just make sure you use your two beach chairs and beach umbrellas each day; it's part of the $13 daily surcharge you'll see on your bill as a resort fee). If a day at the beach isn't enough of a tropical escape, spend some quiet time in the gorgeous garden—then it'll be just you and the birds.

243 rooms. Restaurant. Business center. Fitness center. Pool. Beach. $251-350

★★★★THE RITZ-CARLTON, SOUTH BEACH

1 Lincoln Road, Miami Beach, 786-276-4000, 800-241-3333; www.ritzcarlton.com

Not only can you expect the Ritz-Carlton's signature service here, but this hotel on South Beach offers a few little extras that make a big difference. The hotel features a stunning permanent multimillion-dollar art collection (no need to make your trip during Art Basel Miami anymore) and the world's only tanning butler—a person whose job is to make sure you have just the right amount of sunscreen in all the right places. The hotel itself is awe-inspiring, thanks to its storied history; the building, which sits at the foot of Lincoln Road, was restored from the original 1953 Morris Lapidus-designed DiLido hotel. The guest rooms feature dark cherry-wood furniture highlighted with a pretty deep-blue-and-beige color scheme. Make sure you book an ocean-view room to fully experience the hotel's location. If you miss out on an ocean-view room, then just spend time at the elevated infinity pool, which provides a lovely vista of the Atlantic. Another tiny touch that makes a monumental difference.

375 rooms. Restaurant. Business center. Fitness center. Pool. Spa. $351 and up

★★★★THE SETAI

2001 Collins Ave., Miami Beach, 305-520-6000; www.setai.com

As one of the chicest hotels in Miami, the Setai is the place to see and be seen on South Beach—that is,

---

WHICH HOTELS OFFER THE MOST UNUSUAL AMENITIES?

The Ritz-Carlton, South Beach:
This hotel offers the usual Ritz-Carlton amenities, but goes a step further by offering the services of the world's only tanning butler, someone who will rub lotion on those hard-to-reach places on your back to ensure you get an even tan.

The Setai:
Celebrities hide out in The Setai because the hotel is designed with privacy in mind. They also might be drawn to its two-floor recording studio from Lenny Kravitz or the 10,000-square-foot penthouse suite with its own lap pool.

if you happen to see anyone at all. Because although celebrities flock to this hotel, it is designed so that rooms feel like secluded enclaves, and outside of the pool area, you just might feel as if you were on your own desert island. The Setai spreads out over two buildings and features the smaller studio suites in the refurbished Art Deco building (formerly the Dempsey Vanderbilt hotel) and a modern 40-story glass tower that houses the more expansive suites and privately owned condo suites. Inside, however, it's more Asian-inspired minimalism than Art Deco. You won't find a color that even comes close to Miami teal or coral here; the sleek, angular furnishings ooze deep blacks, jade green and rich teak woods, right down to the hardwood floors in each room and the black granite bathtubs with matching black tiles. But if all the dark and cool colors leaves you a little cold, make for the hotel's restaurant or grill, where you can get your pick of hot cuisines that span the Far East (including Chinese, Thai, Indian, Singaporean and Malay). Who knows? You might spot someone famous chowing down on the delectable fare.

120 rooms. Restaurant. Business center. Fitness center. Pool. Spa. $351 and up

★★★THE SHORE CLUB, MIAMI BEACH

1901 Collins Ave., Miami Beach, 305-695-3100;
www.shoreclub.com

This hip hotel is not for the faint of heart; leggy models and celebrities sometimes dot the landscape by the infinity pools and the white-on-white guest rooms. The Shores is also all about the party and easy access to several bars (by the pool, on the beach, and indoors) so you'll never go thirsty. Dance the night away at the Red Room or indulge in mojitos at the poolside Rum Bar. The rooms are breezy Miami-minimalist and include 400-count Egyptian cotton sheets. Book the private duplex beach house for a separate entrance and your own private pool.

384 rooms. Restaurant, bar. Fitness center. Pool. Spa. $351 and up

★★★SOUTH BEACH MARRIOTT

161 Ocean Drive, Miami Beach, 305-536-7700, 800-228-9290; www.marriott.com

Sometimes, when you're overwhelmed with hip-boutique-this or beachside-that, you just want to run to the embrace of a familiar name. Cue the Art Deco-style Marriott. The hotel, while still technically located on South Beach, is off the beaten path and away from the thick of things near the more-crowded areas of Ocean Drive (i.e., north of Fifth Street). Still, that doesn't mean the hotel is a snoozefest. In the lobby, the Marriott keeps the South Beach vibe alive with some contemporary touches, including funky artwork behind the reception desk and an art sculpture of blown glass. The rooms are by far comfier and larger than you'll find at the other hotels along the beach, and the infinity pools (flanked by towering palm trees) make for a picturesque place to catch some rays. And though it suffers from a lack of identity because of its Marriott moniker, there are hints of rebellion. Exhibit A? An aviary stocked with flora and fauna, including small birds, koi fish and tropical foliage—not your typical Marriott fare.

236 rooms. Restaurant, bar. Fitness center. Pool. $351 and up

★★★THE TIDES HOTEL

1220 Ocean Drive, Miami Beach, 305-604-5070, 800-439-4095; www.tidessouthbeach.com

Attentive service and gorgeous décor is what keeps people coming back to The Tides. South Beach hotel staffs unfortunately have a reputation for being cold and aloof, but at The Tides, you're greeted at the door, everyone remembers your name and almost any request is accommodated. (It's not for nothing that all guests receive a genie-like "personal assistant," assigned to make any request happen.) Probably the best part about staying at The Tides, which was redone in May 2008, are the customized rooms by star interior designer Kelly Wearstler. Internationally known for her signature, Wearstler fuses Hollywood glamour with laid-back beach-chic at The Tides.

45 rooms. Restaurant, bar. Fitness center. Pool. Spa. $351 and up

RECOMMENDED

CANYON RANCH HOTEL & SPA

6801 Collins Ave., Miami Beach, 305-514-7000; www.canyonranchmiamibeach.com

If you like your fitness with a shot of bubbly, plant your yoga mat at Canyon Ranch Miami Beach. Located in the restored Art Deco Carillon Hotel, the property boasts a 70,000-square-foot wellness spa with 54 treatment rooms and a two-story indoor climbing wall. Work up a sweat in one of 40 daily fitness classes, cool off with some oceanfront lounging—the hotel sits on 750 linear feet of beach—and refuel with lamb tataki and rosemary roasted cod from the Grill. A bonus: Unlike Canyon Ranch's Lennox and Tucson locations, CRMB serves alcohol—organic and biodynamic alcohol, of course. Rooms feature kitchens outfitted with KitchenAid and Miele appliances, 400-thread count sheets, deep soaking tubs and plush robes you'll have to drag yourself out of upon checkout.

150 rooms. Restaurant, bar. Business center. Fitness center. Pool. Spa. Beach. $351 and up.

CARDOZO HOTEL

1300 Ocean Drive, Miami Beach, 305-535-6500, 800-782-6500; www.cardozohotel.com

This might not be one of South Beach's most sizzling hot spots, but its owners are what draws guests to this 1939 building. Grammy Award-winning singer and Miami darling Gloria Estefan and her husband, Emilio, bought the property in 1992 for a reported $5 million. Decorated with indigenous, multicultural themes, the hotel is filled with art and sculptures from the Estefans' worldwide travels. But of course, pictures of the Cuban-American chanteuse hang in the bar and you can always request from the library of Gloria Estefan and the Miami Sound Machine hits. The rooms are uniquely decorated, and some feature floor-to-ceiling paintings in the main area. Wrought-iron beds, hardwood floors and simple, white bedding makes for a breezy vibe, while the small bathrooms are well maintained, with ceramic-bowl sinks set on top of marble. Some of the rooms have whirlpool tubs, which is a good thing, considering the hotel doesn't have a pool, though there's a great beach across the street. Afterward, cool off at the bar, which makes one of the best mojitos on Deco Drive.

43 rooms. Restaurant, bar. $251-350

WHICH
RESTAURANTS
HAVE THE BEST
OUTSIDE DINING?

Azul:
The fantastic views of
Biscayne Bay are best
scene from the intimate
covered terrace at this
upscale Mediterranean
restaurant. Start with a
crisp glass of wine from
sommelier Cynthia
Betancourt's extensive
selection and appreciate
the view. The only thing
more beautiful might be
the Chef Clay Conley's
carefully orchestrated
cuisine.

The Porch:
The actual porch is
the place to be but the
sidewalk would be a
relaxing second choice for
this restaurant's breakfast
and lunch fare.

Wish:
Designed by quirky
mastermind Todd
Oldham, this bistro has
just a few striped booths
and skinny bistro tables
inside to complement
the curvy, Art Deco bar.
The restaurant is more
known for its assortment
of outdoor tables in the
umbrella-shaded and
nearly secret garden.

MONDRIAN SOUTH BEACH
1100 West Ave., Miami Beach, 305-672-2662;
www.mondrian-miami.com

The Morgans Group (Shore Club, Delano) heads west
with the opening of Mondrian South Beach. Located
on the western edge of South Beach, the hotel is tucked
into a residential neighborhood dominated by 20- and
30-somethings living the beach life in condo towers. It's
a nice change if you're interested in escaping the tourist-
heavy chaos of Collins Avenue. Rooms channel a deco,
retro vibe with Marcel Wanders-designed wall coverings
and custom-made Dutch Delft tiles, while the bathrooms
are stocked with Korres bath products. Marquis restaurant
Asia de Cuba has been well received, but the Mondrian's
real draw is its bayfront pool. Wanders created a collection of outdoor living room-esque spaces, complete with
an adult-sized sandbox, "kissing corners" and stunning
sunset views.

335 rooms. Restaurant, bar. Business center. Fitness center. Pool.
Spa. $251-350

THE RALEIGH
1775 Collins Ave., Miami Beach, 305-534-6300, 800-848-1775;
www.raleighhotel.com

André Balazs, the hotelier best known for transforming
L.A.'s Chateau Marmont and New York's Mercer, helped
rehab The Raleigh in 2002. The oceanfront hotel has an
artsy, old-school glamour to it and attracts international
trendsetters, who congregate here for Art Basel Miami
in early December. But the attention is nothing new.
In 1947, *Life* magazine named the Raleigh's pool "The
Most Beautiful in America" (you won't stop gaping at its
gorgeous curves and black trim), and it was where Esther
Williams filmed some of her most picturesque films.
Today, the beautiful people still converge at the Raleigh,
art festival or not. And who can blame them? Though
the olive-green and rattan-furniture-filled rooms are
"economy" size, the bathrooms boast Kiehl's products and
beach chairs are free. You don't need to head up to your
room to change out of your bathing suit, either; instead,
use the shower/changing rooms at the hotel's Oasis, a
boardwalk area between the pool and the beach. You'll
want to stay as close as possible to that gorgeous pool.

104 rooms. Restaurant, bar. Pool. Spa. $251-350

W SOUTH BEACH
2201 Collins Ave., Miami Beach, 305-938-3000;
www.starwoodhotels.com

The South Beach scene is as migratory as a flock of birds.
And the W South Beach is the newest bird in the nest.

Opened in 2009, the property is W's first all-condo hotel. Spanish-influenced restaurant Solea and Beverly Hills import Mr. Chow attract a steady stream of local celebs while WET, a.k.a. the outdoor pool area, woos the late-night crowd. Rooms range from 574 to 3,000 square feet. If you want the works, book a three-story bungalow and enjoy your own private plunge pool and a complete outdoor kitchen. *340 rooms. Restaurant, bar. Business center. Fitness center. Pool. Spa. Pets accepted. Beach. Tennis. $351 and up*

WHERE TO EAT

MIAMI

★★★★AZUL

Mandarin Oriental, Miami, 500 Brickell Key Drive, Miami, 305-913-8358; www.mandarinoriental.com

With Todd English-trained chef Clay Conley at the helm and sommelier Cynthia Betancourt in charge of the more than 700-bottle wine program, Azul continues its domination of the city's fine dining scene. Conley adds his own touch with dishes such as "revisited" clam chowder, which is presented in a tiny copper pot on a plate with a strip of confit pork belly and a pile of fried Ipswich clams garnished with malt-vinegar aioli. The gorgeous room has a rosewood floor, white marble open kitchen and fantastic views of Biscayne Bay.

Mediterranean, Asian. Lunch, dinner. Reservations recommended. Bar. $86 and up

★★★THE CAPITAL GRILLE

444 Brickell Ave., Miami, 305-374-4500; www.thecapitalgrille.com

The Capital Grille continues to rule the power-broker scene downtown. Brassy appointments, massive chairs and endless walls of mahogany scream masculinity. The purely professional service, along with the perfectly cooked steaks—the 22-ounce delmonico and porterhouse-style veal chop are signatures—and succulent seafood, both raw and cooked, are the draw for dealmakers throughout South Florida.

American. Lunch, dinner. Bar. Reservations recommended. $86 and up

★★★FRATELLI LYON

4141 N.E. Second Ave., Miami, 305-572-2901; www.fratellilyon.com

Located at the entrance to the Driade showroom in the Design District, this trendy Italian eatery comes from Ken Lyon, South Beach veteran and entrepreneur. A wonderful cheese list and a selection of salumi are further enhanced by an excellent, all-Italian wine list carrying vintages from every region from Abruzzo to Valle d'Aosta. But you don't have to limit yourself to grazing. The kitchen turns out surprisingly good fish and meat dishes—always inquire about the specials of the day, especially if the grilled swordfish with preserved lemon or the roasted lamb with cannelini bean ragu is unavailable. The antipasti includes a selection of marinated vegetables and, under the pizza and bruschetta section, a sizzling gorgonzola fondue served with garlic ciabatta is an auspicious starter. Servers try very hard to please here, so if you're uncomfortable (there are some cold spots in the room, and a few communal tables), just ask for another table.

Italian. Lunch, dinner. Closed Sunday. Reservations recommended. $16-35

★★★MICHAEL'S GENUINE FOOD & DRINK

130 N.E. 40th St., Miami, 305-573-5550;
www.michaelsgenuine.com

Michael Schwartz, who first drew attention as chef-proprietor at South Beach's Nemo more than a decade ago, re-emerged with this über-triumphant locavore spot that landed him back on every well-respected foodie page in the country. His menu gets kudos for the sustainable food, which is cooked in a wood-fired oven, that he serves in four different plate sizes, producing tasty dishes like pork bellies with braised Asian vegetables and French onion soup with organic double-yolk farm eggs. The main dining room has a winding staircase, polished dark woods, striking lighting fixtures and an open kitchen, while a second, plainer dining space next door has an outdoor terrace.

Contemporary American. Lunch, dinner. Reservations recommended. Outdoor seating. Bar. $36-85

★★★MICHY'S

6927 Biscayne Blvd., Miami, 305-759-2001

Chef-owner Michelle Bernstein created this orange-and-white, 60-seat, Upper East Side, shabby-chic charmer with her husband, David Martinez, in 2006 after a charismatic stint at Azul. A hometown girl with an Argentine-Jewish heritage, Bernstein blends classical French training with neo-Spanish and Latin American influences. Dishes range from foie gras mousse with peach marmalade and brioche crisps and jamón-and-blue cheese croquetas with fig marmalade for appetizers to "short ribs falling off the bone" and steak frites (with both béarnaise and au poivre sauces for dipping) for the main event. The menu changes depending on Bernstein's mood—she might just feel like making a tropically flavored snapper française, accenting it with a mojo beurre blanc, or maybe a Peruvian ceviche instead—but the modus operandi stays the same. You can order a half-portion of any dish, and a fabulous wine list yields finds from Spain, France and South America that complement the food. If you can't get enough of this talented duo, try Senora Martinez (4000 N.E. Second Ave., 305-573-5474), a second spot opened by Bernstein and Martinez in the Design District in December 2008.

Contemporary Mediterranean. Lunch, dinner. Closed Monday. Reservations recommended. Outdoor seating. Bar. $86 and up

★★★PACIFIC TIME

35 N.E. 40th St., Miami, 305-722-7369; www.pacifictime.biz

Decorated like the art galleries that line the streets outside—think spare walls, hung with an avant-garde painting or two—Pacific Time continually buzzes with artists and their pals who love to eat. Good thing chef Jonathan Eismann didn't hang up his culinary hat for good. Since closing his groundbreaking pan-Asian shop in South Beach back in 2007, Eismann had been searching for his next hip locale; he found it in the Design District. This new spot blends pan-Asian dishes (duck two ways, salt and pepper skate, pork ribs Chinatown style) and Mediterranean flavors (braised beef short rib with goat cheese and northern beans, grilled lamb chops with yellow tomato vinaigrette; shaved fennel with frisee and preserved lemon-lime) and leaves diners wondering what time zone they're really in. There is a large menu of little plates as well as regular-sized portions, so you can go tapas-style or an every-entrée-to-himself sort of meal.

Asian, Mediterranean. Lunch, dinner, Sunday brunch. Reservations recommended. Outdoor seating. Bar. $36-85

RECOMMENDED

LAS CULEBRINAS RESTAURANT

4700 W. Flagler St., Miami, 305-445-2337; www.culebrinas.com

Unless you want to go elbow to elbow with a stampede of hungry parishioners, don't go to any of Las Culebrinas' five locations on a Sunday. The crowd forms just after church lets out and doesn't let up until closing. Everyone's waiting for the most authentic Cuban food around. From the chickpeas sautéed with chorizo to the pork stuffed with sweet plantains to the rabbit in garlic sauce, this local chain restaurant is an education in Miami's cultural gastronomy. Don't dare leave without a dish of crèma catalana, blow-torched right in front of you at the table. Each location varies in terms of décor and formality; the original spot on West Flagler is perhaps the most casual (and also where the line extends into the parking lot), while the one in Coconut Grove is all white tablecloths and valet parking (and takes reservations). So if you're willing to trade authenticity and the local set for a guaranteed table, opt for the latter location (and call before you go).

Cuban. Lunch, dinner. $16-35

IL GABBIANO

335 S. Biscayne Blvd., Miami, 305-373-0063; www.ilgabbianomiami.com

Thank you, Masci brothers. We know that you meant to retire in Miami after running the Il Mulino empire in New York for all those years, but we're selfishly glad you didn't. How Miami gourmands survived without Il Gabbiano and its epicurean trappings for so long is a mystery. After an onslaught of tasty nibbles like Parmigiano-Reggiano slices, flash-fried zucchini and bruschetta—all compliments of the chef—the meal carries into a parade of indulgence as only Italian food can create. The homemade gnocchi with spinach-flecked Gorgonzola sauce is surprisingly light and the veal Valdostano, stuffed with foie gras, Fontina cheese and prosciutto, then topped with an unforgettable mushroom cream-Cognac sauce, is down-home decadence at its best. Match it all with a vintage from the mostly Italian wine list, which has a great assortment of Super Tuscans, Barolos and other regional reds; but prepare for disappointment if you're a fan of white varietals—there's very little thought invested in them here. Likewise, the décor doesn't amount to much more than a rotation of modern art on geometrically interesting walls, with the artist frequently on the premises trying to make a sale. But that's okay, because it's more fun watching the Masci brothers man their pasta and Caesar salad stations in the dining room anyway.

Italian. Lunch, dinner. Bar. Reservations recommended. Outdoor seating. $86 and up

NORTH ONE 10

11052 Biscayne Blvd., North Miami, 305-893-4211; www.northone10.com

Creative contemporary cuisine plus a sense of humor—yes, that really is a stone crab "hot dog" with pomegranate ketchup—from chef-owner Dewey LoSasso is a welcome find on this trafficky stretch of Biscayne Boulevard. Regulars stop in for house specialties such as smoked salmon croquetas with "damn hot" guava sauce, soba-wrapped crispy shrimp with wasabi butter and kimchee aioli, and coffee-seared ribeye with black pepper vinaigrette. While the menu changes regularly, you can always expect it to draw on local ingredients ranging from snapper and grouper to carambolas and mangoes from the trees in LoSasso's own backyard.

Contemporary American. Lunch, dinner, Sunday brunch. Bar. $36-85

TWO CHEFS

8287 S. Dixie Highway, South Miami, 305-663-2100; www.twochefsrestaurant.com

It started off with two, but after partner Soren Bredahl's departure years ago, there remains only one master of ceremonies. Chef-owner Jan Jorgensen has been feeding grateful south-of-downtown foodies for more than a decade in this large, airy space with neutral tones and an open kitchen. From local products and artisan cheeses to micro-brewed beers and a fine collection of single malt Scotches, Jorgensen stocks the best of everything he can get his hands on. Authentic, honest and never disappointing, the classically trained Danish chef delivers both traditional dishes such as coq au vin (albeit with bacon, white wine, button mushrooms, pearl onions and white truffle scented risotto) and more inventive fare including meatloaf with black bean barbecue sauce, prosciutto-wrapped asparagus and horseradish mashed potatoes. If you're looking to get your hands dirty before you feast, Jorgensen also offers cooking classes at his restaurant in a separate show kitchen. Our personal pick is the Italian Favorites class, where you get to cook up cauliflower fritters, eggplant "involtini" with ricotta and scallions, savory chestnut custard, and monkfish scaloppine with chianti and sage. There are a couple different chefs that lead the cooking classes, so if you're heart-set on having Jorgensen, be sure to check before signing up.

Contemporary American. Lunch, dinner. Bar. $36-85

MIAMI BEACH

★★★★BLUE DOOR FISH

Delano Hotel, 1685 Collins Ave., Miami Beach, 305-674-6400; www.delano-hotel.com

The visually stunning Blue Door is a collaboration between renowned chef Claude Troisgros and China Grill Management restaurateur Jeffrey Chodorow. The Philippe Starck-designed restaurant's white-on-white furniture framed by white gauzy draperies provides the ideal backdrop for the dramatic cuisine, which is rooted in French method but informed by Brazilian culture. The results are crave-inducing bites such as ravioli filled with taro root mousseline and white truffle oil, and pan-seared Chilean sea bass. The outdoor terrace, overlooking the famous hotel pool, is a delightful spot to brunch.

French, Brazilian. Lunch, dinner. Reservations recommended. Outdoor seating. Bar. $86 and up

★★★BONDST LOUNGE

Townhouse Hotel, 150 20th St., Miami Beach, 305-398-1806; www.townhousehotel.com

If sushi rolls that incorporate global ingredients like chili peppers, sun-dried tomatoes and mustard seed sound tempting, head to Manhattan offshoot

BONDST. A fashionable clientele descends upon here nightly to sample executive chef Mike Hiraga's addicting bites, such as spicy tuna rolls with chili mayonnaise and avocado rolls with garlic ponzu oil and green tea salt. There are a few main courses on the menu, but sleek and sexy BONDST, with its black round cocktail tables, long continuous white banquette lining the walls and short white padded stools, isn't built for a drawn-out meal. Instead, South Beach jet-setters come here for a precursor to whatever evening they have planned, or perhaps even a snack in between activities, while locals come for a quick dinner and stay for drinks.

Japanese. Dinner. Reservations recommended. Bar. $36-85

★★★CHINA GRILL

404 Washington Ave., Miami Beach, 305-534-2211; www.chinagrillmgt.com

China Grill (which has locations in New York, San Francisco, London and many other cities) has been holding ground just south of Fifth Street for more than a decade. The most interesting décor element might be its architectural layout, given that the exhibition kitchen is in the center of the restaurant. China Grill's fan base remains loyal to its plum-and-sesame-glazed lamb spare ribs, crunchy calamari salad, and barbecue salmon with Chinese mustard.

Pan-Asian. Lunch, dinner. Reservations recommended. Bar. $86 and up

★★★JOE ALLEN

1787 Purdy Ave., Miami Beach, 305-531-7007; www.joeallenrestaurant.com

This comfort-food brasserie, featuring basics running the gamut from burgers and fries to meatloaf and mashed potatoes, is a haven for residents and folks in the know. It's no longer as hidden as it once was, now that the formerly undeveloped Purdy Avenue area at the beginning of the Venetian Causeway has been built up around it. But the staff is still wink-wink cozy with clientele whether it's your first go-round or you've been coming for years. Homemade soups change daily—the lentil is particularly tasty, though black bean soup is always available if that one isn't; salad greens are sprightly and fresh; and fish and chicken dishes are light and flavorful. The dining room, sided by a long curving bar at one end and divided by a partial wall down the middle, is actually pretty spacious. But the sign on

WHICH RESTAURANTS ARE BEST FOR A LIVELY SCENE?

Michael's Genuine Food & Drink:
Lunch or dinner, this place is bustling. Chef Michael Schwartz makes sustainable food the star of his dishes. He tries to source all local ingredients, such as yellow jack and snapper that he roasts in his wood-fired oven.

Michy's:
Already packed to the gills, Chef Michelle Bernstein's recent judging efforts on the popular *Top Chef* television series have only added fuel to the fire at this red-hot restaurant.

WHAT ARE THE BEST HOTEL RESTAURANTS?

Azul: Located in the posh Mandarin Oriental Miami hotel, Azul continues its domination of the city's fine dining scene. Chef Conley adds his own touch with dishes such as "revisited" clam chowder, which is presented in a tiny copper pot on a plate with a strip of confit pork belly and a pile of fried Ipswich clams garnished with malt-vinegar aioli. The gorgeous room has a rosewood floor, white marble open kitchen and fantastic views of Biscayne Bay.

Blue Door Fish: Though it has been located within the Delano Hotel for years, this French restaurant with worldly influences is as fresh and modern as when it opened. The chef Claude Troisgros offers a Les Classiques menu, as well as a Les Nouveautes menu and you can't go wrong with the selections from either.

Wish: Located in the equally elegant and distinctive The Hotel, this romantic restaurant offers a distinctive décor and a lush outdoor dining area which is the highlight of the experience.

the door allows Joe Allen's intentions to be known: "No strollers allowed." You get the feeling the management wants this to be strictly an establishment for adults, but locals ignore them and bring their children anyway, who fill up on hamburgers with fries or personal pizzas. However, their strollers do wind up waiting outside.

American. Lunch, dinner, Sunday brunch. Reservations recommended. Bar. $16-35

★★★MARK'S SOUTH BEACH
1120 Collins Ave., Miami Beach, 305-604-9050; www.chefmark.com

At Mark's South Beach, chef Mark Militello offers savvy Floridian cuisine, with Caribbean, Asian and local ingredients in signature dishes such as the potato-crusted Pacific oysters with horseradish, and peppercorn/lavender-spiced moulard duck breast with wild rice pecan flan. Cap your meal with a tasting of exotic housemade sorbets. But the food isn't the only attraction here; the restaurant also offers nice outdoor dining.

American. Lunch, dinner, Sunday brunch. Outdoor seating. Bar. $36-85

★★★PHILIPPE
Gansevoort South Hotel, 2399 Collins Ave., Miami Beach, 305-674-0250; www.phillipechow.com

This high-end Chinese restaurant comes courtesy of Philippe Chow, the Hong Kong-trained, 25-year protégé of New York City's famed Mr. Chow restaurant (which has another location in the new W Hotel on Collins Avenue). Geometric angles and a stark color scheme of onyx black, white and orange, make quite a statement. While a neighboring diner might be staring into the glass-enclosed exhibition kitchen, you might be stuck gazing at a blank white wall. Nevertheless, the food makes up for any inconvenience with dishes like Nine Seasons spicy prawns or rock bass sliced into a delicate egg white sauce. Main dishes are portioned for two but first order one of the satays, such as chicken, beef or Maine lobster. Match them with an aromatic white from the wine list, which does yield some reasonably priced finds, or a sparkling vodka martini.

Chinese. Lunch, dinner, late-night. Reservations recommended. Bar. $86 and up

★★★PRIME ONE TWELVE
112 Ocean Drive, Miami Beach, 305- 532-8112; www.prime112.com

Savvy restaurateur Myles Chefetz must have felt prescient when he opened this independent steak house in 2004 in the historic Browns Hotel, originally built in 1915 and one of the oldest renovated properties on Miami Beach. Chef-driven steak houses have since erupted but they're still chasing the popularity that this one, with its original house-like structure, bricked columns, Dade County pine accents, mosaics and broken tile floors, garnered with celebrities and regular folks alike. Or maybe the height that Prime One Twelve has reached has something to do with all the spirits that infuse the fare. You can start with French onion soup with brandy and aged Gruyère or try a bowl of Sherry lobster bisque (although it's so rich, a cup will do you just fine). Move straight on to the prime steaks, which range from the eight-ounce filet mignon to the 48-ounce porterhouse, partnered with cabernet goat cheese butter. Of course there's baked Maine lobster, cracked and stuffed with jumbo lump crab and bay scallops and finished with cognac butter. The wine list is extensive, exceptional and expensive.

American. Lunch, dinner. Bar. Reservations recommended. Outdoor seating. $86 and up

★★★SMITH AND WOLLENSKY

1 Washington Ave., Miami Beach, 305-673-2800, 888-517-8325; www.smithandwollensky.com

Two words: Wine Week. This two-story steak house's claims to fame are the one-week runs during the fall and spring when vintners from all over come in to pour their products. For a nominal fee (along with the regular bill for food), you have unlimited access to dozens of wines for tasting. Of course, this particular S&W is also notable for more than the great quaffs and succulent fare. Perched alongside the Government Cut shipping channel in South Pointe Park, the restaurant is one of the few places on South Beach where you can watch the water while you dine.

American. Lunch, dinner. Reservations recommended. Outdoor seating. Bar. $86 and up

★★★TALULA

210 23rd St., Miami Beach, 305-672-0778; www.talulaonline.com

Husband-wife team Frank Randazzo and Andrea Curto-Randazzo, both award-winning chefs, operate this South Beach bistro with smooth aplomb. You can choose to sit inside the high-ceilinged, brick-walled dining room, which carries a Manhattan-chic feel, or out on the back patio, where you're enclosed by tropical foliage. Either way, you'll savor the chefs' combined culinary efforts. The menu changes frequently and may include grilled foie gras with caramelized figs, blue corn cakes, red chile syrup and candied walnuts or snapper with pignoli risotto, Key West shrimp and anisette-kumquat butter sauce. There's also a seven-course tasting menu, which can be paired with seven wines.

Contemporary American. Lunch, dinner. Closed Monday. Reservations recommended. Outdoor seating. Bar. $86 and up

★★★TUSCAN STEAK

433 Washington Ave., Miami Beach, 305-534-2233; www.chinagrillmanagement.com

Rustically outfitted in brick and warm fire-and-earth tones, this cozy restaurant feeds you family-style. Sure, some attest that it's upscale family-style, but it's family-style nonetheless, with overflowing platters of food making their way around the table. The Florentine 20-ounce T-bone is enough to feed a party of four with leftovers, though it is tasty enough to tempt you to try and clean your plate. Those craving an even richer treat should order the T-bone crusted with blue cheese. Other favorites include the three-mushroom risotto, gnocchi in Gorgonzola cream sauce, country-style chicken and pan-seared yellowtail snapper with baby artichokes. Tuscan always has a prix fixe, three-course menu on offer as well.

Italian, steak. Dinner. Reservations recommended. Bar. $36-85

★★★★WISH

The Hotel, 801 Collins Ave., Miami Beach, 305-674-9474; www.wishrestaurant.com

Designed by quirky mastermind Todd Oldham, this bistro has just a few striped booths and skinny bistro tables inside to complement the curvy, Art Deco bar. The restaurant is more known for its assortment of outdoor tables in the umbrella-shaded garden. Wish's star chef Marco Ferraro is a Calabria, Italy, native whose menu pours forth a multitude of technically proficient and ingredient-intense dishes, such as pan-seared diver scallops with squash, Brussels sprouts, pancetta and maple syrup. Desserts are equally crafty—the vanilla pot de crème is topped with chopped, fresh oranges and pink peppercorns. It's a fragrant yet zesty reminder that while you're dining in what is tantamount to a secret garden, South Beach is just a few steps beyond the orchids.

Contemporary American. Breakfast, lunch, dinner. Closed Monday. Reservations recommended. Outdoor seating. Bar. $86 and up

RECOMMENDED

FRONT PORCH CAFÉ

Penguin Hotel, 1418 Ocean Drive, Miami Beach, 305-531-8300

If you're lucky enough to secure a spot on the actual front porch, cherish it with your life and settle in for the afternoon. This go-to place for breakfast and lunch on Ocean Drive comprises the porch, the sidewalk out front and the lobby of the Penguin Hotel, but the porch is definitely preferable. The healthy cuisine with lots of grains (granola pancakes), fresh fruits (French toast with bananas) and items like omelets with grilled squash, onions and peppers, will leave you feeling satisfied.

American. Breakfast, lunch, dinner. Outdoor seating. $16-35

NEMO

100 Collins Ave., Miami Beach, 305-532-4550; www.nemorestaurant.com

Nemo is a SoFi (south of Fifth) institution as well as a continual draw for tourists. Executive chef Mike Sabin, who has a local and seasonal sensibility with an emphasis on seafood, presents such concoctions as grilled Key West octopus with gigande beans and wok lobster with eggplant in sweet chili pesto. The restaurant is exquisitely designed with warm woods and jewel tones throughout a series of small, interconnected, open-walled dining rooms.

Contemporary American. Lunch, dinner, Sunday brunch. Reservations recommended. Outdoor seating. Bar. $86 and up

SPAS

MIAMI

★★★★★THE SPA AT MANDARIN ORIENTAL, MIAMI

Mandarin Oriental Miami, 500 Brickell Key Drive, Miami, 305-913-8332;
www.mandarinoriental.com

Cross the bridge from Brickell and Eighth Street to Brickell Key and you'll
already feel the piña-colada-in-one-hand-and-sunscreen-in-the-other aura.
At the Spa at the Mandarin Oriental, the effect is amplified with the smell of
incense and the quiet stillness of a private spa suite overlooking the water and
city skyline. True to its name, the Mandarin Oriental takes inspiration from
ancient Asian cultures. Bamboo floors, dark stones and orchids give treatment
rooms an exotic, calm ambience where visitors can escape to from the rush of
downtown traffic. The spa's signature treatment is the Oriental Harmony, an
almost two-hour rejuvenation that begins with a soaking foot bath followed by
a four-handed warm scrub and massage, in which two therapists work together
to balance out your body. The grand finale is a simultaneous head and foot
massage to ensure every inch is revitalized.

MIAMI BEACH

★★★★THE RITZ-CARLTON SPA, SOUTH BEACH

1 Lincoln Road, Miami Beach, 786-276-4000, 800-241-3333; www.ritzcarlton.com

Situated just steps from the beach, the Spa at The Ritz-Carlton, South Beach
brings elements of the ocean into its treatments. Giant starfish line the navy
walls of the spa, and bowls of sand and stones recall the calm waters outside.
Though there are 14 treatment rooms, the spa retains a small, intimate feel
that's reinforced by hallways that keep each area separate. Treatments like the
Oceanic Body Cocktail soak your skin in seawater rich in vitamins and minerals
to relieve muscle fatigue, and make a great prelude to a massage. The signature
rubdown is the Ashiatsu, an Asian barefoot massage performed by a therapist
suspended from bamboo bars.

★★★★THE SPA AT THE SETAI

The Setai, 2001 Collins Ave., Miami Beach, 305-520-6000; www.setai.com

The Setai, one of South Beach's most chic nightlife spots, is all about the VIP
treatment, so it's no surprise that The Spa at the Setai would follow suit. Each
of its private spa suites has an ocean and pool view, a private bath and a steam
room. Sensual accents like dim lighting, candles and bathtubs filled with
flower petals ensure that you leave your cares behind as soon as you step out
of your robe. Taking inspiration from the rituals of the Pacific Rim, the Setai
doesn't rush its own procedures, such as the three-and-a-half-hour Ayurvedic
Rejuvenation Ritual, which features a foot and body polish, purifying envelop-
ment and massage, hair mask and steam bath. Stay for the entire day and enjoy
a three-course lunch in between a series of massages, facials and body treatments—your choice—and emerge once the sun sets relaxed and ready to party.

HIGHLIGHT

WHAT ARE SOME GOOD SHOPS TO VISIT IN THE DESIGN DISTRICT?

EMESHEL

3930 N.E. 2nd Ave., Design District, 305-571-9177; www.emeshel.com
After becoming a hit in Europe, Hungarian crystal designer Emeshel set up its first U.S. showroom in Miami in 2008. The store features incredibly ornate but practical glass and crystal pieces including vibrant emerald vases, oil and vinegar dispensers, ice buckets, trays and candy jars—perfect for a gift or to add some sparkle to your next dinner party. The fact that everything twinkles as it catches the light makes the store a particularly magical window display by night. (The only downside to that, of course, is that you won't be able to inspect the lovely handmade pieces up close.)
Monday-Friday 10 a.m.-6 p.m., Saturday 11 a.m.-3 p.m.

NAZLY VILLAMIZAR DESIGNS

4310 N. Miami Ave., Design District, 786-306-2496; www.nazlyv.com
This emerging designer is so hip, you can only visit her shop by making an appointment first, so be sure to call ahead. The Colombian-born, Miami Beach-bred Villamizar is best known for her custom leather jackets and bags, which feature her signature touches: hand-embroidered finishes, animal-bone buttons and sassy, modern fits (for jackets, that is). By appointment only.

NIBA

39 N.E. 39th St., Design District, 305-573-1939; www.nibahome.com
If you're looking for just the perfect purple vase to anchor your dining room, you could spend all day going from shop to shop, or you could head straight for NiBa. Dedicated to offering a huge variety of accessories, furniture, lighting and other touches for your home, NiBa keeps only a few of each item in stock at a time, and most of the vintage pieces on display are rare originals.
Monday-Friday 9:30 a.m.-5:30 p.m., Saturday noon-4 p.m.

SUSANE R LIFESTYLE BOUTIQUE

93 N.E. 40th St., Design District, 305-573-8483; www.susaner.com
If you are looking for one-of-a-kind furniture pieces, this spot offers a collection of 18th century-meets-today furniture collections. From seating and tables to light fixtures and garden elements, this eclectic mix of furnishings may include Austrian-cut crystal chandeliers, pink French Deco chandeliers, original Eden Roc night tables refinished in high gloss and 1940s slipper chairs based on the style of Chanel.
Monday-Friday 10:30 a.m.-5 p.m., Saturday noon-4 p.m.

WHERE TO SHOP

MIAMI

BAYSIDE MARKETPLACE

401 Biscayne Blvd., Downtown, 305-577-3344; www.baysidemarketplace.com

The lively, open-air atmosphere of Bayside makes it attractive to locals and visitors to Miami. Many folks come for the name-brand stores (ranging from Sunglass Hut to Brookstone and Guess) and local boutique and kiosks, but many stay for the live-band performances, which take place daily. It's for this very reason that this place often resembles a zoo at all times of the day, but especially between noon and 5 p.m., when the sun is up, the bands are hot and tempers are short—the perfect recipe for sultry, on-the-spot dancing.

Monday-Thursday 10 a.m.-10 p.m., Friday-Saturday 10 a.m.-11 p.m., Sunday 11 a.m.-9 p.m.

MIAMI BEACH

ATRIUM MIAMI

1931 Collins Ave., Miami Beach, 305-695-0757; www.atriumnyc.com

Boutique owner and fashion maven Sam Ben-Avraham opened the Miami outpost of his unisex NYC shop in March 2007 and it immediately became a hot spot; after all, the sleek boutique, outfitted in the subdued shades of blond wood and white walls, carries designers such as Alexander McQueen, Stella McCartney, Missoni and Y-3.

Monday-Saturday 10 a.m.-10 p.m., Sunday 11 a.m.-9 p.m.

BASE

939 Lincoln Road, Miami Beach, 305-531-4982; www.baseworld.com

Urban-chic and street-art aficionados gravitate to this mecca of cool. Sure, the trendy threads tap into hip designers like Lorick, Rag & Bone, Rogan, Fred Perry and Helmut Lang, but we'd just as much head here for the lifestyle store's immaculate CD mixes and Japanese vinyl toys.

Sunday-Thursday 11 a.m.-10 p.m., Friday-Saturday 11 a.m.-11 p.m.

BOOKS & BOOKS

933 Lincoln Road, Miami Beach, 305-532-3222; 265 Aragon Ave., Coral Gables, 305-442-4408; www.booksandbooks.com

Books & Books, with its floor-to-ceiling books and magazines, is a must for literary addicts. Buy your favorite title and browse at the café tables and chairs scattered on the sidewalk in front of the store. This bookstore sells mainstream bestsellers as well as indie favorites, and it also regularly hosts book clubs and author events.

Monday-Thursday 10 a.m.-11 p.m., Friday-Saturday 10 a.m.-12 a.m., Sunday 10 a.m.-11 p.m.

FLY BOUTIQUE

650 Lincoln Road, Miami Beach, 305-604-8508; www.flyboutiquevintage.com

The outside may look like any other store, but the inside décor makes you feel like you stepped inside an old steamer trunk filled with wondrous designer-vintage treasures of the '60s, '70s and '80s. In a nutshell, it's consignment store meets Gucci, Dior and Chanel—finds could be anything from a fuchsia Pucci

HIGHLIGHT

WHAT'S IN STORE IN LITTLE HAVANA?

LILY'S RECORDS

1419 S.W. Eighth St., Little Havana, 305-856-0536, 866-673-7343; www.lilysrecords.com
Here, you'll find the best in salsa, merengue, bachata and more, and if dance music is not your style, Lily's also offers rock en español and other traditional Spanish music styles. If making your own music is more up your alley, Lily's also sells instruments common to Latin bands such as congas, bongos and guayos.
Monday-Saturday 10 a.m.-8 p.m.

LITTLE HAVANA TO GO

1442 S.W. Eighth St., Little Havana, 305-857-9720
Want to take a little piece of Little Havana home with you? No problem. Just step into Little Havana to Go and you are all set. From guayaberas, a traditional, button-down Cuban shirt, and domino sets to memorabilia made by local artists and handcrafted ceramic jars by the popular Miami artists the Curras brothers, Little Havana to Go is a good spot for visitors to find authentic Cuban-theme souvenirs.
Monday-Saturday 10:30 a.m.-5:30 p.m., Sunday 11 a.m.-5 p.m.

LOS PINAREÑOS FRUTERÍA

1334 S.W. Eighth St., Little Havana, 305-285-1135
Aisles of fresh Caribbean fruit favorites can be found in this popular fresh fruit store. Mamey and tiny Caribbean bananas are just a few of the treats you taste, alongside highly charged political window displays (Viva La Bush bumper stickers) and audible contempt for Fidel Castro. Grab a glass of the Sunshine State's famous freshly squeezed orange juice and hit the street.
Monday-Saturday 7 a.m.-7 p.m.

MOORE & BODE CIGARS

1336 S.W. Eighth St. Little Havana, 305-433-3327; www.mooreandbode.com
While strolling along Calle Ocho, you may run across some cigar rollers tucked under a canopy awning on the corner of Calle Ocho and S.W. 16th Avenue. Meet the hand cigar rollers of Moore & Bode, founded and run by a husband-and-wife team Sharon Moore Bode and Robert Bode, which offers three blends of tobacco: Miami, Flamboyán and Flamboyán Dark. Watch these artists at work and buy some cigars for an evening out in Miami, or to take home with you (depending on where you are heading back to, of course).
Hours vary.

floor-length dress, to a black-and-red knee-length Diane von Furstenberg frock.
Monday-Sunday 11 a.m.-10 p.m.

LINCOLN ROAD

Lincoln Road, between Lenox and Washington avenues, Miami Beach; www.lincolnroad.org

In the heart of South Beach sits the renowned Lincoln Road, which teems at all hours with a mish-mash of nightclubs, lounges, bars, restaurants and an eclectic collection of boutiques (in this roundup alone, Books & Books, Fly Boutique and more are on this strip) blended with well-known retail shops, like Victoria's Secret and French Connection. The road was originally founded by millionaire developer Carl Fisher, who envisioned Lincoln Road as Miami Beach's equivalent to New York City's Fifth Avenue or Beverly Hills's Rodeo Drive. In the 1960s, the architect Morris Lapidus took it a step further by transforming the two-way driving road into a pedestrian-only byway, stating that, "a car never bought anything." Lincoln Road attracts tourists from around the world and also remains a hot spot for the local Miami and Miami Beach residents. Since it is technically an outside mall, pack the sunscreen, bottled water and sunglasses.

SENZATEMPO

1655 Meridian Ave., Miami Beach, 305-534-5588; www.senzatempo.com

If midcentury modern makes your heart palpitate, make for this shop, which is packed with Eames, Alvar Aalto, George Nelson and Gio Ponti. The vintage pieces tend to be in good condition. You'll also find goods from as early as the 1930s.
Monday-Friday 10 a.m.-5 p.m.

THE WEBSTER MIAMI

1220 Collins Ave., South Beach, 305-674-7899; www.thewebstermiami.com

When Webster first opened in January 2008 at a temporary location at 12th Street and Collins, it was greeted with a ton of hoopla from local press—after all, it's not every day that a boutique promises a 20,000-square-foot haven of runway pieces and labels like Martin Margiela, Proenza Schouler and Miu Miu. In December 2008, the boutique moved into its permanent location with partner Parisian restaurant Caviar Kaspia.
Monday-Saturday 11 a.m.-8 p.m.

EVERGLADES NATIONAL PARK

Looking deceptively like an open prairie, Everglades National Park is actually more than 1.5 million acres of wetlands. Although much smaller than it once was—it previously covered the bottom third of the state—today the Everglades encompasses the southernmost tip of Florida and is the lower 48 states' third-largest national park. Unfortunately, it's probably one of the most difficult of the national parks to explore—much of it is impenetrable, and an experienced guide is often necessary to point things out while navigating its tangled labyrinth of waterways via boat.

Creating what's known as the "River of Grass," large swathes of the park are blanketed with saw grass, a plant with barbed blades and needle-sharp edges that shoot up ten feet from the water. Only clusters of trees and dense vegetation, called hammocks, break up these grassy glades, which eventually give way along the coast to huge, shadowy mangrove swamps interlaced with tranquil, winding water lanes. The Everglades, considered to be the largest subtropical wilderness in the United States, contains a number of fragile ecosystems and boasts more than 300 animal and 700 plant species.

Humans, beginning with Paleo-Indians, have inhabited the Everglades area since 10,000 B.C. From 1500-1750 A.D., five separate tribes and as many as 20,000 Native Americans dominated South Florida. Their numbers dissipated to only several hundred with the arrival of Spanish explorers, and when the English took control of the area in 1763, the remaining few eventually fled to Cuba. With the indigenous populations absent and with European settlers encroaching further north, migrating tribes of Creek and proto-Seminoles roamed the area to hunt, fish and evade the foreigners settling Florida.

Unfortunately, by the late 1800s the Everglades region began to change shape when early settlers and developers deemed the area useless swamp and began to drain the wetlands. At the beginning of the 20th century, land created by dredging, including areas like Miami and Fort Myers, led to even more loss of the fragile wetlands ecosystem. Species that once thrived in the Everglades began to dwindle and the threat of extinction became a reality for animals like the Florida panther, the American crocodile and the West Indian manatee, among many others.

The idea for saving the Everglades was first proposed and lobbied for by landscape architect Ernest Coe. His efforts were successful, and in 1934, Congress approved the creation of Everglades National Park. It was finally established on December 6, 1947.

Today the Everglades is one of the most threatened national parks. Alterations to paths of flowing water from Lake Okeechobee and population growth have caused the disappearance of more than 50 percent of the original Florida wetlands. Rare and endangered species that can't be found anywhere else in the world still face extinction, and large areas of sea grass beds are dying. Strict conservation is this park's only hope.

The most popular time of year to visit Everglades National Park is Florida's dry season in winter, as the summer wet season brings flooding, making much of the park challenging to navigate. The park is best traveled by car or boat, and because of its large size, you'll first want to decide which of the four main visitor centers and main entries will be your starting point. The Everglades contains four visitor centers: The Gulf Coast Visitor Center welcomes travelers on the northwest coast of the park, the Shark Valley Center on the northeast corner is closest to Miami, Earnest Coe Center serves the East Coast and abuts Florida City, and the coastal Flamingo Visitor Center to the south looks onto a plethora of tiny keys.

Starting in the northwest corner of the park and heading south toward Flamingo will allow for sights along the main park road. The park's main entrance, just southwest of Homestead, is the Ernest F. Coe Visitor Center and Park Headquarters (40001 Route 9366, 305-242-7700; November-April, daily 8 a.m.-5 p.m.; May-October, daily 9 a.m.-5 p.m.), where guests can get oriented to the surrounding sites and history through a short film. Next, take the 38-mile main park road, Route 9366, to the Royal Palm Center (check for daily walks and other schedules) at Mile 4. Explore the freshwater slough (along the Anhinga Trail) to get a lesson on saw grass marsh or to see some of the Everglades' abundant wildlife. There are also great opportunities here to stop and see the trees that populate the park—gumbo limbo, strangler figs and hardwood hammocks (Gumbo Limbo Trail)—and the slash pines that once covered modern-day Miami and other towns, visible at the Pinelands at Mile 7. At Mile 12, you can explore the park's dwarf cypress trees, so named because of their stunted stature due in large part to shallow soils. For a more elevated view of the Everglades, Pa-hay-okee Overlook at Mile 13 is a two-story wooden tower that sits on the saw grass prairie and offers views of these shallow grassy waters for as far as the eye can see. Further along at Mile 20, Mahogany Hammock boasts mahogany and poisonwood trees as well as the United State's only paurotis palm trees, typically found solely in Cuba and Central America. At the end of the road, the Flamingo Visitor Center (239-695-2945; mid-November to mid-April, daily 8 a.m.-4:30 p.m.) is a wild and remote part of the southern Everglades that serves as access to Cape Sable and Florida Bay. Traverse the waterfront to observe an array of Everglades wildlife at this marine nursery.

If you choose to begin your tour of the park in the northeast region and head west, toward the opposite coast and a completely different ecosystem, you'll want to navigate along Tamiami Trail (US 41), which will take you from Shark Valley Visitor Center to Gulf Coast Visitor Center. On the northeastern boundary of the park, US 41 passes by Shark Valley Visitor Center (36000 SW Eighth St., Miami, 305-221-8776; mid-December to mid-April, daily 8:45 a.m.-5:15 p.m.; mid-April to mid-December, daily 9:15 a.m.-5:15 p.m.). This home base and starting point for those visiting from Miami or other East Coast cities sits in the valley named for the Shark River, which runs from the middle of the Everglades to the Gulf of Mexico, where sharks are known to congregate at its mouth. Just past the Visitor Center, look for the 15-mile scenic Loop Road that leads to a 65-foot observation tower where you'll be treated to a stunning 360-degree view of the surrounding saw grass prairies that are filled with birds and alligators. Continuing on US 41 past the Big Cypress Visitor Center and the Florida National Scenic Trail (which leads into the 2,400-square-mile Big Cypress National Preserve just north of the Everglades), head five miles down Highway 29. Just past Everglades City, the Gulf Coast Visitor Center (800 S. Copeland Ave., Everglades City, 239-695-3311; mid-November to mid-April, daily 8 a.m.-4:30 p.m.; mid-April to mid-November, daily 9 a.m.-4:30 p.m.) is the gateway to the Ten Thousand Islands, a mangrove archipelago that sits on the Gulf of Mexico. These "islands" are formed by accumulating deposits of leaves and other plant debris that collect in the waterways flowing around mangrove roots, creating the ever-changing number of small land formations that comprise the southwest Florida coast.

HIKING

Because the Everglades Park is largely made up of wetlands and lacks the mountain peaks of many other national parks, the trails here are easy. Because of the park's huge geographic coverage, it's best to navigate hiking and biking trails by distinct area within the park. Each hurricane season can bring damage to the trails, which close until repairs can be made.

SHARK VALLEY TRAILS

BOBCAT BOARDWALK TRAIL

1 mile round-trip

Trailhead: Off Tram Road behind the Shark Valley Visitor Center.

In the park's northeast region, explore the 0.5-mile Bobcat Boardwalk Trail. This self-guided tour cuts through the area's saw grass prairie and tropical hardwood forest. Wheelchair accessible.

OTTER CAVE HAMMOCK TRAIL

0.5 miles round-trip

Trailhead: Off Tram Road a half mile behind the Shark Valley Visitor Center.

Summer rains can cause this rough limestone trail to flood, but when conditions are good, it leads through a quarter mile of tropical hardwood forest.

PINE ISLAND TRAILS

MAHOGANY HAMMOCK TRAIL

0.5-mile loop

Trailhead: 20 miles west of the Ernest Coe Visitor Center.

The Mahogany Hammock Trail is an elevated boardwalk that wanders through mahogany trees and other lush vegetation. Don't miss the world's largest living mahogany tree, seen on this trail. Wheelchair accessible.

PINELAND TRAIL

0.5-mile loop

Trailhead: 7 miles west of the Ernest Coe Visitor Center.

The paved Pinelands Trail meanders through palmettos, pines and perky tickseed and ruellia wildflowers, which grow on a thin layer of soil covering porous limestone bedrock. A handful of jaunts shoot off the Main Park Road. Wheelchair accessible.

FLAMINGO TRAILS

BEAR LAKE TRAIL

3.2 miles round-trip

Trailhead: 2 miles north of the Flamingo Visitor Center.

At the southernmost tip of the Everglades, Bear Lake Trail takes hikers past 50 types of trees before coming to the lake. This hike is a treat for bird-watchers.

CHRISTIAN POINT TRAIL

3.6 miles round-trip
Trailhead: 1 mile north of the Flamingo Visitor Center.
This trail traverses several ecosystems. See airplants (bromeliads) and coastal prairie before reaching Snake Bight. A long trail, it's best to reserve a half or full day if you plan to walk the entire thing.

TRAM TOURS

Shark Valley Tram Tours (305-221-8455; www.sharkvalleytramtours.com) conducts two-hour guided environmental and educational tours year-round along the 15-mile loop through the "River of Grass." Park-trained naturalists point out wildlife, including woodstorks, red-shouldered hawks and alligators, while explaining the Everglades' fragile ecosystem. The tour culminates with a stop at the park's 45-foot observation deck—the perfect perch for 360-degree panoramic views of the Everglades. Rates are $15.25 for adults, $9.25 for children 3–12.

BOATING

Boating, kayaking and canoeing are great ways to take advantage of what the park has to offer since more than one-third of the Everglades consists of water. All equipment can be rented at various points in the park for excursions down trails like the Turn River Trip's cypress swamp or the 99-mile Wilderness Waterway Trail. For guided boat tours, the Everglades National Park Boat Tours (Gulf Coast Visitors Center, 239-695-2591; year-round, daily) has a narrated excursion that travels through the Ten Thousand Islands area. For that quintessential swamp experience, the Everglades Alligator Farm (40351 S.W. 192 Ave., Florida City, 305-247-2628, 800-644-9711; www.everglades.com) has airboat rides year-round through the farm's "back 40" everglades. Admission is $19 for adults, $12 for children 4–11, includes access to the farm (see below); the airboat ride alone is $13.50 and $8.50, respectively.

FISHING

Both freshwater and saltwater fishing for grouper, sea trout, bass, mackerel and other edible species are popular in the park. The best fishing is on the many water flats, channels and mangrove keys, while shore fishing is somewhat limited. Prime spots for freshwater angling can be found from Nine Mile Pond north and along the Main Park Road. Separate freshwater and saltwater licenses are required for park visitors over 16. The best saltwater fishing is along the Everglades' western coast in Monroe County, in Florida Bay to the south and Ten Thousand Islands to the northwest. Check the visitor centers for information on charter excursions.

ALLIGATOR FARM

To see alligators up close without risking life or limb, the **Everglades Alligator Farm** (*40351 SW 192 Ave., Florida City, 305-247-2628, 800-644-9711; www.everglades.com; year-round, daily*) is home to more than 2,000 of the reptiles ranging from newly hatched to fully grown. Stop by during an alligator feeding demonstration or go to the farm's Wildlife Shows, where you can hold baby alligators and snakes.

WILDLIFE

AMERICAN ALLIGATORS AND CROCODILES:

South Florida is the only place in the world where alligators and crocodiles live together. Most people confuse the two similar-looking reptiles, but the difference is simple: adult American alligators are blackish in color, have a broad snout and only their upper teeth stick out when their jaw is closed; American crocodiles are olive brown, have narrower snouts and sport both upper and lower protruding teeth with a closed mouth. The alligator, once in danger of disappearing from the Everglades due to poaching, can easily be spotted, especially in the marl prairies, while crocodiles thrive in the mangrove swamps.

FLORIDA PANTHER:

The larger Everglades mammals, like bobcats, coyotes and bears, are often harder to spot because of their elusive nocturnal natures. Among the rarest of the protected mammals in the park, the Florida panther is numbered at just 30-50 cats. These endangered animals are a subspecies of the mountain lion and mostly make the areas in or around Big Cypress National Preserve their home.

WEST INDIAN MANATEE:

Aquatic life thrives in the Everglades' waters, including more than 300 species of fish in the park's marine coastlines and freshwater areas. One of the best places to spot these animals is in Florida Bay—home to dolphins, sea turtles and the endangered West Indian manatee. This wrinkled and whiskered marine mammal can weigh as much as one thousand pounds and consume 10 to 15 percent of its body weight daily in sea grasses and other plants that grow in the bay.

BIRDS:

Despite the fact that many of the Everglades' birds were slaughtered in the early 20th century for their plumes—wading birds' populations have been reduced by 90 to 95 percent—almost 400 species of birds still pass through or live in the Everglades today. Bald eagles, warblers and barred owls are active in the Mahogany Hammock vicinity; roseate spoonbills flit about the Paurotis Pond mangroves; and red-shouldered hawks, painted buntings and other transient birdlife are found at Eco Pond.

SOUTHEAST FLORIDA AND THE KEYS

In this relaxing region, you'll find a nice respite from the constant city chaos in Miami. The Southeast is peppered with pretty neighborhoods like Coral Gables. But resort towns such as Boca Raton rule here.

Delray Beach started off as an artists' colony and was home to a Japanese settlement of farmers in the early 1920s, but now travelers head there for beautiful beaches, championship golfing and fishing and a historic downtown district. Another resort town, Hallandale Beach, is a quiet spot that's popular among snowbirds from the northern U.S. and Canada who flock to the city during winter.

One of America's most glamorous and storied resort towns, Palm Beach has been the winter haven of choice for the nation's well-heeled for more than 100 years. The Vanderbilts may have given way to the Trumps in recent times, but the town is still an exclusive, monied retreat. Joining the ladies who lunch at restaurants like Café Boulud, a tropical outpost of the acclaimed New York eatery, or sunning oneself on the soft sandy beaches is the best way to spend a day in Palm Beach. Its neighbor, West Palm Beach, has developed as a resort city because of its accessibility to nearby beaches and the Intracoastal Waterway. The rebuilt downtown area is a hot spot for nightlife.

Then there are those famous Florida Keys. Just off the downtown Miami coastline is Key Biscayne, an intimate, secluded and tropical island that's a top spot for Miamians who want a quick city escape.

The longest island in the bunch, Key Largo extends some 30 miles, but is seldom more than two miles wide. The Overseas Highway crosses the first bridge at Jewfish Creek to start its southwestern spread across the keys to Key West. Scattered on the island are marinas catering to the ever-present anglers and skin divers.

Islamorada is made up of 18 miles of coral, limestone and sand on four different islands of the Keys. Sport fishing, diving and snorkeling amid coral reefs and shipwrecks are the main tourist attractions.

Transformed from a little fishing village by developers who invested $15 million in the area, Marathon has become the hub of the Middle Keys. Tourism and sport fishing are the mainstays of its economy. The city is about an hour away from both Islamorada to the north or Key West to the south on the Overseas Highway.

Known for its 19th-century gingerbread-style houses and Caribbean lifestyle made famous by Jimmy Buffett, Key West is the southernmost city in the continental United States. The island is known for its lively gay scene, annual flamboyant Fantasy Fest celebration at Halloween and for being the one-time home of Ernest Hemingway.

WHAT TO SEE

BOCA RATON
BOCA RATON MUSEUM OF ART
Mizner Park, 501 Plaza Real, Boca Raton, 561-392-2500; www.bocamuseum.org

The museum's exhibits include paintings, photography, sculpture and glass.

HIGHLIGHTS

WHAT ARE THE TOP THINGS TO DO IN SOUTHEAST FLORIDA?

HURRAH FOR HOLLYWOOD BEACH

Unlike the spring-breaker-packed beaches in other regions of the state, Hollywood Beach isn't flashy, and it's a favorite sunning spot among locals. It also has a great Broadwalk lined with little restaurants and shops.

VISIT JOHN PENNEKAMP CORAL REEF STATE PARK

Bring your snorkel and scuba gear (rentals are available, too) to this excellent park, which has the largest living coral reef in the continental United States. Explore 25 miles of the marine sanctuary.

SAY HELLO TO FLIPPER AT THE MIAMI SEAQUARIUM

Aside from being the longest-operating U.S. oceanarium, the Seaquarium is known as the backdrop for the '60s TV show *Flipper* and the home of its dolphin star. Today it offers a Flipper Dolphin Show and porpoise-interaction programs.

TAKE A STRANGE TRIP TO STILTSVILLE

In the '40s, a hard-partying crowd erected a bunch of water huts on stilts off the coast so that they could carouse freely. Of course, the police caught on and closed them down. It's now a ghost town, but Stiltsville makes for an interesting boat tour.

There are also lectures and tours, though you can do a self-guided tour of the two gardens, which are peppered with quirky sculptures.

Admission: adults $8, seniors $6, students $4, children 12 and under free. Tuesday, Thursday-Friday 10 a.m.-5 p.m.; Wednesday 10 a.m.-9 p.m.; Saturday-Sunday noon-5 p.m.

GUMBO LIMBO ENVIRONMENTAL COMPLEX

1801 N. Ocean Blvd., Boca Raton, 561-338-1473; www.gumbolimbo.org

Get close to nature at this wildlife center, where families can view four 20-foot-diameter saltwater sea tanks, stroll a 1,628-foot boardwalk through a dense tropical forest and climb a 40-foot tower to overlook the tree canopy. The forest holds several different species growing north of the tropics. The center's staff leads guided turtle walks to the beach to see nesting females come ashore and lay their eggs.

Admission: $3 suggested donation. Monday-Saturday 9 a.m.-4 p.m., Sunday noon-4 p.m.

COCONUT GROVE AND CORAL GABLES

ACTORS' PLAYHOUSE

Miracle Theatre, 280 Miracle Mile, Coral Gables, 305-444-9293; www.actorsplayhouse.org

There's a hint of 1950s nostalgia when you step inside the Miracle Theatre, even though the Actors' Playhouse renovated the space in 1995 upon moving in. That's because the building used to be a movie house, and the bright, big-lettered marquee announcing the night's production, its box-office kiosk and glass doors that lead into the gold-rimmed lobby are all reminiscent of a time when girls in poodle-skirts and boys in leather jackets came through the place on the regular. Today, the 600-seat main stage houses the musical theater company's main productions, and the two smaller theaters upstairs are used for children's productions, script readings and experimental work. Known for its mainstage musical theater productions and its Musical Theatre for Young Audiences program, the company holds a record number of Carbonell awards, the accolade presented to regional theaters in South Florida. Expect over-the-top performances with tunes that'll stay in your head for days, and feel free to bring the kids.

Admission: mainstage production $35-$48, theater for young audiences $15.

GABLESTAGE

Biltmore Hotel, 1200 Anastasia Ave., Coral Gables, 305-446-1116; www.gablestage.org

It's easy to miss the GableStage as you drive by the 1920s-style Biltmore Hotel and golf resort, but to do so would be a shame. The theater group, which was founded in 1979, performs both Shakespeare classics and contemporary works like the Carbonell Award-winning original production Frozen. The troupe's a bit on the avant-garde side, and it doesn't shy away from tackling some heavy issues, such as a dramatic commentary on the Iraq War in Betrayed or a humorous satire on presidential elections in November. Housed next to the Hotel, by the tennis courts, the theater itself is small in size but big on classic elegance. Walk into the auditorium through archways draped in royal blue velvet that echo the cushioned seats. The slightly sunken stage makes for an intimate feel, even if you're sitting in the very back.

Admission: $37.50-$42.50. Hours: Thursday-Saturday 8 p.m., Sunday 2 p.m. and 8 p.m.

NEW THEATRE

4120 Laguna St., Coral Gables, 305-443-5909; www.new-theatre.org

The black box theater, which the New Theatre troupe calls home, originally opened in 1992 as a movie house called Astor Cinema that became known for showing avant-garde, independent features. New Theatre troupe—a venerated local company that's been around since 1986—has kept this spirit alive since it moved into the 100-seat space in 2001, by focusing mostly on contemporary and classic works. But the troupe truly shines with the former: In 2003, the company commissioned and staged the world premiere of *Anna in the Tropics*, which went on to win a Pulitzer Prize. Following the play's success, it went on to play on Broadway and won a Steinberg Award.

Admission: $35-$40. Thursday-Saturday 8 p.m., Sunday 1 p.m.

HIGHLIGHT

WHAT'S THE STORY BEHIND DRY TORTUGAS NATIONAL PARK?

With more than 64,000 acres of land and water, this national park not only includes the remains of what was once the largest of the 19th-century American coastal forts, but also the cluster of seven islands known as the Dry Tortugas. The coral keys, upon which the fort sits, were named "las tortugas" (the turtles) in 1513 by Ponce de Leon because so many turtles inhabited these bits of land. The "dry" portion of the islands' name warns mariners of a total lack of fresh water. Tropical ocean birds are the chief inhabitants, and each year between February and September sooty and noddy terns assemble on Bush Key to nest. Spanish pirates used the Tortugas as a base from which to pillage boats until 1821, when they were driven from the islands. In 1846, the United States, eager to protect its interests in the Gulf of Mexico, began construction of a fort on the 10-acre Garden Key. For more than 30 years, laborers worked on the fort, a rampart that was a half-mile in perimeter with 50-foot-high walls and three tiers designed for 450 guns. Called the "Gibraltar of the Gulf," this massive masonry fort was designed for a garrison of 1,500 men. Only partially completed, Fort Jefferson never saw battle. It was occupied by Union troops during the Civil War. Resting on an unstable foundation of sand and coral boulders, Fort Jefferson's walls began to crack and shift, making it unsuitable for military defense.

In 1863 it became a military prison, confining some 2,400 men. Among them was Dr. Samuel Mudd, who was imprisoned on the island after setting the broken leg of John Wilkes Booth, Abraham Lincoln's assassin. Following two yellow fever epidemics and a hurricane, the fort was abandoned in 1874. In the 1880s it was reconditioned for use as a naval base, coaling station and wireless station; the USS Maine sailed from the fort for Havana, where it was blown up, triggering the Spanish-American War. The fort became Fort Jefferson National Monument in 1935 and was renamed Dry Tortugas National Park in 1992.

The fort and islands are accessible by boat or seaplane trips from Key West. There is camping and a picnic area on Garden Key; campers must bring all supplies, including fresh water. There's a visitor's center and guided tours available. Contact the park ranger at 305-242-7700. For transportation information, call the Greater Key West Chamber of Commerce at 305-294-2587.

FAIRCHILD TROPICAL BOTANIC GARDEN

10901 Old Cutler Road, Coral Gables, 305-667-1651; www.fairchildgarden.org

This 83-acre botanic retreat isn't just another regular South Florida garden. Rare tropical plants and flowers adorn the immense landscape, with extensive collections of palms, flowering trees and succulents. Witness wildlife at the two-acre Richard H. Simmons Rainforest, the butterfly garden and the William F. Whitman Tropical Fruit Pavilion—just some of the exciting "live exhibits." Other treats include the yearly International Mango Festival (held in July) and the annual Members Plants sale (held in October), where green thumbs can buy exotic and local flowers and plants. To prove this is more than your average plant sale, Fairchild puts out a "list of plants" on its website before the big day, with the exact number of each species up for sale. But as with all rare finds, these leafy creatures don't come cheap.

Admission: adults $20, seniors $15, children 6-17 $10, children under 6 free. Daily 9:30 a.m.-4:30 p.m.

LOWE ART MUSEUM

University of Miami, 1301 Stanford Drive, Coral Gables, 305-284-3535; www.lowemuseum.org

You may not think of hitting a college campus to find one of the city's best museums, but you should make a co-ed exception for the Lowe Art Museum. The permanent collection is the star, with impressive examples of Greco-Roman antiquities, Renaissance and Baroque art, as well as more modern works by Dale Chihuly, Roy Lichtenstein and Robert Arneson to name a few. And to ensure that you don't forget you're on college turf, there are exhibits by UM students and faculty on display as well—a window into the possible masterpieces of the future. Lectures, group tours and the occasional "LoweDown Happy Hour" up the educational fun factor.

Admission: adults $10, seniors and students $5, children free. Tuesday-Wednesday, Friday-Saturday 10 a.m.-5 p.m., Thursday noon-7 p.m., Sunday noon-5 p.m.

DELRAY BEACH

DELRAY MUNICIPAL BEACH

Atlantic Avenue at State Road A1A, Delray Beach

This public beach is a nice spot to spread out your towel and catch some sun. Recreational activities include wind surfing, sailing, volleyball and snorkeling. Seagate Beach, located about a half mile south of the Atlantic Avenue and State Road A1A, features water-sports rentals.

THE MORIKAMI MUSEUM AND JAPANESE GARDENS

4000 Morikami Park Road, Delray Beach, 561-495-0233; www.morikami.org

Built in the 1977, this museum celebrates Delray Beach's Japanese community. It includes a gallery, a tea ceremony house, a theater, a bonsai collection and immaculately kept gardens. Check out Morikami Park, which features a one-mile, self-guided nature trail and has picnicking facilities. There's also a museum shop that stocks accessories, clothing, bento boxes and tea sets.

Admission: adults $10, seniors $9, students and children $6, children 6 and under free. Tuesday-Sunday 10 a.m.-5 p.m.

OLD SCHOOL SQUARE CULTURAL ARTS CENTER
51 N. Swinton Ave., Delray Beach, 561-243-7922; www.oldschool.org

This center, composed of two buildings on the National Register of Historic Places, houses the Cornell Museum of Art & American Culture and the Crest Theatre. The former showcases rotating exhibits on national and international fine artwork and crafts relating to American culture, while the latter hosts everything from professional theater to dance shows.

Admission: Cornwell Museum: adults $6, seniors and students 14-21 $4, children 13 and under free; Crest Theatre: price varies by show. Cornwell Museum: Tuesday-Saturday 10:30 a.m.-4:30 p.m., Sunday 1-4:30 p.m. Closed Sunday, May-September. Crest Theatre: hours vary.

HALLANDALE BEACH
GULFSTREAM PARK
901 S. Federal Highway, Hallandale Beach, 954-457-6233; www.gulfstreampark.com

Home of the Florida Derby, this famous racetrack has a walking ring decorated with leading stable colors. Bronze plaques in the Garden of Champions honor great thoroughbreds. There's also a casino on the premises. The Village at Gulfstream Park—a shopping, dining and entertainment destination—was added in 2010.

Admission: varies per event. January-March, Wednesday-Friday; April, Wednesday-Friday, Sunday.

HALLANDALE BEACH
Hallandale Beach Boulevard at State Road A1A, Hallandale Beach, 954 457-1456; www.hallandalebeach.org

The city's namesake beach is a 4.9-acre spot of sand and surf, though there are also plenty of facilities on hand, such as showers, and volleyball and bocce ball courts.

HOLLYWOOD
ART AND CULTURE CENTER OF HOLLYWOOD
1650 Harrison St., Hollywood, 954-921-3274; www.artandculturecenter.org

This arts and culture facility has a theater that hosts dance and performing arts events, plus a gallery, an art school and a sculpture garden. Recent exhibits have featured the works of Nathan Sawaya, whose sculptures are made using Lego blocks.

Admission: adults $7, students, seniors and children 4-13 $4, children 3 and under free; free on the third Sunday of each month. Gallery: Monday-Saturday 10 a.m.-5 p.m., Sunday noon-4 p.m.; theater: varies by show.

DANIA JAI ALAI
301 E. Dania Beach Blvd., Dania Beach, 954-920-1511; www.dania-jai-alai.com

Jai alai is a fast-paced ballgame that originates from the Basque region of Spain, but it's found a sure footing here in Dania Beach, a town just north of Hollywood. This fronton (the name for the sports arena) holds not only the court, but also betting facilities, a sports bar, plenty of seating for spectators, and a card room for poker tournaments.

Admission: free for spectators. Tuesday-Saturday 7 p.m.; Tuesday, Saturday noon; Sunday 1p.m.

DOWNTOWN HOLLYWOOD

Between Johnson and Washington streets, and N. 14th and 22nd avenues, Hollywood, 954-921-3016; www.downtownhollywood.com

Since the late 1970s, Hollywood's quaint downtown has been experiencing a slow revival, eased along by the low-lying, Art Deco-era architecture in the area. Check out trendy, shop-lined Harrison Street and Hollywood Boulevard, which teems with independent restaurants and art galleries. The 10-acre ArtsPark at Young Circle is also a hub for events, such as concerts and outdoor festivals.

HOLLYWOOD BEACH

State Road A1A between Sheridan Street and Hollywood Boulevard, Hollywood

Hollywood Beach is a local favorite for its non-flashy, laid-back attitude. It spans several miles, two of which are bordered by the Broadwalk, a well-maintained promenade where pedestrians, rollerbladers and cyclists tread. Beachgoers will also find charming mom-and-pop restaurants and shops along the Broadwalk, as well as the Hollywood Beach Theater/Bandshell. On the north end of the Broadwalk is Hollywood North Beach Park (State Road A1A at Sheridan Street), a tranquil portion of the beach with lots of space to lay out and catch some sun.

Admission: free. Hours vary.

HOLLYWOOD BEACH THEATER/BANDSHELL

Johnson Street at Broadwalk, Hollywood, 954-921-3404; www.hollywoodfl.org

This seaside alfresco theater is a great place to catch free music programs, which inspire many to dance under the stars. On Monday, check out Theater Under the Stars Series which features live bands playing big band, swing and other dancing music. On Tuesday, enjoy the Dancing in the Moonlight Series featuring dances like the fox trot, cha cha and the twist. If you're more for modern music, head to the bandshell on Wednesday for the On the Boardwalk series which showcases rock and roll, country and R&B among other types of music.

Admission: free. Monday-Wednesday 7:30-9 p.m.

ISLAMORADA

HURRICANE MONUMENT

Mile marker 81.6, Overseas Highway, Islamorada, 305-664-3661

Located across from the library at mile marker 81.6, this is a memorial to 400 veterans of World War I and others killed in the 1935 hurricane while working on the highway. A few veterans are buried in a crypt in the center of the monument.

JUPITER

JONATHAN DICKINSON STATE PARK

16450 S.E. Federal Highway, Hobe Sound, 772-546-2771; www.floridastateparks.org

Located close to where Quaker merchant Jonathan Dickinson was first ship-wrecked, this park offers more than 10,000 acres between Hobe Sound and the Loxahatchee River and includes the 85-foot-high Hobe Mountain with a 25-foot observation tower, pine flatlands and tropical riverfront. Partake in fishing, boating, canoeing (rentals are available onsite), nature trails, bicycling, picnicking, a playground and camping.

Admission: varies per activity. Daily 8 a.m.-dusk.

JUPITER INLET LIGHTHOUSE & MUSEUM

Lighthouse Park, 500 Captain Armour's Way, Jupiter, 561-747-8380; www.lrhs.org

Organized and run by the Loxahatchee River Historical Museum, this museum features tours of the Jupiter Inlet Lighthouse, a red-brick landmark built in 1860. It is one of the oldest lighthouses on the Atlantic coast and houses local historical artifacts and memorabilia. Also onsite is the DuBois Pioneer House, the second-oldest house in Palm Beach County, built in 1898.

Admission: adults $7, children 6-18 $5, children 5 and under free. Tuesday-Sunday 10 a.m.-5 p.m.

KEY BISCAYNE

CAPE FLORIDA LIGHTHOUSE

1200 Crandon Blvd., Key Biscayne; www.key-biscayne.com/capeflorida

On the southernmost point of Key Biscayne stands a true old Florida landmark. The Cape Florida Lighthouse has been a welcoming beacon to South Florida visitors for more than 150 years. This 95-foot-tall structure offers some of the best views of the bay and the natural beauty that surrounds it. Located within the 500-acre Bill Baggs State Park, a trip to the lighthouse isn't complete without hike through the lush paths of the park. Just pack a map (and a snack)—some trials can be long and challenging.

MIAMI SEAQUARIUM

4400 Rickenbacker Causeway, Key Biscayne, 305-361-5705; www.miamiseaquarium.com

They call him Flipper, Flipper, faster than lightning. No one, you see, is smarter than he … South Floridians loved going to the Seaquarium to catch a glimpse of "the original Flipper." From 1963 to 1967, 88 television episodes and two movies starring Flipper were filmed at the Seaquarium. Not only reserved for TV land fanatics, the longest-operating oceanarium in the U.S. will entice everyone with its sea lion, killer whale and dolphin performances, or opt for presentations that feature sharks, manatees, alligators and other wildlife. If you're feeling particularly adventurous, reserve a spot at "the Dolphin Odyssey" with one of the other "faster than lightning" dolphins, where you can swim with them and even enjoy a porpoise ride.

Admission: adults $35.95, children 3-9 $26.95. Daily 9:30 a.m.-6 p.m.

STILTSVILLE

On Biscayne Bay, roughly one mile south of Cape Florida, Key Biscayne; www.stiltsville.org

Picture homes and offices in the middle of a large body of water, propped up by stilts and you've got Stiltsville. Sitting just a mile off the coast, Stiltsville is an oasis of structures that have seemingly grown out of the sea. This uniquely Floridian neighborhood has witnessed its share of history, hosting everything from shady dealings to wild parties and has even been featured in films like Paul Newman's Absent of Malice. Clubs with an "anything goes" atmosphere were built on stilts in the 1940s, and police raids began in the '50s to stop the prostitution and illegal gambling that had taken up residence there. Once topping off at 27 structures, these water-bound huts were the place to see and be seen when visiting the winter resorts at nearby Miami Beach. Today, things are a bit different. There are only seven structures remaining and a majority of the offices are no longer in business. Homes have been deserted, making it more of a ghost town than an offshore party spot. Still, Stiltsville is like nothing you've ever seen and is worth the boat ride.

KEY LARGO

DOLPHINS PLUS

31 Corrine Place, Key Largo, 305-451-1993, 866-860-7946; www.dolphinsplus.com

This research and education center focuses on the interaction between humans and dolphins. You can watch or participate in two-to three-hour programs (reservations required to participate; experienced swimmers only; equipment provided). Participants must be at least seven years old, and anyone under age 13 must be accompanied by an adult. There are three sessions daily.

Admission: varies by activity. Hours vary by activity.

JOHN PENNEKAMP CORAL REEF STATE PARK

Overseas Highway at mile marker 102.5, Key Largo, 305-451-1202, 800-326-3521; www.pennekamppark.com

Just an hour's drive south of Miami, you'll find some of the best snorkeling and scuba diving in the area. John Pennekamp Coral Reef State Park is home to the largest living coral reef in the continental United States. The park has beautiful hiking trails, boardwalks through mangrove swamps and observation decks for bird watching, but the most spectacular part lies offshore. The state park and adjacent national marine sanctuary cover an area of the Atlantic Ocean that is some 25 miles long and three miles out to sea, where fish, coral reefs and marine mammals are carefully protected. Park concessionaires offer all the gear you need to scuba dive and snorkel. You can also sign up for daily boat trips, snorkeling excursions and glass-bottomed boat rides.

Admission: $3.50. Daily 8 a.m.-dusk.

JULES' UNDERSEA LODGE

51 Shoreland Drive, Key Largo, 305-451-2353; www.jul.com

The world's only underwater "hotel" is five fathoms, or 30 feet, deep. Designed to accommodate six divers (introductory diving classes are available and mandatory, if guests aren't certified divers), the Lodge has an entertainment center, fully stocked galley, dining area, bathrooms and 42-inch windows for watching the fish swim by. Available for three-hour or overnight stays.

KEY WEST

AUDUBON HOUSE AND TROPICAL GARDENS

205 Whitehead St., Key West, 305-294-2116, 877-294-2470; www.audubonhouse.com

This neoclassical home of sea captain and wrecker John Geiger contains an outstanding collection of 18th- and 19th-century furnishings and re-creates the ambience of the early days of Key West, when Audubon visited the island. Many of the artist's original engravings are on display. Admission includes a CD for a self-guided tour.

Admission: adults $12, seniors $11, students $7.50, children $5, children under 6 free. Daily 9:30 a.m.-4:15 p.m.

CONCH TOUR TRAIN

303 Front St., Key West, 305-294-5161, 800-868-7482; www.conchtourtrain.com

Visitors who are short on time should opt for this 90-minute tour that loops around Old Town Key West and covers most of the enclave's major sights. The tour will take you to attractions such as the AIDS Memorial Beach, a gorgeous spot with sands imported from the Bahamas, and the unique Mallory Square, which is at the center of Key West's waterfront. Tours typically depart every 30 minutes.

Admission: adults $29, children 4-12 $14. Daily 9 a.m.-4:30 p.m.

CURRY MANSION

511 Caroline St., Key West, 305-294-5349, 800-253-3466; www.currymansion.com

This 28-room Victorian mansion—which doubles as an inn—was built in 1899 for the son of Florida's first millionaire. In the house, visitors can find original Audubon prints, period antiques, Tiffany glass artifacts and Ernest Hemingway's elephant gun. Self-guided tours are available.

Admission: $5. Daily 9 a.m.-5 p.m.

ERNEST HEMINGWAY HOME AND MUSEUM

907 Whitehead St., Key West, 305-294-1136; www.hemingwayhome.com

This Spanish colonial-style house made of native stone was purchased in 1931 by Hemingway, an early visitor to Key West who wrote many of his books here, including *For Whom the Bell Tolls* and *The Snows of Kilimanjaro*. The museum features original furnishings, memorabilia as well as trees and plants from the Caribbean and other parts of the world, most collected and planted by Hemingway. Be on the lookout for the many cats that roam the premises— Hemingway took in a six-toed cat, and some of the 60 or so felines that live on the grounds are descendants of that kitty.

Admission: adults $12, children $6, children 5 and under free. Daily 9 a.m.-5 p.m.

HARRY S. TRUMAN LITTLE WHITE HOUSE MUSEUM

111 Front St., Key West, 305-294-9911; www.trumanlittlewhitehouse.com

This was the vacation home of the 33rd president, who spent 11 working vacations in Key West between 1946 and 1952. The house has been restored to the period with original Truman furnishings. Guided tours are available.

Admission: adults $15, seniors $13, children 5-12 $5, children 4 and under free. Daily 9 a.m.-4:30 p.m.

KEY WEST AQUARIUM

1 Whitehead St., Key West, 800-868-7482; www.keywestaquarium.com

At this small aquarium, check out unique and colorful specimens of sea life from the Gulf of Mexico and the Atlantic Ocean. The touch tank—a real hit with kids—allows you to feel and examine live starfish, horseshoe crabs, sea squirts, sea urchins, conchs and more. You can take guided, narrated tours.

Admission: adults $12, children 4-12 $5, children 3 and under free.

WRECKERS MUSEUM—THE OLDEST HOUSE

322 Duval St., Key West, 305-294-9501; www.oirf.org

The oldest house in Key West, this structure was built in 1830 with a unique "conch" construction. Once the home of sea captain and wrecker Francis B.

Watlington, the museum now houses displays of Key West's wrecking industry, historic documents, ship models, toys and antiques.

Admission: free. Daily 10 a.m.-4 p.m.

MARATHON

CRANE POINT MUSEUM, NATURE CENTER & HISTORIC SITE

5550 Overseas Highway, Marathon, 305-743-3900; www.cranepoint.net

At this nature center, see exhibits on coral reefs, shipwrecks, Native Americans, wildlife and pirates. There is a 1.5-mile nature trail where you can take in views of Florida Bay and the 1950s-era Crane House. Onsite is the Florida Keys Children's Museum.

Admission: adults $11, seniors $9, students 6-12 $7, children 5 and under free. Monday-Saturday 9 a.m.-5 p.m., Sunday noon-5 p.m.

PALM BEACH

HENRY MORRISON FLAGLER MUSEUM (WHITEHALL)

1 Whitehall Way, Palm Beach, 561-655-2833; www.flaglermuseum.us

This 55-room house was built in 1902 by Henry Morrison Flagler, developer of the Florida East Coast Railroad. An opulent monument to America's Gilded Age, this marble palace contains paintings, silver, glass, dolls, lace, costumes and family memorabilia. Special exhibits illustrate local history and the vast enterprises of the Flagler system. On the grounds is Flagler's private railroad car, refinished and refitted with exact reproductions of the original carpeting, drapery and upholstery materials.

WEST PALM BEACH

MOUNTS BOTANICAL GARDEN

559 N. Military Trail, West Palm Beach, 561-233-1757; www.mounts.org

This is the oldest and largest public botanical garden in Palm Beach County. The grounds feature more than 13 acres of tropical and subtropical plants, including herb, palm, cactus and tropical fruit collections.

Monday-Saturday 8 a.m.-4 p.m., Sunday noon-4 p.m.

NORTON MUSEUM OF ART

1451 S. Olive Ave., West Palm Beach, 561-832-5196; www.norton.org

The Norton carries 7,000 works of art and includes permanent collections in 19th- and 20th-century European paintings, American art from 1900 to the present, a distinguished Chinese collection and a sculpture patio.

Admission: adults $12, children 13-21 $5, children under 13 free. Tuesday-Saturday 10 a.m.-5 p.m., Sunday 1-5 p.m. Second Thursday of each month 10 a.m. -9 p.m.

PEANUT ISLAND

6500 Peanut Island Road, Riviera Beach, 561-845-4445, 866-383-5730

Peanut Island is a 79-acre island where John F. Kennedy had a bomb-shelter bunker built for himself during the Cuban Missile Crisis. It is now a full-service recreational park with boat dock, fishing pier, camping and picnicking.

SOUTH FLORIDA SCIENCE MUSEUM

4801 Dreher Trail N., West Palm Beach, 561-832-1988; www.sfsm.org

The South Florida Science Museum houses dozens of hands-on interactive exhibits, plus the expanded McGinty Aquariums. Check out the Egypt Gallery to see a child mummy or visit the "Out of This World" exhibit to touch a 232-pound meteorite. Observatory viewing and laser light shows are presented on Friday evenings. The planetarium show runs daily.

Admission: adults $9, children 3-12 $6, seniors $7.50. Planetarium shows: adults $4, children 3-12 $2, seniors $4. Monday-Friday 10 a.m.-5 p.m., Saturday 10 a.m.-6 p.m., Sunday noon-6 p.m.

WHERE TO STAY

AVENTURA

★★★★ACQUALINA RESORT & SPA ON THE BEACH

17875 Collins Ave., Sunny Isles Beach, 305-918-8000; www.acqualinaresort.com

This place does it all: it's a luxe hotel, a beachfront resort and home to one of Miami's best spas. So it comes as no surprise that the place is crawling with CEOs of multimillion-dollar corporations and condo-dwelling millionaires (most of the building is dedicated to privately owned condos). Guests check in·for the hotel's boutique vibe and prime location along 4.5 beachfront acres and 400 feet of gleaming Atlantic Ocean coastline. The resort offers the luxury of South Beach without all the bustle; it's located in "Florida's Riviera," Sunny Isles, just 15 to 20 minutes north of South Beach. Take advantage of Acqualina's private beach dining—it allows only two tables per night, set up at opposite ends of the resort's sandy shores, a setup that redefines the word "seclusion." Before dinner, treat yourself to an oceanfront treatment by ESPA, such as the relaxing signature salt and oil body scrub. The one guest complaint? You have to be a tech whiz to figure out how to use the complicated lighting system, but that quibble will fade when you stretch out on Italian imported Rivolta Carmignani bed linens after a day being pampered on Acqualina's spacious private beach.

97 rooms. Restaurant, bar. Fitness center. Pool. Spa. Pets accepted. Beach. $251-350

★★★★THE FAIRMONT TURNBERRY ISLE RESORT & CLUB

19999 W. Country Club Drive, Aventura, 305-932-6200, 866-840-8069; www.fairmont.com

This hotel is a peaceful oasis from the streets of car-congested Miami. Surrounded by condo high-rises, two 18-hole Raymond Floyd-designed championship golf courses give this place country-club class. Head into the pro shop, where Arnold Palmer look-alikes hang out, smoking stogies and swapping hole-in-one stories. If you're in the mood to be pampered, indulge at Willow Stream Spa. For some relaxation, lay out by the three pools, one of which has a waterslide and a lazy river. Or head right to your room, a soothing retreat decorated in butterscotch, light greens and chocolate brown. Rooms come with Bose radios, walk-in closets, marble bathrooms with soak tubs and stall showers as well as private balconies overlooking the gardens and golf courses.

392 rooms. Restaurant, bar. Business center. Fitness center. Pool. Spa. Pets accepted. Golf. Tennis. $351 and up

★★★★TRUMP INTERNATIONAL BEACH RESORT

18001 Collins Ave., Sunny Isles Beach, 305-692-5600, 800-461-8501; www.trumpmiami.com

The rooms of this Trump property are spacious and offer great views of the

Atlantic and the Intracoastal Waterway, which is a huge plus. The beautiful balcony panoramas of the oceans are a great distraction from the elegant but somewhat standard hotel furniture indoors. For more of that view, head to the grotto-style outdoor pool area, where there's also a bar and grill, hot tubs, waterfalls and a children's pool. To get the most spectacular vistas of the ocean, snag a poolside or beachside cabana with air-conditioning, refrigerators, televisions and cabana beds. Another perk: It's easy to escape the mania of South Beach (which is a 25-minute drive south) when you're this close to ritzy Bal Harbour and Aventura or kid-friendly Fort Lauderdale.

249 rooms. Restaurant, bar. Business center. Fitness center. Pool. Spa. Beach. $251-350

BAL HARBOUR

★★★ONE BAL HARBOUR RESORT AND SPA

10295 Collins Ave., Bal Harbour, 305-455-5400, 800-545-4000; www.oneluxuryhotels.com

There's nowhere better to be in Miami Beach but oceanside, and thankfully that's every side of One Bal Harbour, whether you're taking a dip in the Atlantic Ocean, enjoying water sports in Baker's Haulover Inlet, or sipping piña coladas in the pool's private cabanas. Landlubbers can relax with a trip to the Guerlain Spa, followed with an exquisite meal at 1 Bleu and drinks at The View Bar. At night, everyone can rejuvenate in one of the hotel's super-chic rooms, whose cushy beds are outfitted with luxe Anichini bedding and each with a terrace overlooking the water.

186 rooms. Restaurants, bar. Business center. Fitness center. Pool. Spa. $251-350

BOCA RATON

★★★BOCA RATON RESORT & CLUB

501 E. Camino Real, Boca Raton, 561-447-3000, 888-491-2622; www.bocaresort.com

Since opening in 1926, this classic resort has been a top destination on South Florida's Gold Coast. Occupying 356 acres fronting the Atlantic Ocean, the resort has a private stretch of beach, two 18-hole golf courses, 30 tennis courts, seven pools, and a 32-slip marina. As if that weren't enough, the resort is also home to a wide variety of restaurants and lounges, as well as the heavenly Spa Palazzo. If you'd rather explore Boca Raton, check in with the concierge about local activities.

1,043 rooms. Restaurant, bar. Business center. Fitness center. Pool. Spa. Pets accepted. Beach. Golf. Tennis. $351 and up

★★★HILTON SUITES BOCA RATON

7920 Glades Road, Boca Raton, 561-483-3600, 800-445-8667; www.hilton.com

Located in a lakeside complex in the heart of Boca Raton, this hotel is surrounded by shopping and dining. It is also just minutes away from Gold Coast Atlantic beaches. Each suite features a separate bedroom and living room, a balcony, a microwave and coffeemaker, and Crabtree & Evelyn's La Source bath products. Guests can mingle at the complimentary reception, or stroll by the small lake on the grounds.

199 rooms. Restaurant, bar. Complimentary breakfast. Business center. Fitness center. Pool. Pets accepted. $151-250

★★★RENAISSANCE BOCA RATON HOTEL

2000 N.W. 19th St., Boca Raton, 561-368-5252, 888-236-2427; www.marriott.com

This Mediterranean-style hotel is five miles east of downtown Boca Raton in an area of businesses and restaurants. It tries to provide an escape from the bustle, though, with an outdoor pool with gently flowing waterfalls, a restaurant and a poolside bar. Guest rooms have granite bathrooms, and some rooms feature pool-facing verandas. The hotel is near Boca's beaches and country clubs as well as Florida State University, so it's a convenient place to stay, whether you're in town for business or pleasure.

189 rooms. Restaurant, bar. Business center. Fitness center. Pool. $151-250

CORAL GABLES

★★★BILTMORE

1200 Anastasia Ave., Coral Gables, 305-445-1926; www.biltmorehotel.com

At this National Historic landmark, the Biltmore transports you back to the '20s. The hotel was built in 1926, but time hasn't faded this grande dame one bit. Walk among the stately columns surrounding the courtyard and the lobby and you'll feel like you're staying at a rich uncle's estate, rather than in a hotel. The Art Deco-inspired rooms blend a tropical vibe with an old-Miami ambience—think Great Gatsby meets Henry Flagler for a mojito in the lanai. If you're looking for more exclusive treatment, book a room on the seventh-floor concierge level, where you'll get access to a private lounge. This South Florida classic does exclusive exceptionally well (it has hosted presidents and celebrities). It's also the place where Johnny "Tarzan" Weissmuller once broke a world swimming record in the 700,000-gallon pool, adding another historic notch in the Biltmore's belt.

276 rooms. Restaurant, bar. Fitness center. Pool. Spa. Golf. Tennis. $351 and up

★★★HOTEL ST. MICHEL

162 Alcazar Ave., Coral Gables, 305-444-1666, 800-848-4683; www.hotelstmichel.com

Under any other circumstance, the word "cozy" might be too trite to describe a hotel, but that's exactly what this 1926 structure (formerly known as the Sevilla Hotel) is. A hand-operated elevator, complete with an attendant, takes you to your floor on one of the three stories. None of the rooms in this small hotel is furnished alike, with English and French antiques scattered throughout.

28 rooms. Restaurant, bar. Complimentary breakfast. $151-250

★★★HYATT REGENCY CORAL GABLES

50 Alhambra Plaza, Coral Gables, 305-411-1234; www.coralgables.hyatt.com

Bathed in a light-pink tropical tint and done up in Spanish-Mediterranean style, this hotel typifies Coral Gables in a stately and grand manner. The hotel recalls the architecture of Spain's The Alhambra (albeit with more modern lines and minus the history). Hanging above the 13-story building is the hotel's large clock, which gets business folks to their meetings on time and vacationers to nowhere in particular at any time. And that's the mix of people you'll find here. If you're one of the suits, don't hole up in the room, because there's plenty to see just outside the lobby doors. The well-situated hotel is within walking distance to Miracle Mile and Ponce de Leon Boulevard, both sweet shopping and nightlife hubs. If you're staying here for pleasure, catch South Florida sunshine at the large, picturesque pool while soaking in the beautiful Spanish architecture, or take some time out by the fountain in the courtyard. It's all the benefits of the Granada, plus Miami's sunny disposition.

242 rooms. Restaurant, bar. Fitness center. Pool. $251-350

★★★THE WESTIN COLONNADE
80 Aragon Ave., Coral Gables, 305-441-2600; www.starwoodhotels.com

One perk of staying at this hotel chain is that you get to rest on the Westin's reliably amazing Heavenly Bed. (The aptly named bed was conceived by former Starwood Hotels C.E.O. Barry S. Sternlicht, modeled after his bed at his Connecticut home.) Throw in the Heavenly Bath (Westin interviewed 1,000 travelers to find a standout bathing experience, and this one includes a therapeutic spa shower and luxurious bath amenities), and you'll really want to stay awhile at the hotel, which sits in the middle of the sophisticated and lively Miracle Mile. Some bi-level loft rooms are available and feature a spiral staircase that leads to an upper bedroom. There is a downside to this special amenity: hauling the luggage up the stairs can be challenging, so make sure to have the bellhop maneuver it for you. The property more often entertains a business crowd, but for those seeking relaxation, the hotel features a 200-foot-long rooftop sundeck, a sizable heated pool and a spa tub—in case the Heavenly Bed and Bath leave you wanting more.

157 rooms. Restaurant, bar. Fitness center. Pool. Pets accepted. $251-350

DELRAY

★★★DELRAY BEACH MARRIOTT
10 N. Ocean Blvd., Delray Beach, 561-274-3200, 877-389-0169; www.delraybeachmarriott.com

The boutiques, cafés and shops of Atlantic Avenue are all within walking distance of this Mediterranean-style hotel on North Ocean Boulevard. Each of the guest rooms provides a coffeemaker and minibar, and some rooms offer ocean views and private balconies. Take a dip in one of the two heated pools (one pool is adults-only), or bask in the sun on the beach. For even more relaxation, try a treatment at N Spa, which offers eight massages and several other body treatments. It also provides a menu of Ayurvedic services for men.

268 rooms. Restaurant, bar. Business center. Fitness center. Pool. Spa. $151-250

HOLLYWOOD

★★★WESTIN DIPLOMAT RESORT AND SPA
3555 S. Ocean Drive, Hollywood, 954-602-6000, 888-627-9057; www.diplomatresort.com

This elegant yet casual resort offers fabulous views of Florida's Gold Coast. Outdoor activities include golf, tennis, boating trips, beach volleyball and swimming in the 240-foot lagoon-style pool or the infinity-edge, bridged pool. Guests who choose to stay indoors will enjoy beautiful rooms awash in light tones—think all-white bedding and tan carpeting—punctuated by chocolate-brown furnishings. The spa is a soothing retreat from the sands and sun, and provides treatments like the 90-minute caviar facial.

998 rooms. Restaurant, bar. Business center. Fitness center. Beach. Pool. Spa. Tennis. $251-350

JUPITER

★★★JUPITER BEACH RESORT & SPA

5 N. State Road A1A, Jupiter, 561-746-2511, 800-228-8810; www.jupiterbeachresort.com

Jupiter has a more natural appeal than its Palm Beach neighbor, and this casual Caribbean-style resort fits in perfectly with the town's laid-back vibe. Rooms are tidy and well-decorated with a mix of modern and Asian/Art Deco touches. The large, comfortable beds have down duvets and feather pillows; you'll have a hard time getting up to go to the private beach. When you're sun sated, dine on seafood at Sinclairs Ocean Grill.

177 rooms. Restaurant, bar. Business center. Fitness center. Pool. Spa. Beach. Tennis. $251-350

KEY BISCAYNE

★★★★THE RITZ-CARLTON, KEY BISCAYNE

455 Grand Bay Drive, Key Biscayne, 305-365-4500, 800-241-3333; www.ritzcarlton.com

Located just outside downtown Miami on the southernmost barrier island in the United States, this resort delivers the intimacy of a private island escape but with the convenient location of a city hotel. In addition to 12 acres of ocean-front property, the resort has a 20,000-square-foot spa and an 11-court tennis center—plus, it's only five minutes away from the Crandon Park Golf Course. The guest rooms feature British colonial furnishings and pastel colors, and face either the shimmering Atlantic Ocean or lush tropical gardens. Luxurious amenities—such as marble-lined bathrooms, goose-down pillows and plush bathrobes—make for a comfortable stay. Cioppino, the resort's signature restaurant, has an Italian-influenced menu with an accent on local seafood.

490 rooms. Restaurant, bar. Business center. Fitness center. Pool. Spa. Beach. Tennis. $351 and up

KEY LARGO

★★★MARRIOTT KEY LARGO BAY BEACH RESORT

103800 Overseas Highway, Key Largo, 305-453-0000, 866-849-3753; www.marriott.com

This resort has comfortable guest rooms decorated with mahogany furniture and tropical prints, granite bathroom countertops and upgraded bed linens. Onsite is a PADI (Professional Association of Diving Instructors) school for guests who want to take scuba-diving lessons, get specialty certifications, or go on daily dive and snorkel trips to the coral reef and marine sanctuary. If you'd rather keep to temperature-controlled waters, there's also a pool on the premises. Volleyball, jet skiing and parasailing are also available.

153 rooms. Restaurant, bar. Fitness center. Pool. Spa. Golf. $151-250

KEY WEST

★★★CASA MARINA RESORT & BEACH CLUB

1500 Reynolds St., Key West, 305-296-3535, 866-397-6342; www.casamarinaresort.com

This sprawling resort is on Kokomo Beach, the largest beach in Key West. Scuba dive, relax by the oceanfront pools and visit the Sunday veranda brunch at Flagler's restaurant. The guest rooms are bathed in light and feature natural shades in the linens and carpeting, accentuated by dark-wood furniture. All rooms have flat-screen televisions and high-speed Internet access. Spa al Mare doles out treatments like deep-tissue massages or body scrubs. A standout is the popular Ocean Breeze Massage, a heavenly oceanside rubdown.

311 rooms. Restaurant, bar. Business center. Fitness center. Pool. Pets accepted. Beach. Tennis.
$151-250

★★★CROWNE PLAZA HOTEL KEY WEST-LA CONCHA

430 Duval St., Key West, 305-296-2991, 800-745-2191; www.laconchakeywest.com

On the southernmost part of the island sits the highest building in Key West.
Built in 1926, it is listed on the National Register of Historic Places. The lobby
features tropical décor with wicker furniture, palm leaf fans, marble flooring
and lots of cozy seating. Guest rooms are decorated with mahogany antiques
and plush bedding, and some rooms have refrigerators. The seventh-floor
observatory offers panoramic views.

16 rooms. Restaurant, bar. Fitness room. Pool. $151-250

★★★DOUBLETREE GRAND KEY RESORT

3990 S. Roosevelt Blvd., Key West, 305-293-1818, www.doubletree.com

This tropical resort is just one mile from the Key West airport. Enjoy hotel-
sponsored water sports at the private beach or try your hand at a game of
badminton. A free hourly shuttle is provided to the airport, beach, golf course
and historic Old Town, so there's no need to rent a car. Guest rooms and suites
feature blue and yellow cottage-style decor and comfortable beds. The deck is
a lovely place to catch some rays, and the pool is a good spot for cooling off.

216 rooms. Restaurant, bar. Fitness center. Pool. Pets accepted. Beach. $151-250

★★★HYATT KEY WEST RESORT & SPA

601 Front St., Key West, 305-809-1234, 800-233-1234; www.hyatt.com

A lush tropical setting with gardens and ponds inhabited by a large variety of
turtles can be found at this hotel in downtown Key West. In the modern guest
rooms, all-white linens get livened up with bright red throw pillows and the
balconies show off great views of the Gulf, especially at sundown. Rooms are
spacious and little things like pillow-top mattresses make them comfortable.
Area attractions and shops are nearby, but for guests who want to stay in and
relax, consider the onsite Jala Spa—treatments are influenced and informed by
the local natural environments, such as the beach and the Everglades.

118 rooms. Restaurant, bar. Fitness center. Pool. Spa. Pets accepted. Beach. $251-350

★★★LA MER & DEWEY HOUSE

504-506 South St., Key West, 305-296-6577, 800-354-4455; www.southernmostresorts.com

Located on the south end of the island and surrounded by foliage is this lovely
little inn, only a few steps from the beach. Guest rooms feature fresh flowers
and are decorated in a tropical, contemporary style. Beds are fitted with luxury
linens, and the roomy bathrooms come stocked with an amenities basket and
plush towels. A continental breakfast and afternoon tea are served in the cozy
parlor. For guests looking for a more vibrant scene, lively Duval Street is just a
few blocks away.

11 rooms. Restaurant, bar. Complimentary breakfast. Pool. Beach. $251-350

★★★LITTLE PALM ISLAND RESORT & SPA

28500 Overseas Highway, Little Torch Key, 305-515-4004, www.littlepalmisland.com

Accessible by boat or seaplane, this private island has white-sand beaches and towering palm trees. Intimate and seductive, the thatched-roof bungalows have rattan furnishings, gauzy canopied beds and are blissfully technology-free, i.e., sans TVs or phones. The resort entices with simple pleasures, like relaxing under the sun, visiting the spa (which features indoor and outdoor massage services) and floating in the freshwater pool. Dinner is served at the onsite restaurant under a tiki-torch-lit, star-filled sky.

30 rooms. Restaurant, bar. Complimentary breakfast. Fitness center. Pool. Spa. No children under 16. $351 and up

★★★MARQUESA HOTEL

600 Fleming St., Key West, 305-292-1919, 800-869-4631; www.marquesa.com

This boutique hotel—whose structure is listed on the National Register of Historic Places—is private and peaceful, and is in the Old Town historic district. Rooms and suites are decorated with antiques and soft pastel prints, maintaining an airy island vibe. Attention to detail, such as rapid replenishing of towels and an always-full ice bucket, keeps guests coming back year after year. Cafe Marquesa serves fine contemporary American cuisine.

27 rooms. Restaurant, bar. Business center. Pool. No children under 13. $251-350

★★★OCEAN KEY RESORT & SPA

0 Duval St., Key West, 305-296-7701, 800-328-9815; www.oceankey.com

Located in Old Town, this resort is in the middle of all the action—it sits alongside Sunset Pier, home of the famous nightly sunset celebrations. Rooms are eclectic and decorated with sleigh-style beds and wicker furniture. Fishing, scuba and sightseeing trips are available at the onsite marina. Next to the marina is the pool area; crash onto one of the cushy lounges and spend a lazy afternoon watching cruise ships pass. Those who would rather enjoy a meal with their view can head to Hot Tin Roof restaurant.

100 rooms. Restaurant, bar. Fitness center. Pool. Spa. $251-350

★★★PIER HOUSE RESORT AND CARIBBEAN SPA

1 Duval St., Key West, 305-296-4600, 800-723-2791; www.pierhouse.com

This Gulf-front resort offers white sand, the Caribbean Spa—with a waterfall Jacuzzi—and several restaurants and bars. Have a drink at the infamous Chart Room Bar, where Jimmy Buffett is rumored to have started his career. The décor here is classic Key West with lime greens and sunset oranges tempered by beige and white walls and furniture. The grounds are landscaped with garden walkways and tropical trees and plants. The pool is well-maintained, and there's a private beach.

142 rooms. Restaurant, bar. Fitness center. Pool. Spa. Pets accepted. No children under 21. Beach. $251-350

★★★THE REACH RESORT

1435 Simonton St., Key West, 305-296-3535, 866-397-6427; www.reachresort.com

Private balconies; sand-inspired décor in shades of beige, white and coral red; and a natural beach make this oceanfront Old Town resort a relaxing hideaway.

HOTEL TIP

WHICH HOTELS ARE THE BEST FOR A QUIET ESCAPE?

FAIRMONT TURNBERRY ISLE RESORT & CLUB, AVENTURA:

When you need a break from the Miami mayhem, this nearby hotel gives you a reprieve. Secluded on 300 acres, the Fairmont gives out relaxation on its golf course, splurge-worthy spa and on the onsite lazy river.

LITTLE PALM ISLAND RESORT & SPA, LITTLE TORCH KEY:

Talk about the perfect escape: To get to this private island, you have to either take a boat or seaplane. Your thatched-roof bungalow also promises to be an oasis, since there are no phones or TVs allowed. Plus, no one under 16 is permitted to stay at the hotel, so peace and quiet is practically guaranteed.

SUNSET KEY GUEST COTTAGES, A WESTIN RESORT, KEY WEST:

Get away from it all at this resort, which sits on Sunset Key, a secluded 27-acre island. You won't have to worry about loud neighbors since you'll get your own cottage. It comes with kitchen and dining areas, so you'll never have to leave your hideaway.

Rooms have tile floors, wet bars, ceiling fans and flat-screen televisions. Diversions include everything from shopping on Duval Street to sunset cruises to dining at the Mediterranean-style Sands Restaurant and Lounge. Guests at the Reach can also head to sister property Casa Marina Resort & Beach Club for spa treatments.

150 rooms. Restaurant, bar. Business center. Fitness center. Pool. Beach. $151-250

★★★SHERATON SUITES KEY WEST

2001 S. Roosevelt Road, Key West, 305-292-9800, 800-452-3224; www.sheraton.com

This all-suite hotel is across the street from Smathers Beach. All rooms have refrigerators, microwaves and coffee makers, and some feature balconies. Rooms are decorated in subdued tones with subtle Caribbean flair. A complimentary shuttle service transports you to and from the airport and historic Old Town Key West. Adding to the tropical setting is a free-form outdoor pool, complete with a cascading waterfall and neatly landscaped greenery. The Beach House Restaurant is also on the premises.

182 rooms. Restaurant, bar. Business center. Fitness center. Pool. Pets accepted. Golf. Tennis. $251-350

★★★SUNSET KEY GUEST COTTAGES, A WESTIN RESORT

245 Front St., Key West, 305-292-5300, 800-937-8461; www.westin.com

The Sunset Key Guest Cottages resort is on a secluded 27-acre island called

Sunset Key. The cottages—which come in one-, two- and three-bedroom options—feature traditional Key West architecture and have kitchens, living and dining areas, CD and DVD players and a beverage and pantry bar. The cottages offer either expansive ocean vistas or garden views. Try the free-form garden pool with whirlpools, or sip a tropical drink at Flippers Pool Bar. There is 24-hour boat transportation to Old Town in Key West.

37 rooms. Restaurant, bar. Complimentary breakfast. Fitness center. Pool. Beach. Tennis. $351 and up

★★★WESTIN KEY WEST RESORT AND MARINA
245 Front St., Key West, 305-294-4000, 800-937-8461; www.westin.com

Overlooking the Gulf of Mexico and next to Mallory Square, this Victorian-inspired resort sits at the northwest edge of Key West's Old Town. Rooms are decorated with upscale Floridian décor, and most have private balconies with water views. The resort marina offers a variety of water sports and a nightly sunset festival along the pier. But just because there is much to do beyond the lobby doors doesn't mean your stay should pale in comparison. Hotel amenities include 24-hour room service, down or hypoallergenic pillows, bathrobes and slippers, and flat-screen televisions.

178 rooms. Restaurant, bar. Business center. Fitness center. Beach. Pool. $251-350

MARATHON
★★★HAWKS CAY RESORT
61 Hawk's Cay Blvd., Duck Key, 305-743-7000, 888-443-6393; www.hawkscay.com

The tropical setting at this resort features a saltwater lagoon and multiple-heated freshwater pools, a children's pool and whirlpools. There's plenty to do with eight tennis courts, a fitness room, a kids' club, golf privileges and water sports. There are also several dolphins at the resort, and you can get close to them through the hotel's porpoise program. After all those activities, relax in your comfortable room, which has a West Indies sensibility that includes a four-poster beds and tasteful wall art.

180 rooms. Restaurant, bar. Business center. Fitness center. Pool. Spa. Tennis. $251-350

PALM BEACH
★★★THE BRAZILIAN COURT HOTEL
301 Australian Ave., Palm Beach, 561-655-7740, 800-552-0335;
www.thebraziliancourt.com

Since the 1920s, the Brazilian Court Hotel has been one of Palm Beach's most dignified addresses. Just a short distance from Worth Avenue's shops, the guest rooms and suites reflect the hotel's dedication to detail. A heated outdoor pool provides a restful spot, while people on the social circuit appreciate the spa and salon services. Sophisticated palates rejoice at the dining offered here, where Manhattan's famed Daniel Boulud has an outpost of his award-winning Café Boulud restaurant.

80 rooms. Restaurant, bar. Fitness center. Pool. Spa. Pets accepted. $351 and up

★★★★THE BREAKERS, PALM BEACH
1 S. County Road, Palm Beach, 561-655-6611, 888-273-2537; www.thebreakers.com

Dating back to 1896, the Breakers earned its moniker from the crashing waves on this resort's stretch of beach. Travelers have come here for more than 100 years to admire the views outside as well as the Venetian chandeliers, hand-painted ceilings and priceless antiques inside. Guest rooms feature traditional furnishings and tech treats such as CD players and PlayStations. The resort includes 10 tennis courts, 36 holes of championship golf, four oceanfront pools, fine shopping, a full-service fitness center and a luxury spa. The five restaurants and four bars serve everything from beachside lobster clubs to foie gras.

540 rooms. Restaurant, bar. Business center. Fitness center. Pool. Spa. Beach. Golf. Tennis. $351 and up

★★★THE COLONY PALM BEACH

155 Hammon Ave., Palm Beach, 561-655-5430, 800-521-5525; www.thecolonypalmbeach.com

This restored landmark hotel first opened in 1947 and has a prime location in the heart of Palm Beach. The elegant interior is richly decorated and furnished but with a comfortable, casual feel. The sunny guest rooms are decorated in a soft color palette, with upscale bedding and pillow-top mattresses. Bike rentals and beach kits are available to if you want to head outside, and a nearby health club is complimentary.

90 rooms. Restaurant, bar. Business center. Pool. $151-250

★★★★★FOUR SEASONS RESORT PALM BEACH

2800 S. Ocean Blvd., Palm Beach, 561-582-2800, 800-545-4000; www.fourseasons.com

This resort unites the best of Palm Beach in one spot. Just minutes from the alluring boutiques of Worth Avenue and the challenges of three championship golf courses, the hotel is set on a tucked-away stretch of golden beach. Though you may prefer to spend your time on the pool deck, where lemon water, chilled face cloths, Evian spritz and fresh-cut fruit will be at your disposal. The guest rooms have a sophisticated décor, with floral prints, pastel colors and casually elegant furnishings. They all come with furnished private balconies overlooking either the pool, gardens or ocean. Southeastern regional dishes are the specialty at the restaurant, while the patio setting of the Atlantic Bar & Grill and the canopied terrace of the Ocean Bistro are perfect for casual meals and cocktails. A spa and well-equipped fitness center round out the experience.

210 rooms. Restaurant, bar. Business center. Fitness center. Pool. Spa. Pets accepted. Tennis. $351 and up

★★★★★THE RITZ-CARLTON, PALM BEACH

100 S. Ocean Blvd., Manalapan, 561-533-6000, 800-241-3333; www.ritzcarlton.com

This luxury resort tucked away on seven oceanfront acres on the southern tip of Palm Beach Island is a blend of elegance and modern convenience. Rooms and suites artfully blend Florida style with European elegance with custom-made Italian mahogany furniture and décor in subdued greens, oranges and tans. There are modern conveniences in the rooms as well, including a 32-inch LCD flat-screen television, DVD player and private balcony. A variety of restaurants showcase the talents of the chefs; try Temple Orange any time of day, or enjoy light fare and delicious drinks at Stir Bar and Terrace. Whichever you choose, end the evening by choosing a selection from the bath menu and requesting that the bath butler have it ready for you when it's time to retire for the day.

270 rooms. Restaurant, bar. Business center. Fitness center. Pool. Spa. Beach. Pets accepted. Tennis. $351 and up

WEST PALM BEACH

★★★PALM BEACH MARRIOTT SINGER ISLAND BEACH RESORT & SPA

3800 N. Ocean Drive, Singer Island, 561-340-1700; www.luxurycollection.com

Located on Singer Island, this property features one- and two-bedroom condos in an elegant setting 10 miles north of Palm Beach. Floor-to-ceiling windows, contemporary art, and marble and polished wood accents are showcased in an oval-shaped lobby. The condo units have all of the conveniences of home, including a full refrigerator, microwave, stove, washer/dryer and Bose stereo. Bathrooms are luxurious and come with Gilchrist & Soames products.

239 rooms. Restaurant, bar. Business center. Fitness center. Pool. Spa. Beach. $251-350

WHERE TO EAT

AVENTURA

★★★BOURBON STEAK, A MICHAEL MINA RESTAURANT

The Fairmont Turnberry Isle Resort & Club, 19999 West Country Club Drive, Aventura 786-279-6600; www.bourbonsteakmiami.com

This glam, 250-seat, Tony Chi-designed steak house marks the first time a restaurant at the club has ever been open to the public, and Aventurians have been busy making themselves into regulars. The menu features wood-grilled steaks with sides like the trio of fries and truffled mac and cheese, as well as other comfort foods like crispy chicken, lobster pot pie and Alaskan king crab.

American. Dinner. Reservations recommended. Bar. $86 and up

★★★CHEF ALLEN'S

19088 N.E. 29th Ave., Aventura, 305-935-2900; www.chefallens.com

One of Miami's first James Beard Award winners and a member of the famous Mango Gang (a group of chefs who practically invented new-world cuisine), chef Allen Susser has turned his long-running establishment (operating since 1986) into a sustainable seafood bistro. The bar offers a 360-degree view into the dining room and the menu features dishes that run the gamut of Caribbean and Latin flavors. For dessert, his legendary soufflés are still, and always will be, worth the calories. Service is as elegant as the mahogany furnishings, and yet the staff remains approachable.

Seafood. Dinner. Reservations recommended. $36-85

★★★★NAOE

175 Sunny Isles Boulevard, Sunny Isles, 305.947.NAOE, www.naoemiami.com

Hidden away in a non-descript strip mall in Sunny Isles, Naoe is as unassuming as its exterior suggests. Still, diners visiting this stretch of South Florida coast should not pass by this gem. Only 17 guests can claim seats in this intimate space, with many lined up along the chef's bar overlooking the open kitchen. Chef/owner Kevin Cory and manager Wendy Maharlika treat diners at this petite Japanese jewelbox as they would guests in their own home. Maharlika holds down the dining room while Cory single-handily prepares every dish that comes out of the kitchen—which means meals can sometimes drag on as he keeps pace with the volume of diners. With food like this, you'll hardly notice. Dinners start with the chef's omakase bento box and then proceed to presentation after presentation of pristine and tender sushi delivered until you call uncle. Though the menu changes daily depending on what fish is freshly sourced from Japan and local harbors, recent dishes included house-made egg tofu with uni and miso-butternut squash soup. House-made 'bbq' eel is sweet and toothy, and comes topped with the chef's own special soy sauce. Speaking of soy sauce, it's the mystery ingredient in the signature ice cream, and it makes for a surprisingly delicious end to the meal.

Japanese. Dinner, Wednesday – Sunday. Reservations recommended. $36-85

★★★NEOMI'S

Trump International Beach Resort Miami, 18001 Collins Ave., Sunny Isles Beach, 305-692-5770; www.trumpmiami.com

Neomi's is all about the tropics, from the flavors on the plate to the vistas off the spacious outdoor patio. The dining room is awash with plush textures and fiery sunset colors, which are softened by white circular light fixtures hanging from the ceiling and curved walls. The kitchen puts out a modern fusion menu that utilizes Nuevo Spanish/Latino influences, resulting in dishes such as foie gras with pistachio and saffron reduction and dried green grapes.

Contemporary American. Breakfast, lunch, dinner. Reservations recommended. Outdoor seating. Bar. $86 and up

★★★OCEAN PRIME

19501 Biscayne Blvd., Aventura, 305-931-5400; www.ocean-prime.com

Aventura Mall's first high-end seafood and steak house resonates with fashion-conscious shoppers who enjoy its convenient locale right next to Nordstrom. The space, from restaurateur Cameron Mitchell, has all the right supper-club accoutrements and attitude. Service begins with a complimentary crudités and continues with white-truffle-and-caviar deviled eggs, before moving on to all manner of steaks, chops and fish fillets, and finishing off with throwback desserts like baked Alaska.

Contemporary American. Lunch, dinner. Reservations recommended. Bar. $86 and up

★★★TIMO

17624 Collins Ave., Sunny Isles, 305-936-1008; www.timorestaurant.com

Beloved by locals, this sophisticated Italian bistro is run by dedicated chef-owner Tim Andriola, a protégé of James Beard Award winner Mark Militello. Though the spot was formerly a Tony Roma's, you'd never know it from the intimate, trattoria-like ambiance and contemporary appointments. A young crowd tends to gather at the bar for items like onion and pepper pizza and a glass of Barbera, but most of the clientele reserves a table for a full-course meal that includes short rib cannelloni with black truffle fonduta and a list of Italian vintages.

Contemporary Italian. Lunch (Monday-Friday), dinner. Reservations recommended. $36-85

BOCA RATON

★★★ARTURO'S

6750 N. Federal Highway, Boca Raton, 561-997-7373; www.arturosrestaurant.com

This formal, family-owned Italian restaurant located in an Italian villa-style building has maintained its commitment to fine service and cuisine. On the inside, this old-school local classic has fresh roses on each table, and live piano music, tuxedoed waiters and candlelight only add to the romantic mood. Housemade pastas dot the menu in dishes such as the spaghetti pescatore and fettuccine al tartufo nero. Make sure to stay for dessert—they arrive atop a rolling cart.

Italian. Lunch (Monday-Friday), dinner. Closed three weeks in July. Reservations recommended. Bar. $36-85

★★★LUCCA

501 E. Camino Real, Boca Raton, 561-447-5822, 888-491-2622; www.bocaresort.com

Located on the ground floor of the Boca Raton Resort & Club, Lucca is an understated, elegant Tuscan-style restaurant that opened under the care of consultant Drew Nieporent, the visionary restaurateur who brought Tribeca Grill, Montrachet and Nobu to New York City. The restaurant boasts floor-to-ceiling windows with beautiful views of the Intracoastal Waterway and Murano chandeliers. Dishes might include osso buco Milanese or a crispy potato-wrapped Key West snapper. There are also a variety of pastas, from roasted pumpkin ravioli to spaghetti and meatballs.

Italian. Lunch, dinner. Reservations recommended. Children's menu. Bar. $36-85

★★★MAX'S GRILLE

404 Plaza Real, Boca Raton, 561-368-0080; www.maxsgrille.com

This modern bistro in Mizner Park—a dining and entertainment hub lined with brick streets, colorful Spanish-tiled buildings and manicured landscaping—offers contemporary comfort food in a see-and-be-seen atmosphere. The open kitchen allows diners to watch their meals being prepared, while the popular outdoor patio is a nice perch from which to people-watch during lunch. At dinner, go for classics like the pasta with a delicious Kobe beef meatball.

Contemporary American. Lunch, dinner, Saturday-Sunday brunch. Reservations recommended. Outdoor seating. Children's menu. Bar. $36-85

★★★MORTON'S, THE STEAKHOUSE

5050 Town Center Circle, Boca Raton, 561-392-7724; www.mortons.com

This restaurant occasionally gets overlooked for being a chain (the original opened in Chicago in 1978). Don't make that mistake. This branch, as the other Morton's, serves consistently well-prepared steaks, seafood and standard steakhouse sides, such as Caesar salad and crisp onion rings. The classy, clubby atmosphere is perfect for striking a business deal or enjoying a quiet dinner for two.

Steak. Dinner. Reservations recommended. Bar. $36-85

CORAL GABLES

★★★CACAO RESTAURANT

41 Giralda Ave., Coral Gables, 305-445-1001; www.cacaorestaurant.com

Chef-owner Edgar Leal mixes pan-Latino flavors in this minimalist eatery where the fare is so visually stunning that it almost trumps the décor. Since 1992, Leal has earned acclaim for successfully pulling influences from Mexico to Margarita Island, Ecuador to Guyana and blending them together for dishes like "vacio" flap steak tiradito with hot chimichurri sauce and Brazilian lobster tail with quinoa risotto and Venezuelan rum sauce. Wine aficionados will love Cacao all the more for its intense interest in presenting boutique vintages from regions all over the globe.

Contemporary Latin. Lunch, dinner. Closed Sunday. Reservations recommended. Bar. $86 and up

HIGHLIGHT

WHAT ARE THE BEST OVERALL RESTAURANTS IN SOUTHEAST FLORIDA?

CAFÉ BOULUD, PALM BEACH

The authority on French cuisine, Daniel Boulud brings his masterful cooking to Palm Beach. Tucked inside the historic Brazilian Court Hotel, Café Boulud elevates traditional fare like steak frites to utter perfection.

CHEF ALLEN'S

Famed chef Allen Susser was one of Miami's first James Beard Award recipients and a member of the Mango Gang, a group that helped lead the new-world cuisine revolution. He continues to turn out winning sustainable seafood dishes.

L'ESCALIER, PALM BEACH

This innovative French restaurant uses fresh seasonal ingredients to make its dishes shine. But the real reason to come here is the vast wine list that would make any oenophile drool.

THE RESTAURANT

Inside the Four Seasons Resort in Palm Beach's signature restaurant you'll find a contemporary and tropically inspired dining room where every seat gets an ocean view, and a menu that melds the flavors of the South, the Caribbean and Central and South America.

★★★CHEF INNOCENT AT ST. MICHEL

Hotel St. Michel, 162 Alcazar Ave., Coral Gables, 305-446-6572; www.chefinnocent.com

Located in the romantic, historic Hotel St. Michel, this restaurant is a great spot for intimate conversation set to the tune of innovative, sophisticated French-American fare. The Art Deco-style dining room gleams with hardwood floors, magnificent plate-glass windows and soft lighting, making it a smart choice for special occasions. There's also live music on Fridays.

Contemporary American. Breakfast, lunch, dinner, Sunday brunch. Reservations recommended. Outdoor seating. Bar. $36-85

★★★LA COFRADIA

160 Andalusia Ave., Coral Gables, 305-914-1300; www.lacofradia.com

A fusion of Peruvian and Mediterranean styles, La Cofradia is an example of balance between décor and cuisine. A lounge in front, filled with leather armchairs, is the perfect setting to meet friends for pisco sours. Chef-owner Jean Paul Desmaison plays up the hallmarks of Peruvian cuisine—purple potatoes, innumerable varieties of corn, "ají amarillo" chiles—but uses his classical European training to raise them to new heights. Try the risotto with ají Amarillo, saffron and lobster or the braised pork with grapes and Pisco for examples.

Peruvian-Mediterranean. Lunch, dinner. Reservations recommended. Bar. $36-85

★★★ORTANIQUE ON THE MILE

278 Miracle Mile, Coral Gables, 305-446-7710; www.cindyhutsoncuisine.com

The creative, new-world menu at this elegant but approachable restaurant echoes the Caribbean, offering island fare accented by tropical fruits, spices, herbs and marinades. Ceviche del mar, West Indian curried crab cakes and sautéed Bahamian black grouper are some of the kitchen's most eagerly devoured signature dishes. The mojitos here have a following of their own, and are often cited by patrons as the best in Miami.

Caribbean, contemporary American. Lunch (Monday-Friday), dinner. Reservations recommended. Outdoor seating. Bar. $36-85

★★★★PALME D'OR

Biltmore, 1200 Anastasia Ave., Coral Gables, 305-913-3201; www.biltmorehotel.com

Located inside the legendary Biltmore hotel, Palme d'Or is a 1920s-era dining room decked out in flowers and tropical foliage, with mirrored columns, ornate light fixtures and a view of the hotel's beautiful, oversized swimming pool. Aside from a long list of inspired à la carte choices, the chef offers a six-course prix fixe experience and a nine-course tasting menu. Each menu can be paired with wine for an additional fee.

French. Dinner. Closed Sunday-Monday. Bar. $86 and up

ISLAMORADA
★★★PIERRE'S

81600 Overseas Highway, Islamorada, 305-664-3225; www.pierres-restaurant.com

This upper-crust Florida Keys enclave serves a balanced selection of New American dishes in a gorgeous, two-story plantation house. There's a pretty veranda, where diners can catch a stunning Florida Bay sunset, and the interior is tastefully decorated with Indian and Moroccan artifacts. The menu includes seafood-inclined contemporary American-Floribbean fare, such as coconut-marinated prawns, grilled yellowfin tuna, and pan-seared foie gras with papaya and mango chutney. Desserts include a rich chocolate bomb cake and banana beignets with Grand Marnier caramel sauce and ice cream.

Contemporary American. Dinner. Closed Monday June-October. $36-85

KEY BISCAYNE
★★★LINDA B. STEAKHOUSE

320 Crandon Blvd., Key Biscayne, 305-361-1111

This upscale steak house is well known in Key Biscayne as a top destination for great meat and seafood. The attractive dining room features soft lighting; comfortable, floral-patterned chairs; soothing pastel colors; and fine artwork. In addition to a selection of Angus beef dishes like filet mignon, prime rib and New York sirloin, Linda B. features Italian-influenced fare like housemade ravioli with ricotta cheese and spinach, and shrimp scampi all'aglio with garlic butter and parsley sauce. Friendly and personalized service puts guests at ease and makes for a truly wonderful dining experience.

Steak. Lunch, dinner. Reservations recommended. Outdoor seating. Children's menu. Bar. $36-85

KEY WEST

★★★CAFE MARQUESA

Marquesa Hotel, 600 Fleming St., Key West, 305-292-1244; www.marquesa.com

This modern American restaurant is in the Marquesa Hotel, in Key West's historic district. Breads and desserts are baked fresh daily and accompany seasonal specialties like lobster and diver scallops with Thai basil sauce, prosciutto-wrapped black Angus filet, and conch and blue crab cakes, all brought to the table by efficient, professional servers. The open kitchen brings life to the intimate 50-seat dining room, which has a casual French brasserie feel. Save room for a sweet treat—the dessert list features decadent items like a key lime Napoleon.

Contemporary American. Dinner. Bar. $36-85

★★★HARBOURVIEW CAFE

Pier House Resort and Caribbean Spa, 1 Duval St., Key West, 305-296-4600; www.pierhouse.com

This restaurant at the south end of busy Duval Street is right on the Gulf and offers great sunset vistas. HarbourView's décor is contemporary with a blue-and-white color scheme and unusual light and dark wood floors. The menu includes a good selection of from-the-sea options, such as conch and crab fritters, and sautéed yellowtail snapper served with herb risotto. Nightly entertainment includes a piano bar and jazz music.

Seafood. Breakfast, lunch, dinner. Reservations recommended. Outdoor seating. Children's menu. Bar. $36-85

★★★LOUIE'S BACKYARD

700 Waddell Ave., Key West, 305-294-1061; www.louiesbackyard.com

This waterfront restaurant serves a seafood-heavy menu and has a spacious outdoor terrace with ocean views. The setting is particularly stunning at sunset, so try to snag an alfresco table shortly before dusk. Standout dishes include sautéed Key West shrimp with bacon and stone-ground grits, conch fritters, and sea scallops in orange-chile broth. Wrap up dinner with an expertly made mojito—the restaurant is known for the mint-rum-sugar concoction—and enjoy the ocean breezes.

Caribbean. Lunch, dinner. Reservations recommended. Outdoor seating. Bar. $36-85

PALM BEACH

★★★★CAFÉ BOULUD

301 Australian Ave., Palm Beach, 561-655-6060; www.danielnyc.com

Southern France meets south Florida at the Palm Beach branch of Café Boulud. Here, Lyon-born chef Daniel Boulud offers the same pitch-perfect French cuisine as that of his New York restaurants, with deftly prepared standards like tuna tartare and steak frites. While the feel of the dining room is formal, it sidesteps stuffiness using a tropical palette of yellows and oranges, illuminated through ample windows and French doors. The restaurant boasts a prime location in the historic Brazilian Court Hotel, just steps from all the shopping

on Worth Avenue.
American, French. Breakfast, lunch, dinner, Saturday-Sunday brunch. Reservations recommended. Outdoor seating. Bar. $36-85

★★★CAFÉ L'EUROPE
331 S. County Road, Palm Beach, 561-655-4020; www.cafeleurope.com

Three thousand bottles of wine, and about two dozen by the glass, await at Café L'Europe. The international menu takes its cues from France, Italy, Asia, Austria and Latin America. Dishes include everything from roasted rack of lamb with a goat cheese potato tart to the classic wiener schnitzel with red cabbage.
International. Lunch, dinner. Closed Monday. Reservations recommended. Jacket required. Bar. $86 and up

★★★CHARLEY'S CRAB
456 S. Ocean Blvd., Palm Beach, 561-659-1500, 800-552-6379; www.muer.com

Located on the picturesque Intercoastal Waterway, Charley's Crab is a perfect spot to watch the sunset over the water while digging into fresh seafood, aged cuts of beef and housemade pasta dishes. A signature is the applejack sea bass, topped with apples and sun-dried cherries, simmered in a sweet bourbon reduction.
Seafood. Lunch, dinner. Reservations recommended. Bar. $36-85

★★★CHEZ JEAN-PIERRE
132 N. County Road, Palm Beach, 561-833-1171; www.chezjeanpierre.com

Choose your preferred dining atmosphere at this many-roomed Palm Beach eatery, whether it be chic and stylish, rustic Mediterranean or an intimate wine cellar. In each setting you'll experience French bistro cooking with a fine balance between traditional and more creative offerings.
French. Dinner. Closed Sunday-Monday mid-July-mid-August. Reservations recommended. Bar. $36-85

★★★ECHO
230A Sunrise Ave., Palm Beach, 561-802-4222; www.echopalmbeach.com

This restaurant brings a dose of contemporary flair to usually staid Palm Beach with an energetic dining room punctuated with vivid colors and striking lighting fixtures and an eclectic menu of dishes influenced by Thailand, China, Japan and Vietnam to match. Besides an extensive sushi bar selection, the menu includes classics like Peking duck, egg foo yong and Hunan cashew chicken—severed with stainless steal chopsticks, of course.
Asian. Dinner. Closed Monday-Tuesday. Reservations recommended. Bar. $36-85

★★★★L'ESCALIER
The Breakers Hotel Palm Beach, 1 S. County Road, Palm Beach, 561-659-8480, 888-273-2537; www.thebreakers.com

The wine list at L'Escalier, an Old World charmer inside the Breakers resort that serves contemporary French fare, includes 1,400 bottles. The resort's collection contains 25,000 bottles, 7,800 of which are on display in the Wine Cellar adjacent to L'Escalier. In other words, if you love wine, this is the restaurant for you. The menu here is innovative yet rooted in French tradition. Seasonal ingredients are sourced from specialty purveyors, and the kitchen delicately adds layers of flavor to the plate, allowing the quality of the ingredients to shine in dishes such as duck breast with caramelized endive and black raisins, and steak au poivre with baby root vegetables, smoked potato croquettes and a fig compote.

French. Dinner. Closed Sunday-Monday. Reservations recommended. Bar. $86 and up

★★★THE LEOPARD LOUNGE

Chesterfield Hotel, 363 Cocoanut Row, Palm Beach, 561-659-5800; www.chesterfieldpb.com

Located in the landmark Chesterfield Hotel, built in 1926, the Leopard Room offers diners distinctive food served in a richly decorated, leopard-themed room featuring black and red accents, leopard skin-patterned carpet and matching menus and dishware. Despite its wild décor, the menu sticks to simple classics like fat slabs of Angus beef, just-caught fish and fresh pastas.

American. Breakfast, lunch, dinner. Reservations recommended. Outdoor seating. Bar. $36-85

★★★RENATO'S

87 Via Mizner, Palm Beach, 561-655-9752; www.renatospalmbeach.com

Dine inside or out at this Palm Beach favorite, where Italian classics like veal Milanese with fresh arugula and tomatoes are served by a friendly and professional staff. The outdoor courtyard and bar is a charming place to settle in and sample just caught seafood such as sautéed black grouper with polenta and spinach.

Italian. Lunch, dinner. Outdoor seating. Bar. $36-85

★★★★THE RESTAURANT

Four Seasons Resort Palm Beach, 2800 S. Ocean Blvd., Palm Beach, 561-533-3750, 800-432-2335; www.fourseasons.com

Inside the Four Seasons Resort in Palm Beach's signature restaurant you'll find a contemporary and tropically inspired dining room where every seat gets an ocean view. The menu melds the flavors of the South, the Caribbean and Central and South America, and comes in prix fixe versions with three, four and five courses. Appetizers include such creations as jumbo lump crab with alligator pear, golden tomato coulis and crispy potato lace, while entrées can include black duck foie gras with wild rice, passion fruit and baby root vegetables.

American. Dinner. Closed Monday. Reservations recommended. Jacket required. Bar. $36-85

★★★RUTH'S CHRIS STEAK HOUSE

661 Highway 1, North Palm Beach, 561-863-0660, 800-544-0808; www.ruthschris.com

Aged beef cooked to perfection has kept Ruth's Chris among America's favorite steak-house chains. The à la carte sides, including sliced beefsteak tomatoes with onions and crumbled blue cheese and creamy mashed potatoes or sweet potato casserole with pecan crust are as satisfying and flavorful as the meat.

Steak, seafood. Dinner. Reservations recommended. Bar. $36-85

PALM BEACH GARDENS

★★★CAFÉ CHARDONNAY

4533 PGA Blvd., Palm Beach Gardens, 561-627-2662; www.cafechardonnay.com

Owned by husband-and-wife team Frank and Gigi Eucalitto, Café Chardonnay offers eclectic American cuisine and an extensive international wine list. The menu takes on global influences from Asia, France and Italy. Dishes include herb and dijon crusted rack of lamb with goat cheese mashed potatoes and lamb jus, and hand cut fettuccine with Maine lobster and diver scallops in a truffle reggiano parmesan cream. Wines are offered in flights of three tastes paired with a selection of cheeses and pâté, as well as "Round-trip" flights— two half-bottles, a dessert wine, cheese and pâté.

American. Lunch, dinner. Outdoor seating. Children's menu. Bar. $36-85

RECOMMENDED

KEY WEST

ANTONIA'S
615 Duval St., Key West, 305-294-6565; www.antoniaskeywest.com

This Old Town restaurant is approximately six blocks from both the Gulf and the Atlantic. Wood walls and flooring, white tablecloths, candles and pretty table settings make up the simple yet elegant décor. All the menu items, including the pastas and desserts, are prepared on the premises.

Italian. Dinner. Bar. $16-35

BAGATELLE
115 Duval St., Key West, 305-296-6609; www.bagatellekeywest.com

Bagatelle is in a historic sea captain's house, built in 1884, in the heart of downtown Old Key West, just a short walk from Mallory Square. Dine on the wraparound porch, which is a great spot for people-watching. A casual menu is offered for breakfast and lunch, while dinner features everything from seared tuna to honey friend lobster tail to whole fried Thai snapper.

American, seafood. Breakfast, lunch, dinner. Outdoor seating. Bar. $36-85

KELLY'S CARIBBEAN BAR, GRILL & BREWERY
301 Whitehead St., Key West, 305-293-8484; www.kellyskeywest.com

Pan American airline's first tickets were sold in this building in 1927. Nowadays, the bar and eatery is owned by actress Kelly McGillis of *Top Gun* fame. The bar, which also has a microbrewery on the premises, remains a destination for its delicious Key lime martinis and beers, while the menu features a variety of fish with different island preparations (grilled with charred tomato relish, blackened with mango salsa, etc.), and steaks (grilled, au poivre or crusted with bacon and gorgonzola) as well as jerked chicken, coconut shrimp and more.

American, Caribbean. Lunch, dinner. Outdoor seating. Children's menu. Bar. $16-35

PALM BEACH

TA-BOO
221 Worth Ave., Palm Beach, 561-835-3500; www.taboorestaurant.com

This Palm Beach staple is the place to see and be seen in town. The menu offers a variety of well-executed American bistro fare, including a variety of steaks, grilled dishes and pizzas. If you want to check out the scene, drop in during happy hour (4:00–6:30 p.m. daily and 9:00 p.m. until close Friday and Saturday) when the drinks are sometimes more than half off and you'll find everything from pizza to oysters to pistachio encrusted lamp lollipops for half price.

American. Lunch, dinner, Sunday brunch. Bar. $16-35

SPAS

AVENTURA

★★★AQUANOX SPA

Trump International Beach Resort Miami, 18001 Collins Ave., Sunny Isles Beach, 305-692-5730; www.trumpmiami.com

A slower pace is evident on the second floor of the Trump International Beach Resort Miami, home of the Aquanox Spa. The coed relaxation rooms let you to wait for your treatments alongside your beloved, and the olive-green suede lounge chairs will have you reclining into serenity in no time. Abstract art covers the walls, and orchids seem to sprout from every surface. If you've traveled from afar and still feel a bit jet-lagged, try the Passport to Bliss, Aquanox's signature 80-minute massage with starfruit-pear exfoliants, a custom foot treatment and a full-body Swedish massage.

★★★★ESPA AT AQUALINA RESORT & SPA

Acqualina Resort & Spa on the Beach, 17875 Collins Ave., Sunny Isles Beach, 305-918-6844; www.acqualinaresort.com

The hotel lobby at Aqualina is a quiet retreat from the bustle of Collins Avenue, but when you step through the hallway into ESPA, the tranquility is taken to an entirely new level. This is the kind of place that avid spa-goers come back to time and again. At ESPA, you are encouraged to arrive at least an hour before your treatment to enjoy the spa's relaxation lounge, crystal steam rooms, showers and ice fountains—and take it from us, it pays to be early. Welcoming you upon arrival is an energizing tropical fruit smoothie, a refreshing cold towel to wipe away the outdoor heat and a lone, lovely orchid. There's no hopping from one treatment room to another here. Each private pavilion is equipped with a shower and heated bed and is set up so that all services can be completed in one room. Most popular at ESPA is the Time treatment, two to four-hour blocks of customized attention. Not sure where to begin? The ESPA Skin Brightener will minimize the effects that pollution, stress and lack of sleep have on your face, while the two-hour Ocean Journey treatment combines a stress relief massage with an algae body wrap to nourish the skin. It's relaxing—like a day at the beach (minus the sand in your hair).

★★★★WILLOW STREAM SPA

The Fairmont Turnberry Isle Resort & Club, 19999 W Country Club Drive, Aventura, 305-933-6930; www.fairmont.com

The Willow Stream Spa at the Fairmont Turnberry Isle Resort & Club is the perfect location for a spa experience. The palm trees, water fountains, terraces and sunny skies at this 300-acre Mediterranean-style resort are soothing backdrops for any treatment. Make your way up the sage green spiral staircase to the second floor treatment rooms; their palm tree-lined balconies are a great place to indulge in the Turnberry Classic Pedicure with orange oil. If you'd rather block out the world for a while, step back indoors and the therapists will draw the black-out curtains for a stress relief customized massage, one of the most popular treatments. The spa, which stresses the importance of clients' "streams" of energy, also offers Vichy Treatments, in which a multi-head shower massages your body with water.

BAL HARBOUR

★★★★THE SPA AT ONE BAL HARBOUR

ONE Bal Harbour, 10295 Collins Ave., Bal Harbour, 305-455-5411; www.oneluxuryhotels.com

Bathed in a neutral beige-and-white palette, the 10,000-square-foot spa is its own calming getaway within the already blissful ONE Bal Harbour. And you can forget about those spas that try to soothe you with sounds of the ocean; this one is the real deal, thanks to its views of the water from the treatment suites. Ease your jet lag with a specially tailored regimen or have your feet massaged in the serene, white-curtain-clad Foot Therapy Lounge, and follow it up with a makeup application to get you ready for Miami Beach nightlife. If your body needs a little love the next morning, detox with a facial or a Harmonising massage—a favorite is the 4-Hand Impériale massage, which features two therapists and results in a whole lot of relaxation.

BOCA RATON

★★★★SPA PALAZZO AT BOCA RATON RESORT & CLUB

Boca Raton Resort & Club, 501 E. Camino Real, Boca Raton, 561-347-4772, 888-491-2622; www.spapalazzo.com

Spa Palazzo reflects the beauty of the Mediterranean in its architecture and seductive design. Modeled after Spain's Alhambra palace, this spa offers services inspired by nature. From eucalyptus and chamomile to honey-coconut-mango, the body scrubs pay tribute to natural ingredients. Body wraps use grapefruit, peppermint, moor mud and algae. Facials cleanse and soothe with botanical extracts, Florida citrus and aromatherapy oils.

KEY BISCAYNE

★★★★THE RITZ-CARLTON SPA, KEY BISCAYNE

The Ritz-Carlton, Key Biscayne, 455 Grand Bay Drive, Key Biscayne, 305-365-4500; www.ritzcarlton.com

You don't have to travel too far from the city to find a tropical island paradise. Just minutes from downtown Miami is a Caribbean-inspired oasis on secluded Key Biscayne. This spa soothes the body and mind with treatments that incorporate healing elements of the land and sea. The extensive spa menu features body therapies, specialized skin care and facials that utilize a holistic approach. Try the Seawater Therapy, which restores and balances the skin with a pure, freeze-dried seawater bath. Wellness services include personal training, body sculpting and kickboxing, as well as classes such as tai chi and yoga.

KEY WEST

★★★★SPA TERRE AT LITTLE PALM ISLAND

Little Palm Island Resort and Spa, 28500 Overseas Highway, Little Torch Key, 305-515-3028, 800-343-8567; www.littlepalmisland.com

Reconnecting with body and soul is the philosophy behind Little Palm Island's Spa Terre. The menu is filled with massages and body treatments, many inspired by Indonesian and Thai techniques and traditions. Spend an hour unwinding with a Swedish, sports or aromatherapy massage, or let heated volcanic river rocks do the work in a hot-stone massage. Tired feet and lower legs are soothed with reflexology, while skin is revived with the detoxifying Caribbean seaweed body mask or the rehydrating cucumber and aloe wrap.

PALM BEACH
★★★★THE SPA AT THE BREAKERS
The Breakers Palm Beach, 1 S. County Road, Palm Beach, 561-653-6656, 888-273-2537; www.thebreakers.com

This 20,000-square-foot facility is a pampering paradise overlooking the Atlantic Ocean. The spa features 17 treatment rooms, eight salon stations, a fitness center with ocean views, an outdoor lap pool with a whirlpool spa and an ocean terrace for alfresco massages. From marine algae body wraps to pomegranate-salt and honey-papaya scrubs, exfoliating and cleansing never sounded so appetizing. The salon offers a full range of beauty services, from waxing and makeup application to hairstyling and coloring.

RECOMMENDED

EAU SPA AT THE RITZ-CARLTON, PALM BEACH
The Ritz-Carlton, Palm Beach, 100 S. Ocean Blvd., Manalapan, 561-533-6000, 800-241-3333; www.ritzcarlton.com

This gorgeous spa is equal parts luxury, whimsy and fun. Mix your own concoction at the Scrub and Polish Bar, read a book in the Self-Centered lounge or sip a martini in the café. Luxurious treatments include a bejeweled collection, which involves using precious stones for facials and body treatments. There are also special services tailor-made for brides, moms-to-be and for the seasons. Book the garden villa for your treatment and shower under the stars.

WHERE TO SHOP

AVENTURA
AVENTURA MALL
19501 Biscayne Blvd., Aventura, 305-935-1110; www.shopaventuramall.com

This mall, the fifth-largest in the U.S., sits smack-dab in the heart of bustling, upscale Aventura. It hosts some of the higher-end stores in the Miami area. Sprinkled between anchors like Nordstrom and Bloomingdale's are Michal Negrin, 7 for All Mankind and Barneys New York Co-Op. There are hundreds of stores—aside from men's and women's apparel—for serious shoppers: home furnishings, kid's clothing, toys and accessories shops.
Monday-Saturday 9 a.m.-10:30 p.m., Sunday noon-8 p.m.

BAL HARBOUR
BAL HARBOUR SHOPS
9700 Collins Ave., North Miami, 305-866-0311; www.balharbourshops.com

It's only the cream of the crop at this alfresco retail space in Bal Harbour, which means you'll find only the most luxurious in jewelry and fashion. The two-story mall is surrounded by lush foliage, which makes you feel like you are shopping in a garden. Bulgari, Chanel, Dior, Giorgio Armani and Louis Vuitton are just the tip of the iceberg from about 80 of the designer shops here.
Monday-Saturday 10 a.m.-9 p.m., Sunday noon-6 p.m.

BOCA RATON
MIZNER PARK
433 Plaza Real, Boca Raton, 561-362-0606; www.miznerpark.org

Mizner Park is a 30-acre shopping and dining village with gardenlike spaces that makes for a unique entertainment experience. There are more than 50 stores from which to choose; restaurants with sidewalk cafés; an amphitheater that hosts outdoor concerts; and an art museum and a movie theater.

Monday-Saturday 10 a.m.-9 p.m., Sunday noon-6 p.m.

CORAL GABLES
BELLINI
50 Miracle Mile, Coral Gables, 305-460-9898; www.bellini.com

Exquisite modern design collides with old-world charm in Bellini's handmade baby and children's furniture. Other handmade trinkets from local artisans, such as hand-painted first tooth and baby's-first-curl boxes, are also peppered throughout the store.

Monday-Saturday 10 a.m.-6 p.m., Sunday noon-5 p.m.

MIRACLE MILE
Coral Way from Douglas to LeJeune roads, Coral Gables, 305-569-0311; www.shopcoralgables.com

Brides, take note: The Miracle Mile, a section of Coral Way, is chockablock with wedding-day bonanzas. The strip comes studded with more than a dozen shops for designer wedding gowns, fanciful invitations, and one-of-a-kind bridal and wedding accessories. And just like in real life (unless your guests are real cheapskates), the housewares follow; the strip boasts a ton of furniture and home-design stores, so you can get your kitchen kitted out by Mia Cucina, your living room set up with the help of Roche-Bobois and your lighting done by Luminaire. Of course, there's more to the Mile, if you don't do domestic: Think homegrown boutiques, spas, restaurants, art galleries and live-theater houses.

PEPI BERTINI
315 Miracle Mile, Coral Gables, 305-461-3374; www.pepibertini.com

Who knew Milan and Miami had so much in common? Milan is an epicenter for fashion and Miami … well, Miami has Pepi Bertini, the city's epicenter for Italian men's fashions. Italian clothing and handmade shirts and suits are the name of the game here, and no guy looking for a well-cut suit vest, tie or dress shirt will leave empty-handed. Just like the garments' cuts, the service here is old-world, so expect to leave feeling warm and fuzzy on the inside and looking sharp and handsome on the outside.

Tuesday-Saturday 9 a.m.-6 p.m.

VILLAGE OF MERRICK PARK
358 San Lorenzo Ave., Coral Gables, 305-529-0200; www.villageofmerrickpark.com

You'll feel like you've entered a villa in Spain as you step into the Village of Merrick Park, which harkens to old Spanish-style buildings. Of course, in no real Spanish villa will you find the likes of Nordstrom, Neiman Marcus, Tiffany & Co. and Swarovski beckoning from all corners. But we'll trade authenticity for a luxe shopping experience any day, if the latter involves lush gardens, tropical foliage and water fountains sprinkled throughout an immaculately kept courtyard. By the time you hit La Perla, Hugo Boss and Pottery Barn Kids, you might want to make a courtesy call to your credit card company and warn them of the damage in advance.

Monday-Saturday 10 a.m.-9 p.m., Sunday noon-6 p.m.

INDEX

FLORIDA

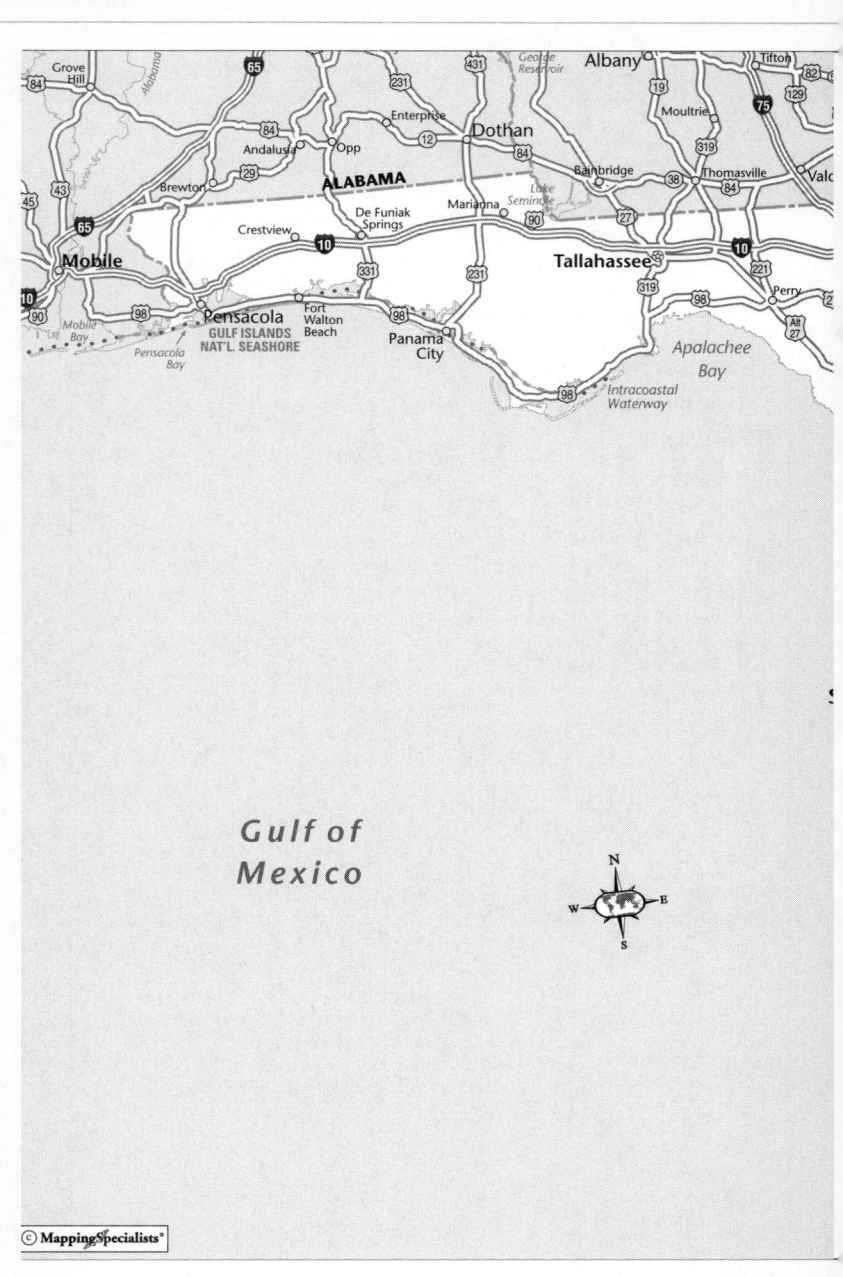

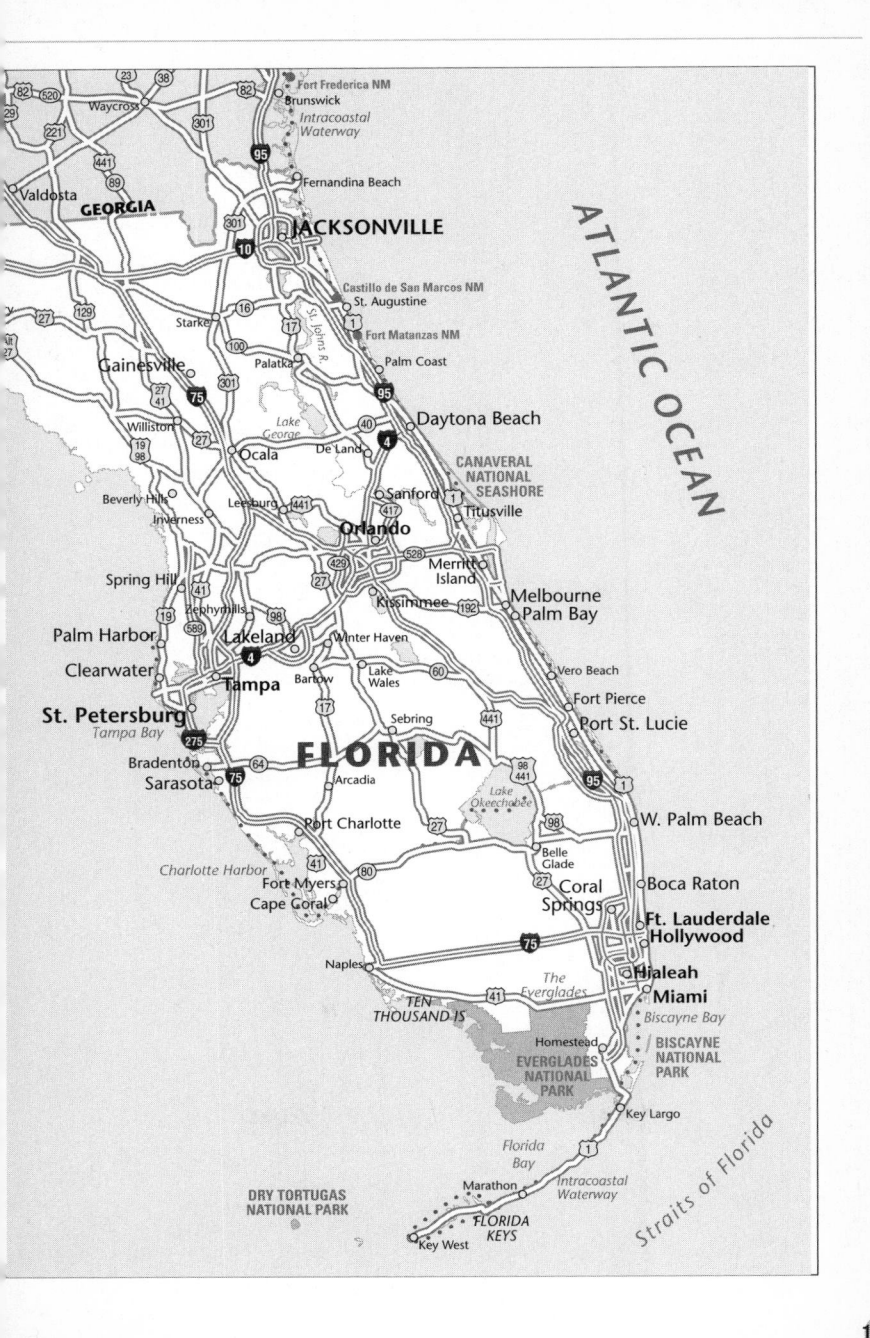

NOTES

NOTES

NOTES

NOTES